THEATRICAL LIBERALISM

Marc Chagall® *Isaac Blessing Jacob* (1931). Digital image © The Museum of Modern Art/ Licensed by SCALA/Art Resource, NY. ©SODRAC 2012 and ADAGP 2012, Chagall®

Theatrical Liberalism

Jews and Popular Entertainment in America

Andrea Most

NEW YORK UNIVERSITY PRESS
New York and London

NEW YORK UNIVERSITY PRESS
New York and London
www.nyupress.org

References to Internet websites (URLs) were accurate at the time of writing.
Neither the author nor New York University Press is responsible for URLs that
may have expired or changed since the manuscript was prepared.

LIBRARY OF CONGRESS CATALOGING-IN-PUBLICATION DATA
Most, Andrea, author.
Theatrical liberalism : Jews and popular entertainment in America / Andrea Most.
pages cm   Includes bibliographical references and index.
ISBN 978-0-8147-0819-4 (cl : alk. paper) — ISBN 978-0-8147-2462-0 (pb : alk. paper)
1. Jews in the performing arts—History. 2. Jews in the performing arts—United States—
History. 3. Jewish entertainers—United States—History. 4. Jews in popular culture—
United States. 5. Theater—New York (State)—New York—History. 6. Musicals—
New York (State)—New York—History. 7. Broadway (New York, N.Y.) I. Title.
PN1590.J48M67   2013
305.892'4—dc23   2012048183

New York University Press books are printed on acid-free paper, and their binding materials
are chosen for strength and durability. We strive to use environmentally responsible
suppliers and materials to the greatest extent possible in publishing our books.

Manufactured in the United States of America
10 9 8 7 6 5 4 3 2 1

To my parents, Arnold and Deborah Most

A Jew is asked to take a leap of action rather than a leap of thought. He is asked to surpass his needs, to do more than he understands in order to understand more than he does. . . . Right living is a way to right thinking.
—Abraham Joshua Heschel, "The Science of Deeds," *God in Search of Man*[1]

Acting is the most exact and exacting of arts. In it nothing can ever be left to chance—to an inspiration of the moment. . . . To wait, in acting, for inspiration to flash upon you is about as sensible as to wait until your house is in flames before looking for a fire escape. Night after night, often for many months, the same words must be spoken, the same actions be performed in the same way. . . . It is, I believe, safe to say that no actor ever produced a truly great effect in acting except as a result of long study, close thought, deliberate purpose and careful preparation.
—David Belasco, "Acting as a Science"[2]

It may be that being a Jew satisfied the frustrated actress in me. It may be that I have dramatized myself as a Jew.
—Edna Ferber, *A Peculiar Treasure*[3]

CONTENTS

ACKNOWLEDGMENTS

I am deeply indebted for the intellectual support I received while writing this book from my colleagues at the University of Toronto in the Department of English, Centre for Jewish Studies, Centre for the Study of Religion, and Centre for the Study of the United States. Grants from the American Council for Learned Societies (ACLS) and the Social Sciences and Humanities Research Council of Canada allowed me time for research and writing and supported major research expenses. My thanks as well to the Department of English for SIG funds, which supported image-research and manuscript-preparation costs. Unless otherwise noted, all biblical quotations are drawn from the *JPS Hebrew-English Tanakh* (Philadelphia, PA: The Jewish Publication Society, 1999).

Courtney Bender, Andrew DuBois, Joel Faflak, Jason Haslam, Pamela Klassen, Greil Marcus, Randall Martin, Katherine Scheil, and Werner Sollors—editors all—helped develop my ideas and sharpen my prose at earlier stages of the project. I am grateful to Columbia University Press, Harvard University Press, and the University of Toronto Press for permission to reprint revised versions of articles, which appeared in their publications. Thanks as well to Sebastian Fabal at the Rodgers & Hammerstein Organization and Troy Schreck at Alfred Publishing; they have always responded quickly and cheerfully to my repeated requests for reprint licenses. Jennifer Hammer's unwavering faith in the project has sustained me through the publishing process. Thanks as well to my copyeditor Mary Sutherland, Despina Papazoglou Gimbel at New York University Press, and Cynthia Crippen for careful indexing.

Generous colleagues read the book at various stages of completion. Elspeth Brown, Natalie Zemon Davis, Paul Franks, Janet Jakobsen, Elizabeth Legge, John Marshall, Richard Rabinowitz, Will Robins, and Sarah Wilson read portions of the manuscript and offered crucial feedback. In her comments on multiple versions of the manuscript, Pamela

Klassen has taught me a great deal about religion and secularism in the United States. I am especially grateful to Neal Dolan, Jonathan Sarna, and Larry Switzky for reading and responding to the final manuscript. Their expertise in the areas of liberalism, Jewish history, and performance theory improved the book enormously. I have also profited from conversations with colleagues, family, and friends over the years that this book was in development. Peter Ackerman, Joyce Antler, Ed Elkin, Robert Gibbs, Louis Kaplan, Mona and Jacques Kornberg, Clea Lewis, Derek Penslar, Anton Piatigorsky, Ava Roth, Melissa Shiff and Anna Shternshis helped me refine my ideas about Jews and popular entertainment.

An extraordinary group of students and research associates assisted me at all stages of the project. Hyun-duk Chung and Nomi Sturm compiled early bibliographies. Ilana Sober and Rachel Adelman helped me make my way through classical Jewish sources on action and acting. Matanya Mali spent months painstakingly locating relevant rabbinic material on Jews and the theater; our sessions on the story of Jacob and Esau reshaped the entire trajectory of the book. A special thanks goes to Alexandra Rahr, who has been instrumental in this project since its inception. As my research assistant for four years, she has spent countless hours in the library unearthing obscure nineteenth century antitheatrical plays, constructing critical histories of major films, checking on footnotes, finding images, securing licensing rights, and offering her insightful suggestions on the many texts in this book. Working with her has been one of the true pleasures of this project. For all credits and copyright notices, please see Credits at the back of this book.

My sister, Jennifer Most Delaney, has been a constant source of support and encouragement, as well as publishing and design advice. My children, Max and Alice, both consummate theatrical liberals, have been an ongoing source of surprise and inspiration. Max used Mel Brooks's *The Two Thousand Year Old Man* as an improbable bedtime lullaby for years while Alice regularly considers dinnertime an opportunity to perform her latest versions of Broadway musical numbers. Without my husband, Alan Ackerman, this book would literally not exist. He taught me a great deal about liberalism, theatricality, and American culture; discussed and debated every stage of the argument with me; read and edited every draft; and supported me in countless ways—both material and spiritual—through the many years this book was in progress. The ideas about action, obligation, and community in this book are deeply rooted in my own childhood experiences. It was my parents, Arnold and Deborah Most, who instilled within me the values of American and Jewish liberalism, and this book is dedicated to them.

Setting the Stage

On Armistice Day, November 11, 1938, Kate Smith introduced a new song, "God Bless America" on her CBS radio program, recorded live at the New York World's Fair. The song was instantly popular. Ms. Smith continued to sing it on every one of her radio broadcasts for the next year; she recorded it with RCA in 1939, the lyrics were introduced into the Congressional Record, and it has long been considered an alternate national anthem.[1] The song remains central to American popular culture today, and experienced a renewed burst of popularity after September 11, 2001, when congressmen, Broadway performers, baseball players, and stock traders all sang the song as a way of asserting their patriotic commitment.[2] "God Bless America" was originally written for the musical revue *Yip, Yip, Yaphank* by Irving Berlin, a Russian Jewish immigrant to America at the turn of the twentieth century, the son of a cantor, and one of the most successful writers of popular theater music in American history.[3] The complete lyrics to the song are as follows:

> While the storm clouds gather
> Far across the sea,
> Let us swear allegiance
> To a land that's free;
> Let us all be grateful
> For a land so fair,
> As we raise our voices
> In a solemn prayer.
>
> God bless America,
> Land that I love,
> Stand beside her and guide her
> Through the night with a light from above.

From the mountains, to the prairies,
To the oceans white with foam,
God bless America,
My home sweet home.

Berlin's choice to become a secular American songwriter rather than a cantor like his father has long been the stuff of American immigrant legend.[4] Indeed, "God Bless America" is one of the songs that has solidified the narrative of the transformation of religious Jew into secular American. But what about those bits about the "solemn prayer" and about God blessing America? How can a song that is a prayer be connected unproblematically with a writer who insisted on a secular identity? Or with a public sphere that is considered secular? What exactly does *secular* mean in this context?

As we can see in the national embrace of "God Bless America" (and of its composer), American popular entertainment forms a central part of established national culture. Songs, plays, and movies express the core values of this culture, through stories that rarely focus directly on God and blessings but rather on the theater itself. In Jewish-created American popular culture, however, the distance between God and the theater is far shorter than one might assume. First- and second-generation American Jews created a popular theatrical realm, one which is commonly understood as secular yet reveals itself on closer examination to be far more Jewish than the word *secular* would indicate. In this world of popular entertainment, Judaic values about freedom, performance, action, and communal obligation exist in productive tension with Protestant liberal ideals. Grounding the history of American popular culture in the multiple religious traditions that informed the worldviews of its practitioners allows us to understand more clearly why Jews were and are so deeply involved in American popular entertainment, how Jews successfully acculturated to America in the twentieth century, and how American liberalism developed and changed in response to the arrival of millions of immigrants from many different religious backgrounds.

Popular scholarly explanations for the persistent relationship between Jews and popular entertainment in America generally argue that the Jews who created Broadway musicals, Hollywood films, superhero comics, or Tin Pan Alley songs were, above all, interested in leaving behind their (or their parents' or grandparents') immigrant roots and traditional religious observance, and assimilating into mainstream American society. The theater and other forms of popular entertainment seem to have offered a clear escape route.[5] In my own work on Broadway musicals, I too have argued that the Jewish creation of popular entertainment offered a way for Jews to acculturate by creating a fantasy America, which was distinctly open to and tolerant of people like themselves. But this fantasy version of America—and the analyses that explicate it—posit the existence of a secular space outside of and untouched by religious ritual and values. This American secular space is seen as a kind of level playing field on which ethnic groups encounter one another and reshape that field to accommodate various forms of difference.[6] This model of an American public sphere fails to take into account the deep-seated religious underpinnings of this form of secularism, the multiple ways in which religious communities express values and beliefs, and the unexpected venues in which those expressions appear.

The terms *religious* and *secular* share a distinct history firmly rooted in the Protestant Reformation and Enlightenment. In the face of advances in science and the rise of liberal political systems in Europe and America in the late nineteenth century, scholars began to describe what became known as the secularization thesis, which argued that with the advent of modernity, the world was becoming less overtly religious.[7] In the past few decades, religious studies scholars have taken issue both with the thesis itself (modern societies have not followed the neat arc defined by the thesis; religious belief and practice has survived and been transformed in the modern age) and with the universalizing assumptions on which the secularization thesis relies. As the scholar of religion Janet R. Jakobsen articulates, secularism cannot be understood as a general category; indeed, she argues, American secularism can be understood only in relation to the Protestant values that shaped so much of U.S. history.[8] Recognizing the Protestant basis for the idea of the universal secular will allow us to distinguish between different responses to Protestantism and different types of secularisms.

This rethinking of the secular is rooted in a reconsideration of the meaning of religion. In his foundational essay, "Religion, Religions,

Religious," Jonathan Z. Smith tracks the use of the term "religion" by explorers and scholars beginning in the sixteenth century, and of the development of the study of "world religions," arguing that the category of religion is "a category imposed from the outside on some aspect of native culture."[9] Tomoko Masuzawa builds on Smith's argument, showing how the notion of religion as a particular aspect of social life, rather than the organizing principle of a civilization, is a uniquely Protestant and modern idea, and the idea of "world religions" is closely linked to the rise of a particular nationalist and imperialist ideology.[10] Robert J. Baird pushes this farther, arguing that "world religions" have long been understood in terms of their resemblance to or difference from Protestantism. Pointing to David Hume's eighteenth-century tract, *The Natural History of Religion,* Baird argues that Hume and other Protestant Enlightenment thinkers grouped together those aspects of a culture's social life that, like Protestantism, emphasized private, individual confessions of faith and called them "religion."[11] Hume was, of course, preceded by John Locke, whose "Letter on Toleration" of 1689 virtually invented the idea of the private sphere by defining religion as an inward matter of faith. Janet Jakobsen and Ann Pellegrini have argued that this new classification system not only created a set of practices called "religions" but also created pressure on non-Protestant groups to reinvent themselves *as* religions in order to achieve rights, freedoms, or social powers.[12] If certain private, individual acts are labeled as religion, then the rest of the culture becomes secular. American secularism therefore is built on a Protestant model, which divides aspects of culture into public and private spheres, and relegates religion to the private sphere.

How does Judaism, which has never neatly conformed to this public-private model, fit into this picture? The contemporary religion scholar Laura Levitt shows how many Jewish communities in Western and Central Europe, which up until emancipation were "self-governing corporate bod[ies]," were transformed in the nineteenth century into collections of voluntary individual adherents to a particular faith:

> What religion offered to Jews in the liberal West was a Protestant version
> of religious community that they could apply to themselves as Jews. . . .
> Although political emancipation was the product of the age of reason,
> the end of the rule of religion, for Jews in the West, this version of the

rule of reason brought with it, ironically, a reaffirmation of religion, and specifically of religion as a kind of faith.[13]

In other words, in order to achieve civil rights, liberalizing Jews redefined themselves as members of a religion, Judaism, which much more closely resembled Protestantism. As Levitt shows, many Jews of Central European descent gladly embraced a new identity in America, which defined them as members of a particular faith, with all the religious and political freedoms granted to such faith groups; the Reform movement modeled many of its practices on mainline American Protestant behaviors. A number of Jewish thinkers in early twentieth-century America were self-consciously critical of Jewish movements built along Protestant lines. Rabbi Israel Friedlaender, an important figure in the early days of the Conservative movement, wrote in 1919:

> It was a fatal mistake of the period of emancipation, a mistake which is the real source of all the subsequent disasters in modern Jewish life, that, in order to facilitate the fight for political equality, Judaism was put forward not as a culture, as the full expression of the inner life of the Jewish people, but as a creed, as the summary of a few abstract articles of faith, similar in character to the religion of the surrounding nations.[14]

Mordecai Kaplan, the founder of the Reconstructionist movement in Judaism, likewise argued in his 1934 manifesto, *Judaism as a Civilization,* that Judaism can survive in the face of science and scepticism only if it re-embraces the concept of Jewishness as a complete way of life, not simply a matter of private faith. Levitt demonstrates how Eastern European Jewish immigrants to America developed not only new religious movements in response to this transformation of Judaism but also a variety of Jewish secularisms.[15] She argues that many Eastern European Jewish immigrants turned to secular Yiddish culture—theater, literature, politics, and art—as a means of achieving the rights and religious freedoms promised by American law while resisting self-definition as a faith group. Some secular Jews likewise turned to Zionism and the Hebrew language for similar reasons. And, of course, some American Jews retained their traditional practices and resisted secularization altogether, while others severed all ties to the Jewish community, intermarried with Christians, and fully assimilated into the mainstream culture.

In Jewish-created popular culture in the non-Jewish public sphere such as the Hollywood films, Broadway plays, and popular novels written by secular American Jews, we find yet another distinctively Jewish response to the pressures of Protestant secularization. These secular Jews can be understood not simply as Jews who have given up religion but as Jews struggling to inhabit a public space shaped by a liberal Protestant conception of faith as an aspect of private life. The quality of this American- and English-language version of Jewish secularization is more elusive than its Yiddish counterpart not only because it is embedded directly within Protestant secular culture, but because it is designed expressly to appeal to members of that culture. At the same time, this form of Jewish secular culture has turned out to be extremely resilient, perhaps because it is so organically American. Although these writers and artists come from a wide variety of Jewish backgrounds, they are united by a liberal Jewish perspective that insists on the potential compatibility of Judaism with American liberalism. Rather than creating alternative secular spaces in which to inhabit a Jewish cosmos, therefore, these artists worked within the existing Protestant secular culture and found ways to reshape it to better reflect their own values, practices, and larger worldview. They wanted to be Americans, so they created works of American popular culture that would allow them to participate in that culture and let them do so on their own terms.[16]

Judaism has always existed for Jews beyond the reaches of the synagogue and organized religious practice, and in the early and mid-twentieth century Judaism continued to shape the worldview of so-called "assimilated" or "secular" Jews, albeit in ways that were not as obviously "religious" or "Jewish" as the observance of holidays or the maintenance of dietary laws. To identify this elusive American Jewish secular culture is not to look for overtly religious or ethnic representations on stage and screen. Rather, this book explores more subtle affinities between Judaism, liberalism, and the theater. The films, plays, and novels discussed here offer complex visions of imagined communities, individual desire, communal responsibility, and sacred space that emerged from the encounter of Judaic and Protestant worldviews that characterized the early- and mid-twentieth-century American Jewish experience.

Furthermore, the Jewish worldview that permeates much of American theatrical culture of the twentieth century reaches far beyond the Jews who created it. Its enormous popularity demonstrates the power of these ideas for many Americans, and shows how religious communities intersect and transform themselves within a pluralist national context. This book focuses specifically on the American Jewish case, and the particular relationship between Jewish-created popular culture and Judaism. But equally fascinating narratives could be told about the Catholic secularism of Irish American drama and the relationship between the Black Baptist church, African cultures, and the development of jazz, ragtime, and tap dancing.[17]

The American literary scholar Sacvan Bercovitch persuasively argued nearly four decades ago in *The Puritan Origins of the American Self* that the apparently secular American public sphere was actually decisively shaped by religious culture, in his view by one particular religious group, Anglo-Protestant Puritans.[18] This book expands on Bercovitch's claim, arguing that other religious groups—in this case, Jews—responded to the Puritan strain inherent in American liberalism in creative and productive ways, bringing their own spiritual and philosophical traditions to the project of developing and expanding the contours of secular liberal society. Puritans were famously anti-theatrical, and the Puritan-inflected liberalism Bercovitch describes is based on the idea of a true self that resides within each of us. The notion of a private essential self inherently deserving of individual rights lies at the core of America's foundational documents—the Declaration of Independence and the Constitution—as well as the many political speeches, Supreme Court decisions, and mass movements that form the established history of American liberalism. But centuries of American literary and popular culture from *The Autobiography of Benjamin Franklin* to *The Great Gatsby* to the films of Woody Allen celebrate a different kind of liberal individual, one who is theatrical, anti-essentialist, mobile, focused on exterior modes of self-presentation, capable of shucking off history and tradition and being repeatedly born anew. Herein lies an apparent paradox: How can a civic culture founded in an anti-theatrical understanding of the self contain and nurture a popular culture that celebrates theatricality? This book unravels that paradox in a journey that takes us from the Hebrew Bible to the eighteenth-century Enlightenment to the

Broadway stages and Hollywood screens of twentieth-century America. This journey raises questions about accepted oppositions such as private and public, religious and secular, interior and exterior, and elite and popular culture. Liberalism encompasses more than legal abstractions and political movements, and is expressed in a surprising variety of arenas. To understand the vibrant force of American liberalism, we will explore the dialectical relationship between its essentialist Protestant roots and the anti-essentialist theatrical impulses that have always been implicit (if generally repressed) in American culture, and which achieved remarkable creative expression in Jewish-created popular culture of the twentieth century.

The Protestant culture Jews encountered in America was not, of course, monolithic. Secular Jewish writers, directors, and performers were in close contact with diverse strains of Protestant thought, which often functioned in direct opposition to one another. Jeffrey Stout in *Democracy and Tradition* notes the competing interests of what he calls orthodox Christians—those whom Bercovitch focussed on whose theology is rooted in the Puritanism of Plymouth Rock—and liberal Protestants, who identify more with the democratic striving for perfection characteristic of Emerson, Whitman, and Dewey. These two types of Protestants express different views of liberalism, which mirror aspects of the essentialist/anti-essentialist paradox. He also identifies a third tradition, blues spirituality, which has its foundations in African American culture and African polytheism, and is far more theatrical in its liberalism than either of the other two. Stout describes the ways in which African Americans and liberal Protestants made common cause in the development of American liberal culture:

> In jazz, rock, and film, as well as in novels, essays, and poems, the spirit of the blues and Emersonian striving for perfection have often reinforced one another, creating a combined cultural force that orthodox Christians have found deeply disturbing but have largely misunderstood as an expression of liberal secularism.[19]

Jewish creators of popular entertainment often operated in similar ways, drawing on aspects of liberal Protestantism and blues spirituality as well as Judaism to create culturally potent forms, which were likewise easily misunderstood by orthodox Christians as expressions of a religiously vacant (and hence debased) liberal secularism. The power of this popular culture resides not in its secular neutrality, however, but in its specific spiritual vision, one that makes use of secular cultural modes to express a morally coherent and passionately felt worldview.[20] First- and second generation American Jewish writers and directors negotiated a position for themselves within and alongside these multiple strains of Protestant American liberalism by reimagining key aspects of traditional Jewish culture as theatrical. In the process, they created a new form of secular Judaism, expressed in a hybrid and enormously successful popular culture, which tapped into the theatricality of American democracy and spoke (and continues to speak) to a broad American public.

Artists of the 1920s, 1930s, and 1940s created compelling images of what it might mean to be a modern liberal American, images that were discussed, debated, rejected, embraced, and transformed throughout the twentieth century. My term for this worldview is *theatrical liberalism*, which combines two complex ideas. The first, "*theatrical*," will be treated in depth in chapter 1. The second, "*liberalism*," is in many ways the subject of the entire book, but its specific use in theatrical liberalism requires some explanation. The liberalism to which I refer is classical liberalism—the set of ideas about individual freedom, capitalism, and representative government that informed the founding of American democracy in the eighteenth century—as opposed to the use of the term *liberal* to mean politically left wing, or a member of the American Democratic Party. This more recent definition of the word "liberal," however, does have an important historical relationship to the development of theatrical liberalism. Indeed, at the same time that theatrical liberalism became synonymous with certain forms of American popular culture, American Jews emerged as a consistently liberal voting bloc, and the epithet "New York Jewish liberal" came to express both a particular political position and a particular kind of popular culture. Classical liberalism, however, refers to a complete system of political, economic, and metaphysical concerns. Theatrical liberalism largely focuses on philosophical questions about the nature of the self and community, and spends less energy on debates about governing structures, law, or free markets, although these issues do arise in individual plays and films via the metaphor of the theatrical community.

Jewish writers and directors of popular culture wrestled with the challenges of constructing a modern liberal Jewish self and imagining a society in which such selves could reach their fullest potential. They probed the boundaries of both Judaism and liberalism to figure out what liberty might mean for a Jew: How free were Jews to fashion selves while remaining within the parameters of an ethical and spiritual tradition that placed limits on individual freedom? Their works raised questions about whether Jewish men and women were equally free to fashion selves, and they explored the ways in which the particular structure of Jewish families and communities shaped possibilities for self-fashioning. Engaging with ideas drawn from Protestant liberalism, Judaism, and acting theory, these writers and directors wondered about the source of the self, which is, after all, the basis for a doctrine of natural rights. Is it a gift from God, a product of race, or history? Or is it defined by one's actions in the world? Similarly, their works questioned whether identity is private or public, unified or multiple, shifting or stable. Making use of theatrical metaphors, they vigorously debated the role of a liberal individual in relation to his or her community. In a world that privileged individual rights over the obligations that form the core of Jewish practice, what would keep liberal Jews bound to one another, if anything? Is liberal individualism morally defensible in Jewish terms?

Hundreds of American plays and films written and directed by Jews in the early twentieth century find common ground in their shared responses to these questions. Four key features distinguish works of theatrical liberalism from other works of American popular culture. First, these works reconstruct the theater as a sacred space, a venue for religious expression, and the performance of acts of devotion, thereby turning theatricality into a respectable cultural mode. All the works discussed in this book are, to a greater or lesser extent, about the theater and the performance of identity. Most are explicitly meta-theatrical, and many are part of a new genre invented to express the worldview of theatrical liberalism—the backstage musical (or backstage play)—which combines the conventions of romantic comedy with the drama of putting on a show. This form offers the ideal structure in which to consider questions of individual choice, self-fashioning, and communal obligation. Second, in celebrating theatricality, these plays and films privilege a particularly Jewish attitude toward action and acting in the world, stressing the external over the internal, public over private. Third, these works strenuously resist essentialized identity categories, promoting a particular kind of individual freedom based on self-fashioning. Theatrical liberalism guaranteed secular Jews the freedom to perform the self, a freedom cherished by a people so often denied the right to self-definition, whether by Christian dogma or racial science. And fourth, that individual freedom is circumscribed by a set of incontrovertible obligations to the theatrical community. In these plays and movies, there is a palpable tension between the liberal rhetoric of rights and the Judaic rhetoric of obligation (*mitzvot*), and the moral weight of these stories turns on the fulfilling of theatrical obligations, even at the expense of individual rights. And while these shows embrace the commercial demands of the free market—indeed their success is most often judged on the basis of their popularity—when theatrical obligations come into conflict with the logic of the marketplace, the obligations take priority. "The show must go on" was the new dogma of the theatrical liberal.[21]

What exactly constitutes a Jewish artist? I focus on those writers with a clear connection to Judaism, through their own education, contact with the Jewish *habitus,* and belief systems of parents or grandparents, or through otherwise living in close enough proximity to a traditional Jewish community to have absorbed clear messages about what constitutes Jewish values and practices.[22] These writers and artists emerged from many different types of Jewish communities. A majority of those who achieved success in the first few decades of the twentieth century were second-generation descendants of Central European Jews: Edna Ferber, George S. Kaufman, Jerome Kern, Oscar Hammerstein, Richard Rodgers, and Lorenz Hart. By the 1920s, 1930s, and 1940s many American-born Jews of Eastern European descent, such as Irving Berlin, Arthur Miller, Leonard Bernstein, and Jerome Robbins, as well as a number of assimilated German Jews like Ernst Lubitsch and Kurt Weill, had entered the sphere of American popular culture as well. But the evidence for Jewish sensibility lies more directly in the texts than in the biographies of the writers. In the texts, the distinctions one would expect of Jews from different geographical and class backgrounds break down in favor of a remarkably coherent set of distinctively American

Jewish cultural ideas. As these cultural ideas became part of the popular culture, they took on a life of their own. I am not arguing for an exclusive claim to theatricality on the part of these Jewish writers and directors; rather, I highlight the affinity between theatricality and certain aspects of Judaism as at least a partial explanation of the Jewish attraction to and success in American popular entertainment. These Judaically inflected ideas are by no means the exclusive property of Jews, and many were later adopted by those with no particular connection to traditional Jewish life.

Theatrical Liberalism begins with a discussion of two key topics, which form the theoretical underpinnings for the book: theater and theatricality. The primary text of chapter 1 is the dramatic narrative in Genesis of Jacob pretending to be his twin brother Esau in order to gain Esau's birthright and his father's blessing. This glance backward at a biblical story may seem surprising in a book devoted to exploring twentieth-century American popular culture. But centuries of commentaries on this ancient story of performance reveal an ongoing discussion about the ways in which Jewish selves are—and ought to be—formed and performed. In chapter 2 we follow the birth and flowering of theatrical liberalism in early twentieth-century America, examining in detail its major ideological and dramaturgical features in a wide variety of films, plays, and other popular entertainment of the 1920s, 1930s, and 1940s and beyond. In the wake of the Great Depression, World War II, the Holocaust and the post-war Red Scare, many artists began to raise questions about the morality and efficacy of theatrical liberalism. Chapter 3 examines the expression of this ambivalence in works that critique and reconfigure the backstage musical and romantic comedy—and the acting style that supported them—as inherently false and naïve. Rodgers and Hart's modernist musical *Pal Joey*, Arthur Miller's "tragedy for the common man" *Death of a Salesman*, and Bernstein, Laurents, and Sondheim's adaptation of a Shakespearean tragedy, *West Side Story*, all express deep disillusion with the values of theatrical liberalism.

In the late 1950s and early 1960s, the values of theatrical liberalism caught the imagination of Jewish social scientists, who found it useful for explaining everyday behavior. At the same time, a newly emerging Jewish ethnic pride led to a celebration of "authentic" Jewishness in popular culture. Chapter 4 explores the tension between these two impulses in the work of Erving Goffman, Sid Caesar's early television sketches, and the musicals *My Fair Lady, Funny Girl,* and *Fiddler on the Roof.* The debates over theatricality and authenticity reached a peak in the later 1960s and 1970s as theatrical activity spilled off of stages and screens, and boundaries between audiences and performers disintegrated. Examining representations of the 1967 march on the Pentagon, the performance theory of Richard Schechner, the film parody *Young Frankenstein* by Mel Brooks, and the essays of Lionel Trilling and Cynthia Ozick, chapter 5 explores how Judaic ideas about idolatry and self-fashioning informed countercultural debates about art, entertainment, and identity. The popular embrace of multiculturalism in the 1980s and 1990s was accompanied by a renewed faith in theatricality, now reimagined as performativity by Jewish scholars such as Judith Butler, Eve Kosofsky Sedgwick, and Marjorie Garber. Chapter 6 constructs a conversation between their academic writing on identity and popular theatrical representations of Jews in multicultural America in works such as Philip Roth's *The Counterlife,* Woody Allen's *Zelig,* and Tony Kushner's *Angels in America.* Long replaced in the popular culture by the secular Judaic values of theatrical liberalism, Judaic texts, rituals, and ideas began to slowly re-emerge into public view at the end of the twentieth century. The book concludes with a brief discussion of the ways in which theatrical liberalism is changing in order to incorporate art and entertainment which once again reimagines the distinction between the religious and the secular in the American public sphere.

1

Jews, Theatricality, and Modernity

It is well known that throughout the twentieth century, American Jews were deeply involved in the creation of American popular entertainment. Never much more than 3 percent of the population, Jews were nonetheless instrumental in the development of the major industries and entertainment forms that provided mass culture to a majority of Americans through much of the twentieth century: Broadway, Hollywood, the television and radio industries, stand-up comedy, and the popular music industry have all been deeply influenced by the activity of Jews. If we look beyond America's shores, we find the same story, although not quite to the same extent, in many centers of European culture.[1] In the modern era, especially in liberal society, Jews were among the foremost practitioners of the modern theater and by the late nineteenth century were explicitly associated both with the theater and with theatricality throughout Europe and North America. This close connection between Jews and entertainment represented a radical departure from traditional Jewish attitudes toward the theater. This chapter explores why, for centuries, Jews were one of the few European cultures without any official public theatrical tradition. We then look at how the particular historical conditions of Jewish modernity in Europe eventually led Jews to become intimately involved with the theater. Finally, we examine the history of interpretation of the biblical story of Jacob and Esau in order to understand the ways in which Jewish thinkers across the ages have responded to the morally ambiguous aspects of theatricality itself, a mode which encompasses both acting on the stage and performance in everyday life.

* * *

For more than 1,500 years, traditional Jewish authorities were notoriously anti-theatrical. In Warsaw, for example, as late as the 1830s local synagogue councils pressured the city's police commissioner to forbid Jews to stage theater performances, arguing that such performances would be "an indecent mockery that leads to demoralization and is strictly forbidden by religious laws."[2] Theater did, nonetheless, achieve a carefully circumscribed place within early modern traditional European Jewish communities, bursting forth on the holiday of Purim, when role-playing, pageantry, costumes, and general hilarity were grudgingly allowed by religious authorities, and in wedding celebrations, where the *badkhn*, or wedding-jester, told stories and jokes, and his accompanying *klezmorim* (minstrels) performed musical numbers for the bride and groom and their guests. Until the mid-nineteenth century, however, aside from the occasional mention of Jewish actors in court theaters (mostly in Italy) and a lively subculture of traveling jesters, musicians, and magicians, nonreligious theatrical activity was almost nonexistent in traditional European Jewish communities. Constrained by a number of factors, including biblical prohibitions against cross-dressing, rabbinic prohibitions against a woman singing (or, by extension, performing) in public, and the general resistance to any form of intellectual or artistic pursuit that fell outside of the study of Torah, public theatrical entertainment unrelated to Purim did not gain a serious foothold in Jewish life until the advent of the modern period and the Haskalah (Jewish Enlightenment).[3]

The rabbis of the Mishna and the Talmud explicitly addressed concerns about the theater in terms of how to regulate Jewish interactions with non-Jews. The theater was assumed to be part of non-Jewish culture, and the rabbis were concerned with delineating how, where, and when Jews were allowed to participate in this often overtly pagan public entertainment. Much of the commentary on the theater, therefore, is located in a tractate of the Talmud devoted to the discussion of idol worship (Masechet Avodah Zera). The Talmud quite clearly forbids Jews from attending the Roman theater for three reasons. First, far from being simply a place of entertainment, the Roman theater was seen as a gateway to a world of idolatrous behavior: the action on the stage might involve human and animal sacrifices, gladiator battles, and actors dressed as gods. The rabbis knew that it was impossible to separate earthly and cosmological concerns in the Roman theater and therefore forbade Jews from participating in, or even watching, these pagan practices.[4] Second, even those theatrical productions that did not involve idol worship were forbidden because they were considered pointless entertainment; it was considered inappropriate for Jews to be seen "sitting with fools" (*moshav leytzim*).[5] Those engaged in frivolity were wasting time that could be spent in studying Torah. Third, the Roman theater involved not just plays and ritual sacrifices but also gladiator shows and other forms of violence. The Talmud explicitly implicates those who watch such bloodshed as being complicit with it.[6]

The level of detail that the rabbis use to explain their prohibitions, however, indicates that Jews were in fact regularly attending the Roman theater. After issuing a blanket prohibition against attending the theater, the Talmud outlines all the different types of theaters, stadiums, and circuses one should avoid, and delineates all the different types of performers who might be considered "frivolous" (such as soothsayers, magicians, clowns, buffoons, actors, and the like), implying close familiarity with a variety of theatrical forms. Indeed, recent archeological evidence not only supports the attendance of Jews at the Roman theater—an inscription in the theater of Miletos, for example, reserves an entire seating area for Jews—but also argues for a Jewish presence in the production of some theater on the basis of a recently identified play from the Hellenistic period titled *Exagogue,* by a Jew named Ezekiel.[7] Hence the need for the prohibition laws. The rabbis also describe a number of loopholes. One might attend the theater, for example, to bear witness to the death of a Jewish man (martyred in the stadium) and thereby prevent his wife from becoming a grass widow (*agunah*), unable to remarry. The Roman theater likewise was one of the few sites where Jews could publicly participate in the political sphere. When the Emperor appeared at the theater, it was not uncommon for members of the populace to demonstrate or present petitions. The rabbis, therefore, acknowledge that one can attend the theater in order to participate in a crowd that "screams" about troubles to the government. And finally, the theaters were important places of business, and Jews were clearly involved in a number of commercial activities surrounding the theater. The rabbis tried to regulate these practices by indicating that one may make money from "frivolity" but not from idolatry. A Jew can, for example, sell concessions at the theater but may *not* be in the business of manufacturing the pedestals for idol worship or ritual garments for the practice of idolatry.

Numerous Talmudic legal codes also made it extremely difficult for Jews in the Roman empire, and later in the lands of Christian Europe, to develop a theatrical tradition of their own. Starting from the biblical injunction: "You shall not copy the practices of the land of Egypt where you dwelt, or of the land of Canaan to which I am taking you; nor shall you follow their laws" (Lev. 18:3), the rabbis of the Talmud denoted a wide variety of prohibited practices, many of which prevented Jews from participating in the theaters of the lands in which they lived or from founding theaters of their own. While some of the commentators see this law as referring to idol worship and the practice of forbidden sexual taboos, others use a "slippery slope" argument, widening the prohibition to encompass daily habits ("*hukot goyim*") that might present a temptation to follow the ways of the non-Jews. An early midrash uses this law not only to forbid Jews from attending the theaters and circuses of non-Jews but also from copying their fashions.[8] Maimonides, one of the most important and respected philosophers in Jewish history and a model for Jewish rationalism in the medieval period, elaborates on the reasons for this ruling, explaining that the *goyim* are not good role models and one should not strive to imitate them. Jews should not desire to wear purple because the *goyim* wear purple, or to dress with weapons in order to look like knights. Jews are supposed to be different, Maimonides insists, so why would one want to copy the hairstyles, fashions, or modes of entertainment of the *goyim*?[9] By the sixteenth century, these interpretations were integrated into the strict legal code of the *Shulchan Aruch*, which forbade particular hairstyles, ways of shaving the head, fashions, and other practices that were considered explicitly non-Jewish. If one were forbidden to dress like the gentiles, it would be difficult to portray a gentile on the stage.[10] Jews were also forbidden to build structures that looked like those used for idol worship because the mere presence of such a building might encourage idolatry. Indeed, the modern Hebrew word for stage, *bamah*, in biblical Hebrew generally referred to an altar used for pagan sacrifices. Theaters and stages were therefore automatically suspect spaces.

The problem of creating a theatrical tradition was further hampered by the laws against cross-dressing and hearing the voice of a woman in public, making it extremely difficult to create a sustainable theatrical tradition if male and female characters cannot be portrayed on the stage together. In many cultures (including that of Elizabethan England), women were banned from acting on the stage, but female roles were still represented—by boys. In the case of traditional European Jewish culture, though, neither option was acceptable. Strict laws of modesty and of separation of the sexes meant that women were not allowed to publicly display themselves in any way. The Talmud assumes that all parts of a woman's body (even her pinky finger) may serve as sexual provocation, and therefore not only should women dress modestly but men should be careful not to look at women who are not their wives. Needless to say, it was therefore impossible for a woman to perform on the stage and abide by Jewish modesty laws. Likewise, women were not and are still not in Orthodox communities allowed to chant prayers or read from the Torah in the presence of men. The voice of a woman (*kol b'ishah*) is considered inherently sexually suggestive and a potentially illicit distraction for men, especially men at prayer. But listening to or looking at women for any kind of pleasure—sexual or aesthetic—is frowned upon in multiple sources, one in *Shulchan Aruch* even insisting that a male should not watch a woman hanging laundry or look at women's clothes (even without a woman in them!) hanging on a laundry line.[11]

But the option of using boys to play female roles is also rendered problematic by traditional Jewish law. The Torah clearly forbids cross-dressing: "A woman must not put on man's apparel, nor shall a man wear woman's clothing; for whoever does these things is abhorrent (*toavat*) to the Lord your God" (Deut. 22:5). Much early rabbinic commentary attempts to explain the strong language of abhorrence in this passage (*toevah* implies an idolatrous act, in this case one with sexual connotations) and deduces that cross-dressing will lead to other sexual sins and thus must be avoided at all cost. The Talmud also explains in detail the kinds of dress that are forbidden for men and women, and extends the prohibition to shaving their hair.[12] Medieval commentators further strengthen the prohibition, expressing concern that dressing as the opposite sex will allow one to infiltrate gender-segregated spaces for the purpose of sexual depravity or that cross-dressing could potentially upend the order of creation. One thirteenth-century Italian rabbi, for example, worries that if a man dresses as a woman, his soul might become confused and in the next life return as a woman, or vice versa.[13]

As we have almost no evidence of theatrical performance in European Jewish communities of the late ancient and medieval period, and therefore no evidence of women performers or boys performing as women, it seems that these prohibitions were both effective and culturally binding, at least in the arena of public performance.

By the early Renaissance, when Purim plays were increasingly gaining in popularity in traditional Jewish circles, the *Shulchan Aruch* loosened the prohibition on cross-dressing somewhat, permitting men and women to wear masks and cross-dress for the purpose of fun on a festive occasion. As long as a clear distinction was maintained between dressing up for "fun" and dressing up for licentious purposes, there was no reason, according to this code of law, to insist on a blanket prohibition against cross-dressing.[14] Purim revelers—all men—enacted the story of Purim by taking on both male and female roles, but men tended to perform female roles in such a way that their maleness was never fully obscured, allowing their everyday clothes and masculine shoes to protrude from the bottom of a dress, or exposing a bit of beard to great comic effect.[15] In this way, they managed to circumvent the law while still gesturing at it. In the eighteenth and early nineteenth centuries, a number of Hasidic scholars began to develop mystical justifications for impersonation along with carefully circumscribed and strategic permission for disguise, imitation, and playacting—but only in the service of spiritual purposes and never simply for the sake of entertainment.[16]

In both Europe and America, the emergence of Jewish culture from this traditional religious context was nearly always accompanied by significant Jewish production of secular theater, and, in particular, plays that explored the ambivalence Jews felt about the shifting identity boundaries characteristic of modern life. In eighteenth-century Berlin, for example, "enlightened" Jewish playwrights (*maskilim*) used characters speaking multiple languages (French, German, Yiddish, Hebrew) to signify particular attitudes toward religious and public life, and to express their support for enlightenment but ambivalence about assimilation.[17] In nineteenth-century Eastern Europe and America, Yiddish-language secular theater, which emerged from the sixteenth- and seventeenth-century tradition of Purim plays but, with the rise of secular Jewish culture expanded to become a full-fledged national theater, was equally obsessed with modernity, religious tradition, and assimilation.

In late nineteenth- and early twentieth-century New York, the Yiddish theater played a role in easing the transition for immigrants from a religious to a secular life: the *rebbes* were replaced by stars and the liturgy by secular melodrama, and Jews who in a previous life might have attended synagogue on Shabbat, now went to the theater. While Jews flocked to the theater on Friday nights, many did not easily make the transition from synagogue to secular entertainment and assuaged their consciences by vociferously condemning the actors on stage for "breaking Shabbes." The early twentieth-century journalist Hutchins Hapgood noted that "[t]he actor who through the exigencies of his role is compelled to appear on Friday night with a cigar in his mouth, is frequently greeted with hisses and strenuous cries of "Shame, shame, smoke on the Sabbath!"[18] On weekends, some theaters offered "semi-sacred" pieces, such as Goldfaden's *Shulamis* and *The Sacrifice of Isaac*, in an attempt to attract more religiously observant customers.[19] Many theaters also offered relevant historical plays during the Jewish holidays, but most of the connections between the plays offered on the Yiddish stage and the traditional liturgy were far more subtle. Plays attempted to fulfill the spiritual needs of the immigrant community in new ways. By providing an outlet for deep emotion (both joy and sorrow), a sense of historical Jewish pride, and an escape from the difficulties of the immigrant experience as well as a medium for moral education and a guide to solving the problems of daily life, the Yiddish plays sustained the immigrants spiritually while helping to transform them psychologically into modern American Jewish citizens.

Indeed, Jewish modernity itself can be understood as a kind of theatrical endeavor. Wherever Jews were forced by historical circumstances to adopt double roles and to use performance as a survival strategy, there we see the twin roots of Jewish modernity and Jewish theatricality. Gershom Sholem, for example, argues that we can locate the beginning of modern Jewish self-consciousness in the experiences of those Spanish Jews of the fifteenth and sixteenth centuries forced to live as Marranos—Christians in public, Jews in private.[20] Arguing that Jewish modernity begins with the Sabbatianism that first took root in the diaspora of Spanish Jews after the expulsion in 1492, Scholem writes: "within the spiritual world of the Sabbatian sects . . . the crisis of faith which overtook the Jewish people as a whole upon its emergence from its medieval

This poster from the Thalia Theater advertises a production of *Di Alraytniks*, a comedy of assimilation, alongside *Exodus from Egypt*, a more religious play. (The Dorot Jewish Division, New York Public Library, Astor Lenox and Tilden Foundations.)

isolation was first anticipated" (84). Sabbatianism sacralized "necessary apostasy"—essentially formalizing in religious terms the paradoxical Marrano condition of believing one thing while practicing another. Scholem sees both historic and metaphorical parallels between Sabbatian split consciousness and the modern sense of self developed by the *maskilim* of Berlin. This distinction between "inner" and "outer" selves was later turned into a more general maxim for Russian Jewish modernization by the poet Judah Leib Gordon when he exhorted his fellow Jews to be a "man abroad and a Jew in your tent."[21] That theatrical sense of playing a role in public increasingly pervaded the writing of modernizing Jews and indeed became its defining feature.

* * *

The doubleness inherent in modern Jewish life laid the groundwork for the emergence of new or dormant Jewish attitudes toward performance and theatricality. The Jewish interpretive tradition has always accommodated a plurality of perspectives; although the dominant strain of interpretation around performance preached a severe anti-theatricality, secondary voices have always existed, which are less absolute in their attitudes. The Jewish embrace of theatricality in the modern era led not only to the development of secular Jewish popular entertainment but also to the recovery of these secondary voices and the development of new interpretations of theatricality in core texts of the Jewish tradition.

Performance, impersonation, and disguise are key elements in many biblical narratives. In order to test his brothers' remorse at selling him into slavery, for example, Joseph stages an elaborate ruse when his brothers come to him as supplicants in Egypt (Gen. 42). Tamar dresses as a prostitute to ensnare Judah (Gen. 38). In a last-ditch effort to reassure himself before war with the Philistines, Saul disguises himself in order to persuade a last remaining seer to tell his fortune (1 Sam. 28:8). David successfully escapes the Philistines by pretending to be a madman (1 Sam. 21:13), and later, when he has become king, David is himself tricked by a theatrical stunt when his advisor Yoav directs a "wise woman" to perform the role of a grieving widow in order to convince David to let his son Absalom return to Jerusalem (2 Sam. 14). The Scroll (or *Megillat*) of Esther, included in the *Ketuvim* ("Writings") in the Hebrew Bible, became the source of the earliest modern Jewish theatrical tradition largely because of its melodramatic story of performance and disguise. King Ahashverus calls upon Vashti, his queen, to dance for him and his courtiers, and she refuses. He deposes her and holds a compulsory beauty contest to select a new queen. Upon entering the palace and being chosen queen, Esther hides her identity as a Jew, withholding this information until the crucial turning point of the plot, when she dramatically reveals her identity and foils the evil designs of the king's courtier, Haman, who wants to kill all the Jews.

But of all the theatrical moments in the Bible, none is more riveting and fraught with moral ambiguity than the story of Jacob. In a tour de force performance, Jacob convinces his father, Isaac, that he is actually his brother Esau, and in consequence receives his father's blessing, inherits the covenant God made with Abraham and Isaac, is renamed Israel, and ultimately becomes the progenitor of the twelve tribes and the father of the Jewish people. The covenant between the Jews and God can, in other words, be traced back to a single successful theatrical performance. Throughout the ages, commentators have worked hard to explain and justify Jacob's personal history and morally ambiguous behavior. Some ancient and medieval interpreters condemned him, seeing the story of his life as retribution for his youthful act of performance;

others excused him, finding fault with those around him instead. In the early modern period, Jacob became an increasingly important figure of analysis, both for Hasidim and for *maskilim*. Jacob's ability to inhabit multiple selves and to play more than one role made him particularly sympathetic for Jews facing the challenges of modernity. By the mid- to late-twentieth century, Jacob became a favorite stand-in for the liberal individual, interpreted by critics as representing both the essential and anti-essential models of self that form the paradox of American liberal individualism.

The story of Jacob and Esau (Gen. 25 and 27) begins with Isaac's wife Rebekah's long-awaited but difficult pregnancy. The babies struggled in her womb, causing her great suffering. Rebekah appealed to God, who told her that two nations were in her womb and that "the older shall serve the younger." Soon after, she gave birth to twins. The firstborn was covered with hair and thus named Esau. The second emerged holding on to the heel of the first and was thus named Jacob. When the boys grew up, Esau became a hunter, a man of the outdoors. Jacob was a quiet man who preferred to stay in the tent. Isaac favored Esau while Rebekah preferred Jacob. One day, Jacob was cooking a stew when Esau returned from the fields. He was very hungry and demanded some of "that red stuff" Jacob was cooking. Jacob bargained with Esau, "First, sell me your birthright." Esau, starving, agreed ("I am at the point of death, so of what use is my birthright to me?"). Esau swore to give Jacob his birthright, showing how little it meant to him, and Jacob then gave Esau stew and bread.

Years later, Isaac's eyes began to fail, and he worried that he might die soon. So he told Esau to take his bow, go into the field, hunt some game, and prepare a stew for him so that he might give him, Esau, his blessing before he died. Rebekah overheard this, and, as soon as Esau left the house, she told Jacob to fetch two goats from the flock so that she could make the stew that Isaac liked, which Jacob would then bring to his father so that Isaac could bless him before he died. Jacob, either intuiting Rebekah's intention or devising his own plan, responded that Esau is hairy and he is smooth-skinned. If his father touches him, won't he know that he isn't Esau and end up in a lot of trouble? Rebekah responded that she would take any curse unto herself, but just obey her. Jacob did what his mother asked. Rebekah then gave Jacob Esau's clothes to wear, put the skins of the goats on his arms and neck so he would feel hairy, and gave him the stew to take to Isaac.

Jacob, dressed as Esau, approached his father Isaac, who asked "which of my sons are you?" Jacob responded that he was Esau, the firstborn. Isaac seemed suspicious and asked him how he managed to succeed so quickly at hunting an animal and making a stew. Jacob responded that God gave him good luck. Isaac asked him to come closer, so he could feel whether or not this boy was really Esau. Jacob did so, and as Isaac touched him, he said, "The voice is the voice of Jacob, yet the hands are the hands of Esau." After a few more hesitations and questions, Isaac was apparently convinced and gave the blessing to Jacob. Jacob left his father's room and some time later Esau burst in with a stew and offered it to his father in exchange for a blessing. Confused, Isaac asked, "who are you?" Esau replied that he was, of course, Esau, at which point Isaac began to tremble, asking who it was that he had blessed before. Realizing he had been deceived, Isaac nonetheless insisted that the first "must remain blessed." Esau burst into tears and asked for a second blessing. He received a lesser blessing, and left his father's room, furious and threatening to kill his brother. Rebekah overheard this and sent Jacob away to her brother Laban's house, where Jacob stayed for many years.

This rich narrative offers numerous windows on to the moral status of theatricality in the Torah. The first puzzling moment in the story comes at the beginning, with the naming of the twins. Esau is named for the way he looks—his hairy red mantle, but Jacob is named for the very first action he performs—holding onto his brother's heel as he emerged from the womb. In Hebrew related words share a three letter root. "Jacob" is the Anglicized version of *Yakov*, which contains within it the word for "heel," *ekev*. Why did Jacob hold Esau's heel? Most commentators assume that he was trying, unsuccessfully, to hold Esau back; that from before the moment of birth, Jacob was trying to gain Esau's firstborn status. But if we look at other places in the Bible where the words *Yakov* and *ekev* are used, we find that embedded within the name itself is a commentary not just on Jacob's actions but on his character. The word *ekev* first appears in Genesis 3:15, in the Garden of Eden story in relation to the snake, who is punished for tempting Eve by being forced to slither on the ground and to strike at the heel (*ekev*) of woman. The name *Yakov* therefore evokes the duplicitous behavior of the snake. In other places in the Bible, the

root *ekev* indicates overreaching and circumventing, and is often translated as crooked or devious. When Esau discovers what his brother has
done (Gen. 30:36), he cries, "Was he, then, [rightly] named Jacob that he
might supplant me twice?" The word Esau uses to indicate supplant is
yakveini, yet another word built on the same root as *ekev* and *Yakov*. In
Hosea 12:2, the story of Jacob and Esau is retold, and the name *Yakov* is
likewise equated with the notion of supplanting or overcoming: "In the
womb he tried to supplant (*ekev*) his brother." In the book of Jeremiah,
the root *ekev* becomes even more problematic. Jeremiah uses the example
of the story of Jacob and Esau to warn the Israelites: "Beware, every man
of his friend! Trust not even a brother! For every brother takes advantage
(*akov yakov*), every friend is base in his dealings" (Jer. 9:3). A few chapters
later, Jeremiah continues in the same vein, arguing that "Most devious
(*akov*) is the heart; it is perverse—who can fathom it?" (Jer. 17:9). Everyone, Jeremiah indicates, will act in a deceitful fashion, just as Jacob did.
Pushing the analogy even further, Jeremiah uses the word *akov*, closely
related to *Yakov*, to mean crooked and devious. Whether Jacob's name led
to his actions or his actions gave him his name, the relationship is clear:
Jacob/*Yakov* is someone who attacks from behind (like the snake at the
heel), circumvents and overreaches, and behaves in a crooked and deceitful fashion.

How strange then that Jacob/*Yakov* should be described in Genesis
25:27 as an *ish tam,* which can be best translated as a straightforward or
innocent man, a man of integrity! The Jewish Publication Society (JPS)
Hebrew Bible translates this line: "Jacob was a mild man who stayed in
camp" but the word *tam* carries multiple meanings. Only a few chapters
earlier Abimelech uses this same word to successfully defend himself
against charges of adultery: "When I did this, my heart was blameless
(*tam*) and my hands were clean" (Gen. 20:5). How is it possible to be
both *tam* and *Yakov*, blameless and devious? Jacob is clearly a complicated character, a man of many faces. A few chapters later, Jacob
receives yet another name. Alone in a camp, he wrestles with a mysteri-
ous being all night. As dawn is breaking, the creature asks Jacob to let
him go. But Jacob answers:

> "I will not let you go, unless you bless me." Said the other, "What is your
> name?" He replied, "Jacob." Said he, "Your name shall no longer be Jacob,

but Israel, for you have striven with beings divine and human and have prevailed." (Gen. 32:24–28)

Jacob yet again receives a blessing, but this time, he wants to be absolutely sure the blessing is meant for him. When the angel asks, "what is your name?" Jacob answers truthfully and straightforwardly.[22] At that point, he receives not only a blessing, but a new name. He is now renamed Israel (*Yisrael*), which literally means "wrestled with God." To receive a new name upon encountering God is already a familiar trope in the Torah. Both Abraham and Sarah were renamed when God affirmed the covenant with them (both received an addition of the letter "hay," a portion of God's name; Abram became Abraham and Sarai became Sarah). But unlike Abraham and Sarah, Jacob's name change is incomplete. He is renamed Israel at this point in the story, but he is referred to interchangeably as Jacob or Israel throughout the rest of the narrative. Jacob retains *both* names, and the multiplicity of character is implied by this. He is a man who both wrestles with God and who achieves his goals through circuitous, possibly even devious paths. He is an *ish tam*, a simple or innocent man, and yet he is also a complex character who wrestles with angels, takes on multiple roles, and still prevails. When Jacob asks the angel his name, the angel replies, "Why do you ask this?" (*lamah zeh tishal?*). Rashi, the most important of medieval commentators, appears to embrace multiplicity, explaining that the angel really means: "We have no permanent name. Our names change according to the service we are commanded to do in the mission upon which we are sent."[23] In acquiring multiple names, then, Jacob becomes like the angels, without a fixed identity, changing his role in response to particular situations or missions. In this case, multiplicity is a feature of those close to divinity.

Many commentators have also wondered why Jacob's performance is so effective. When Jacob enters Isaac's room, he says "Father," and Isaac is immediately suspicious, perhaps because Jacob's voice does not sound exactly like Esau's, perhaps because Isaac cannot believe that Esau could have managed to hunt, kill, and clean an animal, and cook a stew so quickly. Isaac asks which son stands before him and how he managed to succeed so quickly. Jacob has a ready answer to both questions. Lacking sight, Isaac engages his other senses—sound, touch, taste and smell—in order to assess the veracity of Jacob's statements. Isaac asks his son to come closer so he can feel him, to determine if he really is Esau. Isaac marvels at the fact that the son's hands feel like Esau's but the voice sounds like Jacob's. He is not yet convinced, however, and asks again, "Are you really my son Esau?" and then tastes the stew and smells Jacob's clothes. Isaac remarks that "the smell of my son is like the smell of the fields that the Lord has blessed" (Gen. 27:27). This smell finally convinces Isaac and he blesses Jacob. Rashi notes that these "blessed fields" smell like apples and that they therefore refer to the Garden of Eden, that "the fragrance . . . came in with Jacob," implying here that Rashi approves of Jacob's presence in this scene.[24] Then the question arises, how did Jacob, who was, after all, wearing Esau's clothes, end up smelling like the Garden of Eden? And why does this smell convince Isaac to bless him? Pirkei d' Rabbi Eliezer, a ninth-century source, offers a fascinating "backstory" for the clothes that Jacob wears, arguing that they were, indeed, the original clothing that God made from the discarded skin of the snake for Adam and Eve in the Garden of Eden.[25] These clothes were passed from Adam and Eve to Noah, Ham, and Nimrod, ending up briefly with Esau before being given by Rebekah to Jacob for this momentous performance (and later to Joseph, as the multicolored coat).[26] According to Pirkei de Rabbi-Eliezer, it is the scent of this "original clothing" that convinces Isaac. As we have seen, Jacob's name already associates him with the original snake. When he wears the skins fashioned in the Garden of Eden (and possibly derived from the snake) and impersonates his brother, he fully inhabits the seductive, devious, and theatrical identity implied by his name. At the same time, it is the smell of the clothing that convinces Isaac that the son who stands before him deserves a blessing. Did the clothes smell that way when Esau wore them? Or does the smell accompany the "one to be blessed"? It is possible that this smell *reveals* something to Isaac more complex than the identity of the man wearing the clothing. Perhaps Jacob has been transformed by his act of impersonation into a more complex being, a combination of Jacob and Esau, of *Yakov* (with the cunning of the Edenic snake) and "*ish tam,*" a being who is inherently deserving of blessing and capable of fulfilling it.

This may help to explain why, once the truth is revealed, Jacob gets to keep the blessing. When Esau appears and Isaac realizes what he has done, we learn that Isaac is seized by a violent trembling (Gen. 27:33). He then declares: "I blessed him; now he must remain blessed!" If the blessing were meant for someone else, why must Jacob "remain blessed" once Isaac has blessed him? Why does a "false" ritual lead to a "true" blessing? What is the relationship here between performance and reality? For reasons that remain unexplained, Isaac cannot "undo" the blessing, even if it was procured under false pretences. Jacob's performance, even if it was duplicitous, has nonetheless achieved a real change in the world. This story raises the possibility that specific kinds of performance have a reality of their own—that in playing Esau, Jacob actually becomes Esau, at least for the duration of his performance. Commentators struggle with this moment in the text, and sages such as the medieval scholar Ramban (Nachmanides) insist that God was speaking through Isaac when he blessed Jacob. Isaac may have been unconvinced by the performance but unable to speak against God's will, and therefore Jacob's blessing sticks. Others point to the fact that Rebekah had received a prophecy of Jacob's pre-eminence when she was pregnant, and that the performance is necessary to be sure that God's will is done. And still others wonder why human intervention—especially of a duplicitous sort—would have been necessary to achieve God's will. Couldn't God insure that Jacob received the birthright without all of this drama and deception? But perhaps the drama and deception is actually part of the point: perhaps what Jacob receives along with the blessing is knowledge of his own multiplicity, the realization that his role in the great narrative of Jewish history will be a complex one. Performance serves a purpose here. It alters reality: it creates the conditions in which prophecy can be fulfilled, and it transforms a "simple" man into a complex heroic character.

Nonetheless, Jacob did have to lie to secure this blessing, and this lapse is the source of great concern. Did Jacob act correctly or did he sin in participating in this performance? The earliest commentaries and analyses of his actions, found in the Bible itself, unequivocally condemn his actions. If we return to the original story, we find the first mention of performance or deceit in Genesis 27:11–12, where Jacob expresses to Rebekah his concern with the plan: "If my father touches me, I shall appear to him as a trickster and bring upon myself a curse, not a blessing." He is worried about being perceived as a "*mitataya*," translated by the Jewish Publication Society Bible as trickster. This word is used only three other times in the Bible, in each case referring to the mockery of God inherent in idolatry. In Jeremiah 10:15 and 51:18, the prophet says of idols "They are delusion, a work of mockery" (*ta-tu-im*, from the same root as *mi-ta-taya*). In 2 Chronicles 36:16, once again in reference to the prophecy of Jeremiah, the followers of the king Zedekiah are accused of "mocking the messengers of God . . . and taunting (*mi-ta-te-im*) his prophets." Jacob is concerned that he will be seen as one who mocks, or trivializes, those who are true messengers of God, and worse, that being a performer is somehow equivalent to being an idolator. This helps to contextualize Rebekah's response, in which she assuages his fears and assures him that if any curse results from this performance, she will take it upon herself. She knows that Jacob is destined to be the leader of the Jewish people, and therefore, far from mocking God's prophecy, this performance will fulfill it.[27]

Some ancient commentators on this story clearly saw Jacob's performance as deception, a sin for which Jacob was later punished. In Genesis 29, Jacob is in love with Laban's daughter Rachel and works seven years in order to marry her. When he awakes the morning after his wedding, he discovers that he has married Rachel's older sister Leah instead. Jacob confronts Laban about this deception and Laban replies, "It is not the practice in our place to marry off the younger before the older," a comment which many interpret as a rebuke to Jacob for over-reaching his older brother. The early midrashic source *Genesis Rabbah*, for example, expands on this moment:

> After waking up in the morning, and finding he had been deceived [by Leah], he said to her, "Deceiver, daughter of a deceiver! Did I not call you Rachel and you answered me?" She replied, "Is there a master without students? Did your father not call you Esau and you answered him?"

Jacob has, it seems, received his just desserts. Likewise, when he is later deceived by his own children, who tell him that his cherished son Joseph was killed by a wild animal, he also gets a taste of his own medicine.[28]

Talmudic and medieval commentators differ on whether Jacob actually lied; most could not stomach a forefather who was so flawed and found ingenious ways to excuse his actions. One common choice was to demonize Esau in order to emphasize Jacob's righteousness. The ancient rabbis interpreted the struggle between the twins in Rebekah's womb, for example, as a kind of "running": when Rebekah passed by the entrance of a Torah academy, Jacob would run and struggle to come out; when she passed by a temple of idolatry, Esau would do the same (*Gen Rab* 63:6).[29] Others interpreted Esau not only as a trapper of animals but also a deceiver of men. Still others found support in the text for labeling Esau a rapist, a murderer, and an idolator.[30] But while Esau's character may help to explain Jacob's actions, it is not sufficient to excuse them. Rashi, therefore, parsed and punctuated the key sentence in the text where Jacob claims to be Esau in such a way that Jacob was actually telling the truth. When Jacob first enters, Isaac asks, "which of my sons are you?" Jacob responds with three words: *anokhi Esau bechorecha*, generally translated, "I am Esau, your firstborn." Rashi repunctuates the response and fills in missing information: In response to Isaac's question, Jacob responds "*anokhi*," which literally means "I" but is interpreted by Rashi to mean "I am the one who is bringing you your meal." Then Jacob goes on to say "*Esau bechorecha*," which literally means "Esau, your first born," but by Rashi is understood as an explanatory comment: "Esau is your firstborn." Rashi implies that Jacob might have known that Isaac would misunderstand, but he technically did not lie. Another medieval commentator, Ibn Ezra, also offers an interpretation of this line, suggesting that Jacob said "*anokhi*" quietly (so that Isaac couldn't hear him) and the rest loudly.[31] Or Hachaim, a Moroccan kabbalist of the eighteenth century, argues that Jacob *is* Esau, and therefore is not *representing* or *performing* Esau but rather is legally asserting his rights. Because he bought the birthright from Esau, he is the one to be blessed, he *is* "Esau" and therefore is not lying. Furthermore, Or Hachaim insists, Jacob was actually doing only what his mother told him to in dressing up as Esau. He is, in essence, acting admirably by respecting his mother and her position as a prophet.

Hasidic scholars of the eighteenth and nineteenth centuries resisted these technical or grammatical excuses for Jacob's behavior. Instead, they were influenced by the romantic and mystical notion that Jacob could somehow "become" Esau for truly moral reasons. In *Pri Tzadok*, for example, Tzadok HaCohen of Lublin connects Jacob's actions to a mystical notion of "*tikkun olam*" by grounding his commentary in the kabbalistic version of the creation story. In the Lurianic Kabbalah, God creates the world through a series of contractions, which leads to the breaking of God's "vessels of light" and the scattering of holy "sparks" or "shards" throughout the material world and throughout history. *Tikkun,* "the repair of the world," occurs through the collection and reassembly of these sparks, via the practice of ritual commandments and the doing of good deeds. Tzadok HaCohen writes that even in the darkest souls—such as the soul of Esau—there are sparks of God's light. He argues that Jacob, in "becoming" Esau, is doing a heroic deed, entering into the dark self of another in order to collect these sparks. Elsewhere, in commentary on *parashat Rosh Hodesh, Pri Tzadok* seems to make the case that lying itself can be a good thing under the right circumstances. The Torah, he argues, must be accepted in naïveté, but once one studies the Torah closely, one becomes a master of shrewdness, a skill that can be used for good or evil. Rabbi Yisrael of Koznitz, another Hasidic scholar of the late eighteenth century, takes a similar point of view. Instead of Jacob entering into Esau, however, he argues that a part of Esau has entered into Jacob when he buys the birthright, and therefore, once again, Jacob is telling a kind of truth when he claims that he is Esau. In both cases, the scholars acknowledge that Jacob is performing but ascribe to that performance a kind of holy truth.

While some modern and contemporary commentators echo the earlier perspectives, most find Jacob to be a more sympathetic, and even proto-modern figure. Moses Hyamson, an English-born rabbi who taught at the Jewish Theological Seminary in the early twentieth century, seems particularly concerned with the ways in which Jacob's actions are viewed by non-Jews. In *Sabbath and Festival Addresses* (1936), Hyamson asks: "How frequently is the taunt flung in our teeth: Your ancestor Jacob was a cheat?" His sermon aims to show how both Rebekah's and Jacob's motives were pure, even if the performance itself was questionable. Through the ruse of Jacob's disguise, he argues, Rebekah aims to demonstrate to Isaac that he has been mistaken in his estimation of Esau. In this case, while the performance does not exactly justify the ends, it is at least understandable. In his Torah commentary (1974), the Reform rabbi Gunther Plaut focuses more on Isaac, the audience, than on Jacob, the performer. He sees Isaac as a kind of modern spectator, willingly suspending disbelief. Isaac, Plaut claims, wants to be deceived, he wants to think that Jacob is Esau; he wants to be misled. He knows in his heart that Esau cannot carry the burden of the covenant, and therefore Rebekah and Jacob's performance actually proves to be an enormous relief for him, offering him a way out of confronting Esau directly with his shortcomings. The Rabbinical Council of America's (Orthodox) Sermon Manual from 1975 is likewise surprisingly positive about Jacob's performance, arguing that God deliberately gave Jacob good acting skills and cunning in order that he could cope with the shrewdness of Laban, his future father-in-law and furthermore— with both post-Holocaust and Zionist allusions—asserting that Jews have survived by the twin skills of recognizing cunning and practicing it when necessary.[32] Harold Bloom, in his foray into biblical criticism in *The Book of J* (1990), admiringly compares Jacob to an Enlightenment figure: "J's Jacob is a man of feeling, of acute sentimentality, a prophet of sensibility, almost of a sort that would be typical in the eighteenth-century European Enlightenment."[33] In her love of disguise, deception, and theatricality in the Jacob story, Bloom's highly skilled and ironic author-figure J (whom Bloom argues is a woman) compares favorably with Shakespeare: "These greatest of writers are allied in their obsession both with wordplay and with coverings" (ibid., 215).

Jacob is also an enormously useful figure for those interested in reconciling Judaism with the concerns of post-modernism. The philosopher Emanuel Levinas and the literary critic Avivah Zornberg offer extended readings of Jacob's performance, and while they reach different conclusions, they both see this act of performance as central to Jewish ethics. Both critics highlight formerly overlooked commentaries in making their arguments. In his 1964 lecture, "The Temptation of Temptation," Levinas sees the "*temimut,*" or integrity, associated with Jacob (remember Jacob is described as "*ish tam*") as the basis for penetrating to the very heart of Jewish ethics.[34] In his lecture, Levinas reads closely a portion of the Talmudic Tractate Shabbat (88a and 88b), which comments on the revelation at Mount Sinai in Exodus 19, in order to develop an understanding of the relationship between Western philosophy and Judaism (an idea he calls "the temptation of temptation"). The core of the lecture rests on the centrality of *temimut,* the integrity or innocence of Jacob. The temptation of temptation, according to Levinas, describes the condition of Western man, embodied in protagonists such as Ulysses or Don Juan, who are eager to experience everything. In this Western narrative, "one must be rich and a spendthrift and multiple before being essential and one" (ibid., 32). But Levinas is unconvinced of the moral integrity of this privileged philosopher, who "takes risks in security" and is "simultaneously outside everything and participating in everything" (ibid., 34). He sees the Western desire to know before acting, to test the waters before jumping in, as seductive yet problematic. At the same time, he recognizes the problems inherent in naïve or childlike faith, based not in experience but in ignorance. The question he poses is: Is it possible "to escape the temptation of temptation without . . . reverting to childhood. . . ?" (ibid., 36). Is there another opposition to the temptation of temptation that is not simply naïveté?

To answer this question, Levinas turns to the Israelites' acceptance of the Torah on Mount Sinai with the words "*na'aseh v'nishma*" (we will do and we will hear), a phrase that we discuss in detail in chapter 2 when we explore the central role of action in theatrical liberalism. Here it is important only to note the apparently reversed order of the verbs— ought not one to hear what is expected before agreeing to do it? Levinas relates a midrash, which proposes that when God offered the Torah to the Israelites, he held the mountain over them, saying "If you accept the Torah, all is well, if not here will be your grave." Was the Torah offered under threat, then, or was it chosen freely? Levinas insists that the Torah, which invents the notion of free choice, cannot itself have been freely chosen on the basis of available evidence. The acceptance of the Torah therefore must come *before* the possibility of free choice. The action of acceptance (*na'aseh* / we will do) *precedes* the understanding of what one has accepted (*nishma* / we will hear or understand). Only in practicing the commandments of the Torah do the Israelites later come to self-consciously accept it of their own free will (much later, according to the Talmud, during the time of Esther). This counterintuitive integrity, which expresses itself in "doing" before "understanding," begins to gesture at what Levinas means by *temimut*.

Levinas then shows how the Talmud responds to the many critics of the Jews, who argue that the Jews were naïve in accepting the Torah before they knew what was in it. One rabbi observes that in committing themselves to doing before hearing, the Israelites were privy to the secrets of the angels. Far from being naïve, Levinas observes, they were divinely inspired. In another story, a Sadduccee, coming upon a rabbi deep in study, says to him, "You should have listened in order to know whether you were able to accept, and if you were not able to accept, you should not have accepted." The rabbi replies, "It is written about us who walk in integrity (*teimat / temimut*): 'The integrity of the upright guides them' and about those who walk upon tortuous paths, it is written 'the crookedness of the treacherous destroys them'" (Prov. 11:3). What constitutes integrity (*temimut*) here? According to Levinas, here we have the basis for all Jewish ethics, an explanation that brings us back to the paradox of Jacob's dual selves (the *ish tam* and the crooked traitor):

> "We will do and we will hear" does not express the purity of a trusting soul but the structure of a subjectivity clinging to the absolute: the knowledge which takes its distance, the knowledge without faith, is *logically* tortuous; examining prior to adherence . . . is, above all a degeneration of reason, and only as a result of this, the corruption of morality. (ibid., 47–48)

The moment of acceptance, of "we will do," is, for Levinas, the only ethical way of responding to a direct confrontation with another: "To hear a voice speaking to you is *ipso facto* to accept obligation toward the one speaking." The acceptance of obligation precedes any kind of fully conscious understanding of the nature of that obligation. That will come later; indeed all the rest of Jewish history is commentary, discussion, and argument in the service of understanding. But this moment is an absolutely engaged lucidity, a *doing,* a moment of what he calls "angel's knowledge." This innocence without naïveté, uprightness without stupidity, is what Levinas calls *temimut.* And *temimut* is, as he points out, the essence of Jacob. Far from being a contradiction, Levinas shows how the conjunction of "*ish tam*" and "*Yakov*" lies at the heart of what Israel will become: "Jacob, the man of integrity, the most upright of men, *Ish Tam,* is also the man aware of evil, crafty and industrious" (ibid., 48). Jacob is multiple and complex, an *actor.* He possesses multiple names and embodies the kind of integrity that can only come from simultaneously knowing and not-knowing, from innocence that is not naïveté. For Levinas, Jacob's performance as Esau, along with the many other events of his life, offers an example of the only kind of integrity possible in a post-Holocaust, post-modern Jewish ethics. At the same time, Levinas's definition of integrity gets at the heart of American and American Jewish ambivalence regarding theatricality. Americans are constantly experiencing a fall from grace and then regaining their innocence. This innocence, like that attributed to Jacob by Levinas, is an innocence without naïveté, a knowing innocence.

Levinas sees Jacob's *temimut* as a modern, even post-modern form of innocent integrity that allows Jacob not only to engage in a "crafty" performance to gain his father's blessing but also to engender a people able to accept the obligation of Torah before knowing the nature of that obligation. Avivah Zornberg, in *Genesis: The Beginning of Desire* (1995), reads the characterization of Jacob as "*ish tam*" as a kind of non-characterization, a smoothness or innocence that Jacob must leave behind in his proto-modern struggle to define his own identity.[35] For Zornberg, the story of Jacob's performance is one of leaving *temimut* behind, of moving from sincerity to authenticity, a narrative she explicitly links to Lionel Trilling's *Sincerity and Authenticity*.[36] As Zornberg notes, Trilling describes the biblical Abraham as a character about whom we cannot use the word "sincere." For Trilling, "sincerity" is an invention of the early modern period and does not make sense in relation to characters from the ancient world who had little sense of theatricality, of the possibility of multiple selves. Zornberg disagrees. Like Bloom, she sees Jacob as a fundamentally modern character and argues that "*ish tam*" might best be understood as "sincere man." Up until the moment of his impersonation of Esau, Zornberg argues, Jacob has worked to insure a direct correspondence between who he is and who he appears to be (Trilling's definition of sincerity). This helps to explain why Jacob is so worried that his father may consider him a trickster, a dissembler. Referring to the word Jacob uses, *ke-metateia*, which can be interpreted as one who jests about or mocks one's relationship to God, Zornberg argues: "[W]hat Jacob dreads is not being found out, but being perceived by his father as 'one who jests,' as fundamentally unserious about his relation to his father and, essentially, to himself" (Zornberg, 149). In other words, Jacob is concerned about being perceived as insincere (*not* "ish tam") not only in his own being but in his relationship to his father and to God.

Rebekah acknowledges that Jacob's worries are unfounded, however, because, according to Zornberg, the act of impersonation will lead not to insincerity but to a kind of freedom that will allow Jacob to leave behind his sense of himself as an "*ish tam*," a sincere person, and discover instead his true self, to emerge from the experience a more authentic character. Performance, in this reading, creates a moment of liberal freedom in which Jacob can "detach [him]self from imposed conditions, from the roles assigned by birth and social rank," enter the risky world of ambiguity, equivocation, mimicry, and "gain access to a new authenticity of self" (ibid., 154). Zornberg argues that "what happens in the 'action' of the encounter (with Isaac) is that Jacob, as distinct identity, 'simple man,' . . . disappears from the scene. Up to this point, he has been referred to by name, redundantly; now, Jacob becomes a pronoun . . . [This] evokes the disappearance of the old self-constructed Jacob, and the birth of a new hybrid being" (ibid., 171). Embracing Hasidic interpretations of the story, Zornberg insists that Jacob, in many important ways, *becomes* Esau—or some sort of hybrid being, part Esau, part Jacob—when he crosses the threshold into his father's room.[37] To cross the threshold from his mother's world to his father's, like being born, is to enter a space of doubt: "To be born is to leave the simplicity, the 'sincerity,' of life-with-mother and to cross a threshold into a world ruled by 'appearance, art, illusion, optics, necessity of perspective and error'" (Zornberg, *Genesis*, 174).[38] When Jacob re-emerges from his father's room, after receiving the blessing, he is a new person. Zornberg cites Pirkei d'Rabbi Eliezer's description of Jacob at this moment:

> When Jacob left his father's presence, he left adorned like a bridegroom and like a bride in her ornaments. And there descended on him reviving dew from heaven, and his bones were covered with fat; and he, too, became a champion fighter and athlete. (ibid., 178)

The hybridity of impersonation has become naturalized in Jacob's very body (he is both bridegroom and bride). The performance has effected a real change in the world (he becomes fat). In receiving some of Esau's characteristics (the physicality of the hunter or athlete) in conjunction with his own, Jacob exudes "a radiant awareness of new possibilities that spring from deep within the self" (ibid.). Through the impersonation and the blessing, Jacob has "emerge[d] into greater wholeness" and is finally true to himself (ibid., 179).

For Zornberg, performance enables Jacob to discard *temimut* and achieve authenticity. Theatricality here is a tool, a potentially dangerous activity, which allows for the temporary loosening of social conventions ("becoming a pronoun," without a fixed name) in order that Jacob may discover and embrace his true self. Once that true self emerges, Jacob's skills at impersonation and powers of theatricality are no longer necessary and hence are discarded, like the *temimut*, in favor of a more authentic mode of being. Authenticity trumps theatricality. Zornberg's idea of *temimut* contrasts sharply with Levinas's (and with Trilling's, who is deeply suspicious of authenticity). Although Jacob does indeed "become a pronoun" during the scene of impersonation, it is important to note that he ultimately regains his name following the scene and retains it even when he receives new names. His authenticity is, perhaps paradoxically, multiple and complex. In many ways, then, the Jacob who emerges bears more resemblance to Levinas's definition of integrity / *temimut* (innocence without naïveté) than Zornberg's authenticity.

But the point here is not to decide in favor of one interpretation or another but to notice the tension between them. Levinas celebrates Jacob's performance *as* integrity, as a symbol of the conjunction of engaged action *and* wise innocence that will come to characterize the Jewish relationship to Torah. Zornberg views performance as a device, a morally suspect but necessary moment of freedom on the route to discovering one's authentic self. These two modern perspectives on the Jacob story take us to the heart of the Jewish liberal debate over the moral challenges of constructing a self in a free society. In the eyes of modern commentators, Jacob becomes a model for the shaping of a modern Jewish self, but which Jacob? Both the crafty (but well-intentioned) trickster and the dissembling (but authentic) idolator make regular appearances in works of American Jewish popular entertainment. These two versions of Jacob struggle for dominance in Jewish narratives of theatrical self-making in the twentieth century. The moral status of theatricality and authenticity shift repeatedly over the course of the century, buffeted by historical events, intellectual trends, and the changing position of Jews in American life. Early in the century, however, the model of craftiness combined with integrity that characterizes Levinas's Jacob powerfully takes center stage in the constellation of works that define theatrical liberalism.

2

The Birth of Theatrical Liberalism

There was once a vulgarian who went to the synagogue on one corner of the street when he wanted to weep, and to a bawdyhouse on the other corner when he wanted to be gay. But once, when he wanted both to weep and be gay at the same time, he put up a theatre in the middle of the street that combined synagogue and bawdyhouse into one.[1]

Jewish immigrants to the United States in the late nineteenth and early twentieth centuries landed in urban environments undergoing enormous social and cultural transformation. On the one hand, in the settlement houses, immigrant aid societies, and public schools that immigrants encountered every day, the purveyors of the Social Gospel preached a liberal Protestantism that worked to improve the educational, work, and living conditions of the urban poor and focused attention on a very particular type of assimilation to Protestant American norms. On the other hand (and often in direct opposition to the values of the Social Gospel), powerful mass entertainment industries were just beginning to emerge in vaudeville, motion pictures, and the popular press, ready to sell their products to a population already beginning to embrace what the historian Warren Susman called "the culture of personality."[2] Jews brought to this fertile environment their own particular worldview, a deeply theatrical sense of self, and an intense desire to succeed in the New World. This perfect storm led to the creation of a new form of American culture, that of theatrical liberalism, which combined salient features of Protestantism, liberalism, Judaic rituals and attitudes, and the inherent theatricality of a nation in formation. Characterized by a revolutionary embrace of theatricality as a viable social mode, the prioritizing of external action over internal intention, the celebration of self-fashioning as a uniquely American form of freedom, and the construction of a theatrical community based on obligation rather than rights, theatrical liberalism emerged as the hybrid expression of a modern liberal and Jewish worldview.

The Wicked Stage Transformed

One of the most Jewish and most successful theatrical works of the 1920s, *The Jazz Singer*, by Samson Raphaelson, performed on Broadway in 1926 and made into the first "talking picture" starring Al Jolson in 1927, explicitly depicts the theater as the place where religion goes in modern secular America.[3] In this play and film, we encounter Jacob (Jakie) Rabinowitz, the first Jacob of the modern American stage, and one who literally embodies the struggle between the theatricality and authenticity of his biblical forebear. Jakie becomes the American Jack Robin by performing on the vaudeville stage. This causes a rift between him and his immigrant father, an Orthodox cantor on the Lower East Side. Jack tries to convince his father that his choice to be a jazz singer is not so different from being a cantor:

> CANTOR: I taught you to sing to please God, but you sang to please your-self. One minute you were singing in the synagogue and the next minute singing in the street. . . .
>
> JACK: You're right, Papa. I am the same. You did teach me to sing songs of prayer. And I sang them here for you. But when I got out on the street with the other kids, I found myself singing the same songs they sang. And they're very much alike—our songs—and the street songs [*He sings "Ain Kelohenu," a Hebrew prayer tune. And then, suddenly, to exactly the same tune and with exactly the same plaintiveness but with a new rhythm . . . he sings a popular song.*][4]

When asked to replace his father in the synagogue instead of performing on Broadway, however, Jack at first argues for the higher calling of the stage: "Show business is different from anything else," he says, "The finest actors keep right on working, even if there's a death in the family. The show must go on . . . It's like a religion" (ibid., 96). Although Jack does agree to grant his father's wish, it is his ultimate conversion to the stage that is most typical of plays and movies of the time. There is a distinctly religious quality to these secular narratives; the theater is described as an all-consuming passion, a tradition, heritage, and way of life to which its adherents owe undying allegiance. There are countless rituals and myths that shape this religion, and a complex value system that determines the morality of those who operate within it.

We have come to accept this theatrical religion as commonplace, even clichéd. Some might toss it off as yet another example of bowing to the "temple of art." But there is nothing particularly sacred about the *art* here; in fact, the vaudeville show Jack appears in is a distinctly commercial enterprise and even the producer acknowledges that, aside from Jack's powerful rendering of his blackface "mammy" songs, the show isn't much good. But Jack argues not for his individual performance but for the theater itself as a new object of devotion. The religious content in stories about the theater tends to be overlooked or underplayed because the stories are treated as unequivocally secular works of popular culture, not to mention ephemeral, trivial, and undeserving of serious intellectual attention. Furthermore, these early backstage musicals undermined the conventional moral standards of religious Americans of the time—all those scantily clad women, young people leaving their families to go on the stage, showgirls in dubious relationships with wealthy men, actors pretending to be something they are not. Indeed, many battles were fought between self-appointed censors from religious organizations and the producers and writers of these shows and films over the apparently immoral nature of theatricality. But although the battles were often framed as a struggle between moral, religious folk and secular, immoral, and money-hungry businessmen and artists (which, in their ugliest characterizations, were represented simply as a battle of Christians vs. Jews), they may be more productively imagined as a battle between competing worldviews, differing visions of what constitutes religion and its corresponding secular culture.[5]

Christian culture has always regarded the theater with ambivalence. The story of this ambivalence was given historical shape and significance by Jonas Barish, a Jewish intellectual born in the precise time and place (New York City, 1922) when theatrical liberalism began to take shape, in his magisterial exploration of attitudes toward theatricality in European culture, *The Antitheatrical Prejudice*. In a survey spanning thousands of years, Barish shows how Christendom simultaneously embraced and

rejected the promises of the theater, using it for displays of religious pageantry, turning it into a key symbol of religious difference during the
Reformation, and transforming it into a figure for the public sphere in
early modern liberal thought. Anti-theatricality in Western culture can
be traced all the way back to Plato, who was famously hostile to impersonation. As Barish notes, Plato's hostility to the theater became "the cor-
nerstone of an anti-theatrical edifice" that has shown remarkable resil-
ience in two millennia of European culture. While epithets from other art
forms tend to be used in a positive manner (an "epic" struggle, "lyrical"
beauty, a "musical" voice, etc.), he notes that

> terms borrowed from the theater—theatrical, operatic, melodramatic,
> stagey, etc.—tend to be hostile or belittling. And so do a wide range of
> expressions drawn from theatrical activity expressly to convey disap-
> proval: *acting, play acting, playing up to, putting on an act, putting on a
> performance, making a scene, making a spectacle of oneself.*[6]

The Roman Catholic Church for many centuries tolerated theatrical
spectacles that emerged from religious activity (medieval church drama
and passion plays), and the rites of the Church itself were overtly theatrical, performed with elaborate costumes, sets, music, and gestures. With
the rise of Calvinism in the sixteenth century—which explicitly rejected
Catholic theatricality—religiously based anti-theatrical movements
gained momentum in many parts of Western Europe. The legitimization
of the secular Elizabethan stage created a Puritan backlash that ultimately
led to the brief closing of the British theaters in 1642. Like the rabbis we
encountered earlier, Puritan pamphleteers labeled actors hypocrites,
considered the creation of an alternate world on the stage tantamount to
idolatry (competing with God for the gift of creation), fulminated against
cross-dressing on the stage, and generally accused the theater of encouraging lewd and lascivious behavior.[7] According to the Puritan pamphle-
teer William Prynne, God determined the character of each person, and
it would be sinful, and hypocritical, to attempt to alter one's character
through playacting: "He enjoy[n]es all men at all times, *to be such in shew,
as they are in truth: to seeme that outwardly which they are inwardly;* to act
themselves, not others."[8] Absolute sincerity is the mandate of every good
Christian, and the stage was seen as a sinful impediment to that goal.

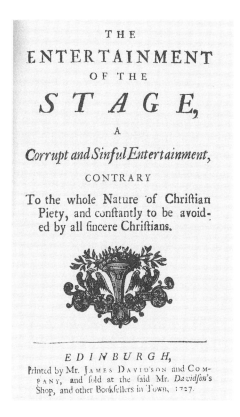

A typical Puritan anti-theatrical tract from G. Anderson, *Mr. Law's Unlawfulness of the Stage Entertainment* (1727). (New York: Garland Publishers, Inc., reprint, 1974).

Lingering Puritanical influence, combined with the fact that the British theater was connected to the monarchy, led to skeptical reactions to theatrical activity in the newly formed American republic. In 1778 the Continental Congress passed an edict condemning the stage and demanding the dismissal of any government official "who shall act, promote, encourage, or attend such plays."[9] Massachusetts banned plays of any kind until 1792, and even supporters of the stage, who prized the democratic social encounters it made possible, condemned the moral laxity of actors and associated the theater with prostitution.[10] Interestingly, from the earliest days of the republic, Jews were deeply involved in defending the American theater. Two early nineteenth-century figures, Mordecai Manuel Noah and Isaac Harby, were influential in the English-language secular theater and in the face of Protestant disapproval, Harby published a "Defence of the Drama" in 1828, which argued for the theater as a civilizing force and a beneficent moral influence.[11]

As the American Republic came of age in the nineteenth century, attitudes towards the theater shifted along with political movements. Democratic politics quickly became (and remain) a remarkably theatrical enterprise, as demonstrated both in Washington, D.C. in the rags-to-riches autobiography of Abraham Lincoln, and in the mid-nineteenth-century theaters themselves, as demonstrated in the meteoric rise of actors like Edwin Forrest, whose nationalist sentiments provoked the infamous Astor Place Riot.[12] The American ideology of socioeconomic mobility similarly led in the nineteenth century to an exploration of the theatrical skills necessary to fashion a new, upwardly mobile self, talents celebrated in P. T. Barnum's autobiography but treated with more suspicion in Herman Melville's 1857 cautionary tale, *The Confidence Man*. Coined in the United States in 1849, the "confidence man" served as a symbol of the instability inherent in a new meritocratic democracy and came to stand for the anxieties caused by a culture obsessed with self-fashioning. As Melville shows, in a nation that favored mobility and welcomed immigrants, one could never be sure what class people came from, who their families were, and if they were to be trusted. P. T. Barnum's *Autobiography,* published in 1854, which explained with pride his personal success at conning the public, was coolly received by most readers, and Mark Twain was similarly ambivalent about the colorful con men he depicts in *Huckleberry Finn* (1885).[13] Actors, often seen as a particular breed of con man, received suspicious treatment in nineteenth-century American fiction such as *Franklin Evans* by Walt Whitman, a temperance novel in which theater, actresses, and alcohol work together to destroy the moral fiber of the central character.[14] The dangers of the stage for young women were particularly stressed in these stories. *Little Women,* by Louisa May Alcott, describes the sisters' experience with parlor theatricals with cautionary suspicion, and her novel *Work: A Story of Experience,* contains an extended section in which the central character, Christie, goes on the stage and is changed for the worse by the experience. Anna Cora Mowatt's *Autobiography of an Actress; or, Eight Years on the Stage* likewise deals with the dangers the stage poses to a young woman.[15]

American high society continued to be biased against actors even when other prejudices against the theater began to soften. While high society theater audiences often enjoyed stage spectacles, they rarely consented to admit professional performers into their ranks. And even though *attending* the theater became more acceptable over the course of the nineteenth century, many of the plays presented ironically warned audiences against the lures of *performing* on the stage. An overview of popular plays and melodramas of the period reveals a persistent sense that performing on the stage is seductive, sinful, and vulgar, and that those who practice the theatrical arts are neither respectable nor trustworthy. The theater is represented in countless nineteenth- and early-twentieth-century plays as an especially dangerous place for young women, whose virtue would be sullied by the very act of appearing on the stage. In the 1906 play *The Chorus Lady*, for example, a pair of sisters narrowly escape moral disaster on the vaudeville stage; the happy ending occurs when both end up back in the safety of a country village.[16] In *Rollo's Wild Oats*, similarly, a young and innocent chorus girl, Goldie, is celebrated when she stops the show and prevents her lover from continuing with his dreams of theatrical success.[17] A holdover from this anti-theatrical style, the early sound film *Applause* (1929) likewise features a down-and-out burlesque actress who saves her daughter from the stage by sending her to a convent.[18]

Jews were often implicated in this anti-theatricality. As Barish argues, anti-Semitism and anti-theatricalism share many common features.[19] The popular anti-Semitic image of the Jew as a diasporic cosmopolitan, one who fits in everywhere but belongs nowhere, led to numerous comparisons between Jews and actors. In *The Gay Science*, Friedrich Nietzsche identifies what he sees as a peculiar and insistent relationship between Jews and performance, claiming that the Jews are "a people possessing the art of adaptability par excellence" and equating acting with the condition of being a Jew: "what good actor today is *not*—a Jew?" he asks.[20] In late eighteenth-century France, the questions of Jewish citizenship and of the rights of actors were debated simultaneously.[21] Jewish rootlessness was likewise conflated with theatricality in European and American novels of the nineteenth and early twentieth centuries (George Eliot's *Daniel Deronda* and Henry James's *The Tragic Muse* are two of the best known), and both were viewed with suspicion by many nineteenth-century dramatists as well. The power of the nineteenth-century theater director to influence actors and audiences was often conflated with anti-Semitic attitudes as well. One example (among many) of this phenomenon is *Trilby,* adapted by the American playwright Paul M. Potter from Du Maurier's novel of the same name. This play centers on the actions of the evil Svengali, a Jewish maestro who snatches a young innocent French girl from her fiancé and forces her, through the powers of hypnosis, to perform as a singer on the stage.[22]

A more ambiguous example is Edmond Rostand's 1897 play *Cyrano de Bergerac,* whose central character is unable to pursue his romantic desires due to the size of his nose. He chooses instead to write and direct romantic scenes for another, vicariously engaging in seduction by becoming a kind of theater director. *Cyrano* opened in the midst of the Dreyfus affair, and Rostand was a vocal supporter of the wrongly accused French-Jewish officer Alfred Dreyfus. While Cyrano is certainly not an explicitly Jewish character, he possesses many features of the theatrical Jew, in this case given a positive spin, perhaps as a means of arguing for the nobility of the spurned Dreyfus. Socially hampered by a large nose, Cyrano writes odes to the lovely Roxanne, but gives them to the more physically appealing musketeer "Christian" to deliver. Cyrano writes Christian's lines, directs him in how to recite them, and at one point even plays the part of Christian himself (under cover of darkness), all in order to vicariously experience the love of Roxanne.[23] Even when embraced by as noble a figure as *Cyrano,* however, theatricality is still suspect and ultimately self-defeating. Neither Cyrano, Roxanne, nor Christian achieve their desires, and Cyrano is able to reveal to Roxanne his true feelings—and himself as the true author of Christian's words—only when he is on the verge of death.

With the entrance en masse of first- and second-generation Jewish writers, directors, and producers into the world of American entertainment, however, attitudes toward the theater and theatricality in America underwent a radical shift. Theatrical life was transformed from the "wicked stage" to a celebrated, respectable, and quintessentially American cultural mode. An enormously successful new form—the backstage drama (or backstage musical)—emerged to articulate this new ethos, and plays about actors, or about putting on a show, became an extremely popular and long-lasting feature of American popular culture.[24] In the musical number "Life Upon the Wicked Stage," from the Hammerstein and Kern operetta *Show Boat,* for example, a showboat actress comically bemoans the fact that the anti-theatrical connection between stage performance and sexual immorality is, alas, mistaken:

> Life upon the wicked stage
> Ain't ever what a girl supposes;
> Stage door Johnnies aren't raging
> Over you with gems and roses.

"The wicked stage," it turns out, is not so wicked after all. Ellie laments that, contrary to what a girl supposes, while one may depict vice in the theater (she tells us later that she can "play a hussy or a paramour"), the actress retains her virtue, much to her chagrin. While life on the stage does not necessarily lead to a better sex life off stage, however, it does offer something else which more than compensates for this lack:

> I admit it's fun to smear my face with paint,
> Causing ev'ryone to think I'm what I ain't,
> And I like to play a demi-mondy role, with soul!

For Ellie, the reward of acting is the soulful pleasure of performance itself. Indeed, she rhymes "role" with "soul," implicitly connecting the internal with the external performance in a way that is typical of the works of theatrical liberalism. At the end of the song, she claims

> If some gentleman would talk with reason
> I would cancel all next season.
> Life upon the wicked stage
> Ain't nothin' for a girl!

But her chorus immediately disputes this, responding, "You'd be back the season after!" The theater may not offer Ellie the life of decadence and glamour she desires and which the nineteenth-century guardians of moral virtue abhorred, but it does offer something even more powerful. The freedom to "cause everyone to think you're what you ain't," is not dispensed with lightly.

While for centuries the theater was seen by most Americans as opposed to the values of good Christians, plays and films of the early twentieth century began to feature positive comparisons between the theater (or "show business") and a moral life. Conversion to the ethos of the stage was a staple of the backstage musical in the 1930s. A typical Warner Brothers musical of the era, *Dames* (1934), for example, features the Puritanical and anti-theatrical Ezra Ounce, who leads a crusade against the very theater in which his nephew and niece are performing, only to be converted to the delights of the stage by the end.[25] In George S. Kaufman and Edna Ferber's comedy *Stage Door* (1936), the central character Terry describes her commitment to the stage: "It was almost a spiritual thing, like being dedicated to the church."[26] Similarly, in both Ben Hecht and Charles MacArthur's movie *Twentieth Century* and Ferber and Kaufman's play *Royal Family*, wavering converts are convinced to return to the stage when given the opportunity to perform in explicitly religious (albeit Christian) passion plays.[27] Richard Rodgers and Lorenz Hart's hit musical *Babes in Arms* (1937) proposes the theater as the route to a more Emersonian-style salvation: putting on a successful show is a sign of self-reliance that will prevent the kids of Seaport, Long Island, from being sent away to a work camp where they will be "public charges."[28]

Show Boat, in all of its various incarnations—the novel by Edna Ferber (1925), the fabulously successful stage musical with music and lyrics by Jerome Kern and Oscar Hammerstein (1927, as well as four Broadway revivals), and the two Hollywood films—retells American history, from the 1870s to the 1920s, as a story about the theater and, in doing so, reinvents theatricality as a respectable mode of American national and spiritual expression.[29] Just as in the backstage film musicals, the story of *Show Boat* foregrounds the battle between the forces of Protestant anti-theatricality and the more liberal, freedom-loving, and tolerant world of stage actors. In Ferber's novel, the mother Parthenia Ann Hawks (Parthy) is described as belonging to "the tribe of Knitting Women; of the Salem Witch Burners; of all fanatics who count nature as an enemy to be suppressed; and in whose veins the wine of life runs vinegar."[30] When presented by her husband, Andy, with the idea of living on a showboat, "the Puritan in her ran rampant. He would disgrace her before the community. He was ruining the life of his child" (ibid., 47). Likewise, in one of Parthy's first scenes in the play, she makes clear her feelings about the theater in a tirade to her husband, now Captain Andy, the director of the showboat:

PARTHY: An' you—you think more of your show boat troupe than you do
of your own daughter's upbringing—Well, thank God, her mother
had a good Christian bringin' up in Massachusetts. Where I come
from, no decent body'd touch this show boat riff-raff with a ten foot
pole—let alone have their daughters mixed up with them.[31]

Parthy makes it clear that despite the fact that the family lives on the
boat, she does not want her daughter becoming an actress: "You stick
to the pianner, young lady—no playactin' for you—." And yet, despite
her apparent reliance on long-established American moral codes, in the
context of *Show Boat,* Parthy's "religion" represents an immoral obsta-
cle not only to the freedom of the characters to live, work, and love as
they choose but to the very liberal ideals on which America is founded.
Parthy's views are mocked in the novel, and she is given no songs in
the musical. Instead, audience/reader sympathy is quickly won by the
theatrical characters, including the two stars in Parthy's own family, her
husband, Captain Andy, and their daughter, Magnolia. It will ultimately
be Captain Andy, a firm believer in the moral and spiritual power of
theatricality, whose values will lead the showboat, Magnolia, and the
nation into a new age.

The end of the 1927 Warner Brothers film version of *The Jazz Singer*
makes a more direct comparison between the theater and the synagogue, and both are acknowledged as spiritually edifying. Furthermore,
the progression from one to the other is represented not as a fall from a
higher moral position but as a natural development of Old World Jewish values. Torn between replacing his father at synagogue on the eve of
Yom Kippur and performing opening night in his first Broadway show,
Jakie finally decides to honor his father and return to the Lower East
Side. He passionately chants the Kol Nidre service as his father dies.
We see the ghost of the father tap Jakie on his shoulder, bestowing a
last paternal blessing on the performing Jacob before departing into the
afterlife. At the same time, Jakie's producer and co-star girlfriend listen
to the service through a window. The girlfriend directly compares his
chanting to his stage performances. The intertitle reads, "a jazz singer—
singing to his God." Jakie sings the final climactic note of Kol Nidre,
and the film cuts immediately to an intertitle that reads, "the season
passes—and time heals—and the show goes on," and then immediately

The ghost of Jakie's father gives him a final blessing as Jakie chants Kol Nidre in
The Jazz Singer.

afterward to Jolson's famous star turn as Jack Robin in blackface singing "Mammy," with his beaming mother in the front row of the audience. "The show goes on" is an ambiguous intertitle here—which show?
Is the synagogue service "going on" in Jakie's plaintive mammy songs?
Or vice versa? Is this a progressive narrative, in which, as in Zornberg's
interpretation of the Jacob story, Jakie's "performance" as an observant
Jew secures his father's blessing and allows him to emerge into his more
authentic self as an American jazz singer? Or does Jakie more directly
resemble Levinas's definition of an *ish tam*? Like his biblical forebear,
does Jacob become a man of integrity through his ability to perform
without naïveté *both* the Kol Nidre (which gains his father's blessing)
and the mammy songs (which gains him his mother's approbation, and
his future as an American)? As the film ends, it becomes clear that in
Raphaelson's America, at least, performance and religion are insepara-
ble. Indeed, the most moral choice for Jakie is to choose both.

Samson Raphaelson was well aware of the radical argument about
religion and performance he was making in the play. In his Preface,
which was reprinted in the program book for the film, he wrote:

In this, my first play, I have tried to crystallize the ironic truth that one of the Americas of 1925—that one which packs to overflowing our cabarets, musical revues, and dance halls—is praying with a fervor as intense as that of the America which goes sedately to church and synagogue. The jazz American is different from the dancing dervish, from the Zulu medicine man, from the negro evangelist only in that he doesn't know he is praying.

Both the exotic practices of the "dancing dervish . . . Zulu medicine man . . . and negro evangelist" and that of "jazz Americans" involve a kind of spirituality that is passionate, emotional, and difficult to contain, aspects of the "blues spirituality" discussed earlier. Raphaelson goes on to make the explicit link to Jews: "Jazz is Irving Berlin, Al Jolson, George Gershwin, Sophie Tucker. These are Jews with their roots in the synagogue. And these are expressing in evangelical terms the nature of our chaos today" (Raphaelson, *Jazz Singer,* 10). In both this preface and in his representation of Jack Robin as a blackface minstrel in the play itself, Raphaelson explicitly defines secular Jewish theatricality as a kind of passionate religious expression, showing how both the audiences and performers of jazz musicals are expressing a religious sensibility which is as fervent as more conventional religious practice ("going sedately to church and synagogue") and more effective in expressing the "chaos" of modern life. Jewish jazz, according to Raphaelson, shatters the rigid boundaries between religious and secular, private and public life: cabarets, musical revues, dance halls, and even, as Raphaelson has Jakie argue, the streets themselves, are the sites of passionate religious practice, if only we could recognize them as such.[32]

In 1936 Warner Brothers produced an eight-minute animated spoof of *The Jazz Singer.* The song "I Love to Singa," on which the cartoon was based, was written by Harold Arlen and Yip Harburg (both Jewish songwriters) for Al Jolson's final starring role with Warner Brothers in the 1936 film *The Singing Kid.* The cartoon features "Owl Jolson," the youngest member of a vaguely German immigrant family of musical owls, who has been banished from his home because he insists on singing jazz music rather than the classical music that his father ("Fritz Owl") reveres and at which his siblings excel (they emerge from their eggs as fully formed opera, violin, and flute virtuosos). Dejected and

"Owl Jolson" receives first prize from "Jack Bunny" as his family proudly looks on in *I Love to Singa.*

alone, Owl ends up auditioning for a radio talent show (hosted by "Jack Bunny") with his infectious rendition of "I Love to Singa." His bereft mother hears him on the radio and immediately tows the rest of the family down to the radio station, where they arrive just in time to see young Owl win first prize in the talent contest. The formerly strict Old World father is completely won over by Owl's delightful performance, and the cartoon ends with the whole family reunited and happily dancing and singing in a vaudeville-style rendition of the title song.[33] The cartoon indicates not just how popular and well-known *The Jazz Singer* was in the 1930s, but also how the conflict between theater and religion at the heart of that story had been resolved in a few short years. No longer is "Owl Jolson" faced with a choice between the two: unlike in *The Jazz Singer*, in which Cantor Rabinowitz must die before Jakie can move into the secular world of the theater, in this rendition, the whole family is happily converted to the world of the stage. By 1936 the battle had been won; theater represented the new sacred arena of American popular culture.

Action and Acting

In the opening scene of the Hecht/MacArthur film *Twentieth Century*, the star director Oscar Jaffe (John Barrymore) teaches a lingerie model, Lily Garland (née Mildred Plotka, and played by Carole Lombard, née Jane Alice Peters) to act. The process is slow, methodical, and painful. First, she must learn to enter a room with the proper bearing and composure. She must speak with the right accent and tone. Then she must walk across the stage in the correct manner and stop in a particular place before speaking her next line. Lily has difficulty remembering when and where to walk and to speak, and so Jaffe demands chalk and begins to draw lines on the stage indicating exactly where she should be at each moment in the play. Toward the end of the scene, a shot from above reveals a stage completely covered by white chalk lines. Lily must also learn how to scream in agony when her character learns that her lover is dead. She can't do it. Finally, Jaffe helps her along by sticking a pin into her backside at the appropriate moment. It works, Lily screams convincingly, and she is soon on her way to becoming a Broadway star. This method of building character involves little discussion of emotion and certainly no discussion of the actor's own internal psychological motivations. The acting philosophy of *Twentieth Century*, which references not only standard popular acting styles of the 1920s and '30s but also specifically the style of the hugely influential director David Belasco, is simple and straightforward: walk here, say this, a little louder, now walk there, look behind you, sit down, moan softly.[34] Do it over and over again until you feel it, understand it, and can convey it to those sitting in the very back row of the balcony.[35]

Glancing through a prayer book in my synagogue one Shabbat morning, I found a set of penciled-in notes, a reminder a congregant, or perhaps a nervous bar mitzvah boy or novice prayer leader had jotted down, indicating how one should recite the *musaf amidah*, the set of prayers that conclude the morning Shabbat service. A paraphrase of the instructions (a set of behaviors, which are regular practice in any traditional synagogue): "Rise. Take three steps forward, then three back. Bow slightly. Sing altogether. Say this part to yourself. Mumble aloud. Repeat. Rise up on toes three times. Bend knees and bow slightly. Say this part only between Sukkot and Passover. Step backwards and for-wards, sway to the right, the left and bow forwards. Sit down." Similarly detailed instructions can be found in the Passover Haggadah: "Distrib-ute pieces of the bottom matzah. Take a piece of matzah and break it into two pieces. Add the bitter herbs, dip it into the charoset, and eat it while reclining to the left." How do you light candles on Hanukkah? First, be sure your head is covered. Put the candles into the menorah from right to left, and light them from left to right, using not a match, but a separate candle, called a shamash. There are two blessings to say each night, and an additional blessing to say on the first night.

This kind of detailed instruction about how to act Jewishly is not lim-ited to rituals related to praying in synagogue and observing holidays. One can find explicit, detailed instructions for daily behaviors of all sorts. How does a Jew wash hands before eating? Use a cup, not the faucet. Pour water on each hand three times, alternating hands each time. Then say the blessing, while drying your hands. If you are washing as part of the Friday evening Shabbat dinner, bless the wine first, then wash, then bless and cut the bread. No one should speak until the bread is blessed, but humming is permitted. An observant Jew can find in the Talmud instruc-tions on just about any action a Jew might do in the course of everyday life, including having sex: "There must be close bodily contact during sex. This means that a husband must not treat his wife in the manner of the Persians, who perform their marital duties in their clothes."[36]

For Oscar Jaffe in *Twentieth Century*, acting in the theater demands, above all, close and careful attention to the details of everyday behavior. So does Judaism. Like the Jewish impresario David Belasco, on whom the character of Oscar Jaffe was based, Jaffe knows that if Lily practices enough, and does so with the proper spirit and attitude, eventually she will be a great actor.[37] For Abraham Joshua Heschel, one of the most important American Jewish theologians of the last century, practicing is also key: "A good person is not he who does the right thing, but he who is in the habit of doing the right thing."[38] Heschel argued for the importance of *acting* Jewishly, even if one doesn't understand exactly why or doesn't feel spiri-tually moved to do so. "Judaism insists upon the deed and hopes for the intention" (ibid., 403). Action is the first step to spiritual illumination, not the last.[39] Inverting a famous line from Proverbs, Heschel insists "The way to pure intention is paved with good deeds." From doing will eventually come understanding: "It is the act that teaches us the meaning of the act" (Heschel, *God in Search of Man*, 404). Acting on the stage and acting Jewishly clearly have many affinities, and this common ground provided a space for secularizing Jews to maintain a familiar stance toward everyday behavior while simultaneously dispensing with the overtly religious rituals that formed obstacles to acculturation to the American way of life. In the self-consciously theatrical world of many early-twentieth-century plays and films, a good performance was the measure of a good actor. What an actor did on the stage is what mattered; what an actor believed—who an actor *really was*—was of little interest.

Theatrical liberalism privileged this external and public version of a self, the acting self. Americans have long wrestled with questions about where the "truth" of a self lies, and while action in the world has often been seen as a sign of good internal character, for most Protestants that internal, private faith is the driving force that animates action (rather than the other way around); faith, and the kinds of character traits that allow for and support Christian faith, determine one's chances of salvation and move one to act morally in the world. This Protestant divide between action in the world and private faith deeply influenced early liberal thinkers and helped shape American attitudes toward freedom of religion. For John Locke, for example, religion was largely a matter of faith, and faith is a private, not a state, matter. Separating church from civil government in this way allowed Locke to argue for civil rights not only for various kinds of Protestants but also for Jews, because a Jew's faith was not—in his liberal philosophy—the concern of the civil sphere. When Jewish thinkers began to engage with liberal ideas, they revealed the ways in which Enlightenment notions of religious toleration imperfectly fit the lives Jews actually lived.

The eighteenth-century Jewish philosopher Moses Mendelssohn responded to Locke by exploring the tension in Judaism between action and faith. In *Jerusalem* (1783), Mendelssohn wrote: "Among all the prescriptions and ordinances of the Mosaic law, there is not a single one which says: *You shall believe or not believe.* They all say: *You shall do or not do.* . . . Nowhere does it say: *Believe, O Israel, and you will be blessed; do not doubt, O Israel, or this or that punishment will befall you.*"[40] Mendelssohn acknowledges that faith is required for one to accept the obligations of a Jewish life, but he points out that professions of faith are not required in and of themselves.[41] He points to the same key defining moment for Judaism that Levinas highlighted in his discussion of Jacob, when Moses, after receiving the Ten Commandments on Mount Sinai, recited them aloud to the assembled Israelites at the foot of the mountain. The people then agreed to the terms of the covenant with God, saying, "*na'aseh v'nishma*," the exact Hebrew translation of which is "we will do and we will hear."[42] This phrase has been the source of centuries of discussion among Jews because of the apparently reversed order of the verbs. Shouldn't we hear first and do afterwards? On the contrary, states Heschel. *Na'aseh v'nishma*, we will do and we will hear, argues for the importance of following laws, of acting, of living a life according to Jewish law, *in order to* learn or "hear" why, in order to develop greater understanding of the divine, and in order to bring the world closer to redemption.[43]

Up until the modern period, to be a Jew therefore was not primarily to profess a particular set of beliefs but to act Jewishly in everything one did, from the foods one ate to the clothes one wore to the ways in which one interacted with other members of the community to the role one took in caring for one's house, crops, livestock, or the earth itself. As Tevye says, in the beginning of *Fiddler on the Roof*, "Here in Anatevka we have traditions for everything, how to eat, how to sleep, even how to wear clothes."[44] Thousands of Jewish immigrants arrived on America's shores with the direct, lived experience of a traditional society deeply concerned with the ethical and spiritual implications of everyday behavior. John Dewey noted in *A Common Faith* (1934) that Jewish immigrants were among the few Americans who, in the early twentieth century, had a self-conscious connection to a religious civilization that permeated all aspects of daily life, and that was not limited to private, interior confessions of faith:

> There are a few persons, especially those brought up in Jewish communities in Russia, who can understand without the use of imagination what a religion means socially when it permeates all the customs and activities of group life. To most of us in the United States such a situation is only a remote historic episode.[45]

Accustomed to a culture which asserted the primacy of ritual and deed over declarations of faith, these immigrants confronted in early twentieth-century America the oppositional force (and seductive energy) of a liberal political and social model that granted them freedom of belief and freedom of speech, but not necessarily the cultural freedom to *act* in accordance with those beliefs. For the most part, no civil law in America circumscribed the practice of Jewish rituals like kashrut, Sabbath observance, or the covering of heads. But the overtly secular, tacitly Protestant cultural and social sphere shaped the contours of modern American life, from the calendar and daily cycle to the proper place and time for religious practice to the forms and content of public education to attitudes toward social life, eating, fashion, relations between the sexes and between parents and children. This transparent overlay of Christian social practice in America made it almost impossible to become fully accepted Americans without giving up public signs of religious difference.[46] Most American Jewish writers and thinkers of this generation departed from traditional Jewish practice, but even the most assimilated of them did not completely embrace a worldview that relegated religious action exclusively to the private sphere.[47] Rather, Jewish writers and performers shaped a new kind of American public sphere, one which relocated the Jewish spiritual obligation to act in the world from an Old World religious context to a legitimately American arena, the world of popular entertainment.

In Jewish-authored plays, films, and novels of the early twentieth century, then, *acting* becomes a central moral and dramatic subject. But not just any kind of acting—this is self-conscious and theatrical acting. There is a strong Jewish tradition of acting with deep self-consciousness: centuries of debates on the how, what, where, when, and why of doing particular actions have kept Jews always aware that the actions they perform are not spontaneous expressions of personal faith (although these actions may inspire this sort of passion) but rather carefully rehearsed rituals laden with historic and symbolic significance.[48] Just as Heschel insists that "we do not have faith because of deeds; we may attain faith through sacred deeds," the plays, films, and novels of theatrical liberalism argue for the power of acting to shape belief and feeling. In Rodgers and Hammerstein's *The King and I,* for example, the female lead, Anna, teaches her son to banish fear by whistling. In the song "Whistle a Happy Tune," the external performance of bravery actually effects an internal change from fear to confidence:

> I whistle a happy tune,
> And every single time
> The happiness in the tune
> Convinces me that I'm
> Not afraid![49]

Show Boat similarly dramatizes the power of acting in one of its opening songs, "Make Believe." Gaylord Ravenal, a dashing gambler, and Magnolia, Andy and Parthy's daughter, have just seen one another on the dock. Magnolia insists they should not be speaking because they have not been introduced. Ravenal, an experienced gambler, is well versed in the theatrical arts. He suggests that they "make believe [they] know each other," arguing in song:

> If the things we dream about
> Don't happen to be so,
> That's just an unimportant technicality.

Ravenal dismisses any anti-theatrical prejudice against playacting as a "technicality" and wholeheartedly engages in a serious game of acting. When Magnolia, eager to be an actress, jumps into the game, he pushes further, suggesting they pretend that they have "fallen in love at first sight." Gaylord sings:

> Only make believe I love you,
> Only make believe that you love me.
> Others find peace of mind in pretending
> Couldn't you? Couldn't I? Couldn't we?

Magnolia responds eagerly and innocently, but she has not yet fully come to understand the power of acting to shape her world. They are, after all, just pretending:

> If we put our thoughts in practice
> We can banish all regret
> Imagining most anything we choose.

> We could make believe I love you,
> We could make believe that you love me.

Magnolia's *interior world* is driving the game (She "put[s] [her] thoughts in practice") and she therefore believes she remains in control. She assumes that *external* acting is far less important than *internal* motivations. The phrase "make believe," however, is a telling one. To act in a play is to "make" a belief that did not previously exist. Acting the part of lovers quickly leads to a change in their thoughts and feelings:

> MAGNOLIA & RAVENAL: Might as well make believe I love you,
> RAVENAL: For to tell the truth, I do . . .
> [*Ravenal reaches up and kisses Magnolia's hand. They stand and gaze at each other.*]

In "make believe," acting creates faith, not the other way around. And in countless similar songs and scenes in backstage musicals, lovers, aspiring performers, eager idealists are encouraged to *act* and from this acting emerge new visions, new love, new worlds.

The climactic scene of act 1 in *Show Boat*, which calls into question the racial identities of the leading man (Steve) and lady (Julie) of the *Cotton Blossom*, also turns on the "truth" of acting, and the power of behavior to shape belief. With the boat docked in Mississippi, near her hometown, Julie is in great danger of having her mixed-race background exposed and, as Steve is white, both risk being arrested for miscegenation. During an afternoon rehearsal, a jealous stagehand sneaks off with Julie's photo and takes it to the sheriff. Soon a company member rushes into the theater to inform everyone that the sheriff is headed their way. Steve and Julie, who are both on stage rehearsing the parts of the romantic leads, spring into action. Steve whips out a pocket knife, seizes Julie's hand, and runs the knife across her finger, drawing blood. He then puts her finger in his mouth and sucks the blood as the rest of the company watches in confusion and horror. The sheriff arrives, and tells Captain Andy he is harboring a case of miscegenation. He exposes Julie as half-black (which comes as a surprise to the white members of the company), and notes she is married to a white man. Steve then steps up and responds:

STEVE: You wouldn't call a man a white man that's got negro blood in him,
would you?

VALLON: No, I wouldn't. Not in Mississippi. One drop of nigger blood
makes you a nigger in these parts . . .

STEVE: Well, I got more than a drop of nigger blood in me, and that's a fact.

VALLON: You ready to swear to that in a court of law?

STEVE: I'll swear to it any place. [*Takes a step forward, one hand out-
stretched*] I'll do more than that. Look at all these folks here. Every
one of them can swear I got nigger blood in me this minute. That's
how white I am.[50]

When questioned, the members of the company swear to the truth
of Steve's claim, and the couple are spared legal action. Drawing on and
critiquing the irrationality of racial laws, the scene offers a stark commentary on the relationship between external action and internal truth.
Julie and Steve both look white and yet one turns out to be "black" and
hence denied rights and privileges in the state of Mississippi.

This determination of racial identity is based not on any external
performance, or even on any obvious physical traits, but on truths
deemed to be deeply embedded within the person, truths of the
"blood" that must be taken on faith since all blood is, of course, red. In
their best (and last) performance on the *Cotton Blossom*, Steve and Julie
decide to act. They literalize, in a visual, dramatic, and self-conscious
way, the faith-based theories about "one drop of blood" by having Steve
ingest Julie's blood, on stage, in front of an audience (a double audience,
since the audience for the play *Show Boat* is also watching). Steve has
done what the laws deny is possible—he has changed his racial identity
through performance and, in so doing, has undermined the very faith
on which the law depended. Now he is "black." Or at least he is black for
now, for as long as he performs this part his fellow company members
can, in good faith, insist that he "has Negro blood in him." The sheriff is
convinced of Steve's blackness; we are not. But it is the audience's belief
system this action is meant to change, not the sheriff's. In externalizing
the process of racial identification, Steve's action is meant to raise questions in the heavily race-influenced minds of 1927 audiences about not
only the folly of racial science but also about the complicated relationship between acting and truth.[51]

Steve (Donald Cook) sucks the blood from Julie (Helen Morgan)'s finger in the 1936 film version of *Show Boat.*

The vaunted power of acting, which is "false," to change reality, which is "true," in 1920s and '30s popular culture led to a great deal of anxiety among cultural critics, and religious and political leaders. Hollywood especially became the target of those who lamented the rising status of acting, which its critics saw as a growing interest in cheap imitation, insincerity, and moral laxity and which was, more often than not, blamed on Jews.[52] In the Warner Brothers musicals produced just before the intervention of the Production Code, we see dramatized the struggle between the theatrical impulses of the Hollywood movie industry and America's anti-theatrical heritage. In films like *Gold Diggers of 1933, Dames,* and *Footlight Parade,* a censor or moral arbiter is at first staunchly opposed to the theater, and then converted to the joys and delights of popular entertainment by the end.[53] While theater itself is wholeheartedly celebrated in the early Warner Brothers musicals, however, a palpable concern remains about the blurry line between acting and deception. This ambivalence is most commonly illustrated by opposing pairs of chorus girls. The wide-eyed innocent, played in most Warner Brothers musicals of the era by Ruby Keeler, just wants to sing and dance. She has not been infected by the phoniness of the stage. She does not dye her hair platinum blonde. In each case, she falls in love with her co-star (Dick Powell) offstage, and the love they sing of onstage is therefore "true." At the same time, the films also feature less wholesome chorus girls who lie and deceive in order to advance their own interests. In *Gold Diggers of 1933,* the chorus girls gleefully gull a pair of uptight Boston Brahmins and while their intentions are good (they are trying to insure Ruby Keeler's character can marry happily), their deceptive methods are depicted as decidedly unsavory. In *Dames,* the chorus girl Mabel tricks the upstanding but gullible Horace into backing a show and then blackmails him mercilessly. And the plot of *Footlight Parade* gleefully unmasks an actress who pretends to be "high-class"; she is ultimately discarded by the leading man in favor of his sincere and faithful secretary. Unlike Ruby Keeler's characters, who remain innocently unaware of the potentially corrupting force of the stage, acting in the theater appears to have infected these girls with phoniness and a tendency to lie and deceive. These films appease their critics by striking a careful balance between the wholesome joys of theatrical entertainment and the potential moral risks of the stage.

The German-Jewish director Ernst Lubitsch, on the other hand, had no such qualms, and his early sound films, perhaps more than any others, secured the position of theatricality in 1930s popular culture. Born the son of a Jewish tailor, Lubitsch began a career on the stage in his teens, receiving his early theatrical training in Max Reinhardt's Deutsches Theater. He worked as an actor in early silent films, often playing Jewish comic stereotypes. The silent films he directed were enormously successful in Germany, and Mary Pickford convinced him to emigrate to America in the 1920s, where he achieved even more remarkable success in Hollywood, directing a steady stream of hits for nearly twenty years. Lubitsch served briefly as head of production at Warner Brothers in the 1920s, where he acquired the rights to *The Jazz Singer.* He found his niche in the emerging Hollywood musical, and became famous for his sophisticated and stylish films. Thriving in this new genre, Lubitsch produced comedies almost exclusively, and the comedy of manners became his greatest success, both critically and at the box office. Made for adults, characterized by skillful implication and elegant sexual wit, these films embodied the ironic and urbane style that became known as the "Lubitsch touch." His style was distinctive and considered "European" or "cosmopolitan" because of his disregard for American sexual mores. But the "Lubitsch touch" is best described as a passionate embrace of acting as the most interesting, most effective, and most ethical way to construct a self. Lubitsch worked with a string of talented writers, nearly all of them Jewish, and together they created an alternate universe in which a particular mode of adroit and self-conscious performance grounds the characters in a moral system that turns a blind eye to sexual impropriety and "minor" breaches of law like stealing or drinking in public—but insists on absolute fidelity to the laws of the stage.[54] Lubitsch was deeply invested in theater and artifice, but his films tended to explore not actors per se but the impact that acting, and the particular theatrical skills actors practice, can have in the social world of the street, the drawing room, and the bedroom. Even in the one film that takes a company of actors as its central characters—*To Be or Not To Be*—the bulk of the story focuses on what happens when those actors make use of their talents in a "real world" situation, when acting is taken as not just an artistic pursuit but as a way of life.

Lubitsch's most brilliant collaborative effort—with Samson Raphaelson, who also wrote *The Jazz Singer*—was *Trouble in Paradise* (1932), which offers an elegant and passionate argument for acting as a higher truth within a most unlikely setting, the shady world of con games and bank robberies. Focusing on the love and career of two con artists, the film demonstrates the seductive power of brilliant acting and critiques those who extol sincerity but ultimately behave hypocritically. The film opens in Venice, with a "Baron" (aka Gaston, Herbert Marshall) and a "Countess" (aka Lily, Miriam Hopkins) at dinner. She convincingly performs the role of an aristocratic lady, but as the scene progresses it becomes clear that neither the Baron nor the Countess are what they seem to be. The Countess receives a phone call from a friend whom she pretends is another aristocrat, but when the film cuts to the person at the other end of the phone line, we see the "Countess's" down-and-out roommate. A robbery is discovered in the hotel, and the Countess informs the Baron that she knows about his illegal activities, that he has stolen the missing wallet from the room down the hall. "Baron," she says, "you are a crook. You robbed the gentleman in 253-5-7- and-9. [Pause.] May I have the salt?" The Baron tells her in return that she is a thief, that she has snatched the stolen money from him. The accusations escalate, becoming increasingly incredible. In the course of their brief encounter, it turns out he has taken her brooch ("one very good stone"), she has taken his watch ("it was five minutes slow but I regulated it for you"), and when he finally reveals that he has stolen her garter without her suspecting it, she leaps on him, shouting "Darling! Tell me all about yourself. Who are you?"

Thus begins a passionate and resilient love affair. They love one another not for their honesty or sincerity but for their ability to trick, deceive, and con. And yet this love is, within the ethical parameters of the world of the film, true love. At the end, after a madcap adventure in which they attempt to con a fabulously wealthy and beautiful heiress, neither is punished for their illegal activities. On the contrary, they are rewarded with a happy ending. The only person ultimately punished is the heiress's banker, who is revealed to have been stealing from her for years. The difference between them? The banker insists on his sincerity and constancy ("I have enjoyed the confidence of this family for more than forty years"). His protestations of virtue make him a hypocrite. Gaston and Lily live in an utterly different moral universe, one in which acting, becoming someone else, is a celebrated life skill. Their crimes are inconsequential as they steal only from very rich people who don't suffer from their losses. The film therefore is not promoting stealing and deception but rather arguing for acting as a higher truth. The self-conscious performance of the crooks leads not only to true love but to a kind of honest passion that sincerity and confidence (which the banker professes) could never achieve. For Lubitsch, and for many other writers of popular theater and film of the time, the truth of a person cannot reside inside: How can one ever know what lies inside? The truth resides in *action;* the only way to judge character is to observe what people *do.* The only way to *be* someone is to *act.*

Performance and Freedom

Stephen Sondheim, Burt Shevelove, and Larry Gelbart's 1962 musical *A Funny Thing Happened on the Way to the Forum* revolves around the efforts of the central character, a Roman slave named Pseudolus (played on Broadway with unmistakably Jewish-inflected comic cadences by Zero Mostel), to obtain his freedom.[55] The Plautus-derived plot of the play follows Pseudolus as he schemes to marry off his young master, Hero, to the girl of his dreams, Philia, and thereby buy his (Pseudolus's)

ticket to freedom. Pseudolus imagines, casts, designs, directs, and performs the madcap theatrical performance that will allow him to achieve
his goal. Early in the show, Pseudolus dreams about achieving his freedom in a duet with Hero titled simply "Free." The song consists of a
series of questions posed by Pseudolus to Hero about the many roles he
could perform if he were free:

> PSEUDOLUS: Can you see me as a Roman with my head unbowed?
>   Sing it good and loud!
> HERO: Free!
> PSEUDOLUS: Like a Roman having rights and like a Roman proud?
>   Can you see me?
> HERO: I can see you.
> PSEUDOLUS: Can you see me, a reformer fighting graft and vice?
>   Sing it soft and nice!
> HERO: Free!
> PSEUDOLUS: Why, I'll be so conscientious that I may vote twice!
>   Can you see me?
>   Can you see me?[56]

How does Pseudolus imagine freedom? He asks, over and over again,
"Can you see me?" As the song develops, the roles Pseudolus will play
when he is "free" pile up: poet, artist, lover, patriarch, citizen, man. For
Pseudolus, freedom *is* performance; to be free is to have the right *to be
seen as*, to play, whatever role he desires. This tendency toward performance is already indicated in his name, which, like that of the biblical Jacob/Yakov contains within it the implication that he is inherently
skilled at lying and deception (Pseudolus literally means "lying one"
or "false one"). At the same time, the song indicates the ways in which
Pseudolus, the undisputed star of the show, is *already* a performer and
therefore already free. Pseudolus, the (Jewish) slave, directs Hero, the
(Roman) master, throughout the play, telling him how to dress, how
to behave, where to look, where to go, how to *act*. In this song about
Pseudolus's freedom, it is Pseudolus who tells Hero how to perform the
word "free": "sing it good and loud," "sing it soft and nice." Pseudolus is
an expert not only on the freedom of performance but on the performance of "free":

PSEUDOLUS: When a Pseudolus can move, the universe shakes,
>   But I'll never move until I'm free.
>   Such a little word, but oh, the difference it makes!
>   I'll be Pseudolus, the founder of a family,
>   I'll be Pseudolus, the pillar of society,
>   I'll be Pseudolus the man, if I can only be—
HERO: Free!
PSEUDOLUS: Sing it!
HERO: Free!
PSEUDOLUS: Spell it!
HERO: F-r- double—
PSEUDOLUS: No, the long way!
HERO: F-r-e-e!
PSEUDOLUS AND HERO: Free! (ibid., 35–36)

Hero, a fine upstanding Roman citizen, does not know how to spell "free" such that it will coordinate with the syncopated beat of the music and give the duet the necessary climactic finish. Pseudolus must direct him; he understands how to perform "free." *Forum* presents us with a comic vision of citizenship in a Republic, which is clearly a thinly veiled version of the American Republic. The song and the play are one big Jewish joke about Jews, the theater, and the broad American audiences for whom this theater is designed. In teaching Hero to perform "free," and thereby to grant him citizenship, Pseudolus is tutoring Hero (and the audience) in a particular worldview that equates theatrical performance with the right to choose one's own identity. The ironic twist here, of course, is that for Hero to speak the word "free" to Pseudolus is also *performative.* A master sets a slave free by *saying* that he is free. When the master Hero sings "free" correctly, he not only gives the slave Pseudolus his citizenship, but he also grants him the right to define himself via theatrical performance.

In *A Funny Thing Happened on the Way to the Forum,* and countless other Jewish-created comedies of the early and mid-twentieth century, theatricality represents the freedom to escape oppression and parochialism by inventing and reinventing the self, and to be judged solely on the quality of one's self-fashioned self-presentation. Theatrical liberalism represented for Jewish writers not only a spiritual calling but also a means by which to model a self, to integrate into American society, to gain the freedoms inherent in social and economic mobility, and to insure the widest possible application of these freedoms for all Americans. In exchange for the long-sought-after rights promised by liberalism, Jews privatized their religion, transforming Judaism from a complete way of life to a private faith, thus transforming themselves into viable citizens of these new republics. But in doing so, a new quandary arose. For centuries, European Jews had married within their own communities and led lives largely separate from their Christian neighbors. Traditional Jews defined themselves as a displaced nation and God's chosen people, carrying out a sacred task until the arrival of the messiah and the long-awaited return to Jerusalem. But as Jews began to leave traditional communities, enter the public sphere of European and American culture, and adopt the dress, habits, and citizenship of mainstream Christian society, this national and religious identity was destabilized and the question of "who is a Jew" became a pressing one both for modernizing Jews and for the Christian societies into which they were integrating. Multiple possibilities for communal self-definition arose: Zionist, socialist, Yiddish secularist, cultural humanist, assimilationist (i.e., French, German, American), and many others.

Anxious about the integration of Jews and Christians in modern metropolises, and the increasing difficulty of distinguishing between assimilated Jews and non-Jews, liberal Christian societies and governments looked for ways both to assimilate Jews and, at the same time, to articulate markers of Jewish difference. By the late nineteenth century, European and American Jews were popularly regarded not as a nation (since national identity conflicted with the project to incorporate Jews as citizens of the United States and other liberal democracies) but as a race.[57] The rise of racial science in America and Europe in the mid-to-late nineteenth century created a hierarchy of peoples (with "white" Anglo-Saxons at the top and "black" Negroes at the bottom), and offered security to those at the "top" of the race-defined ladder made anxious by the instability of identity in liberal cosmopolitan society. The rhetoric of race played a major role in the response to Jewish immigrants in America around the turn of the century. In the heavily racialized American society of the early twentieth century, Jews were labeled Hebrews (or Semites, or sometimes Orientals), a distinct race situated somewhere in the middle of the racial hierarchy, not "white" but also not quite "black," and whose physical, psychological, and intellectual features were assumed to be transmitted genetically. Individual American Jews, whether or not they participated in Jewish religious or communal activities, and whether or not they self-identified as Jews, were considered to be racially marked. In a nation divided by race, racial status played a major role in the distribution of rights and privileges, and race was a central feature of discussions over immigration and citizenship policy.[58] While many Jews at first embraced racial self-definition as a mode of identification that asserted belonging while demanding little in the way of communal or religious obligation, with the rise of nativist immigration policies and American anti-Semitism in the 1920s and 1930s it quickly became clear that "off-white" racial designations (or indeed any labels imposed by outsiders) were dangerous for Jews and could prevent them from achieving full civil rights in America.[59] With the rise of Nazism in the early 1930s, the trap of a race-based identity became horribly apparent.

In response, American Jewish writers and artists utilized non-racial and anti-essentialist models of identity in order to argue forcefully against the snare of racial self-definition. In doing so, they unwittingly drew upon an eighteenth- and nineteenth-century ideal of self-formation initially embraced by German Jews eager to gain political rights. The German Enlightenment produced a new ideal for the rising middle class, a secular and aesthetic mode of self-creation through education known as *bildung*, in which success in social and political life was awarded on the basis of merit and achievement, as opposed to noble birth. As David Sorkin has shown, Jewish emancipation in nineteenth-century Germany was deeply intertwined with this notion of *bildung*, and Jews implicitly accepted a situation in which they would "regenerate" themselves via *bildung*—in other words, educate themselves in Enlightenment values and discard "backward" Jewish practices in exchange for citizenship or at least a measure of civil rights.[60] Understandably eager for emancipation, a generation of German Jews passionately embraced the principles of *bildung*, in effect re-creating themselves as secular, highly educated, cultured members of the German middle class.[61] This embrace of *bildung* became a defining feature of middle- and upper-class Jewish life not only in Germany but in other liberal republics (especially France and England); it eventually made its way to the United States, where Jews quickly became among the most avid consumers and purveyors of higher education and all forms of high culture. With the wholesale adoption of racial science and the rejection of the notion of personal self-formation, the rewards promised by *bildung* turned out to be specious in Germany, but they remained real in the United States, where the Jewish embrace of self-formation was reinforced and encouraged by the ideals of perfection inherent in the Emersonian—and inherently theatrical—strain of liberalism.[62] The model of an American liberal self, which is consciously constructed, proved irresistible to Jews eager to refashion themselves as Americans, and by the mid-twentieth century this notion of self-formation was a defining feature of Jewish success in America. In theatrical liberalism, as in Enlightenment thought, *bildung* is a ticket to freedom: in guaranteeing the agency to *create* the self anew, theatrical liberalism gives actors the ability to escape oppression, to embrace multiplicity, and to determine one's own identity definitions in response to the challenges, threats, and seductions of modern American life.

A remarkable amount of American comedy created by Jews features characters who are running for their lives. These characters escape their enemies and achieve freedom not by outrunning or outshooting their oppressors but by transforming themselves into someone else. The ability to create and re-create a self is fundamental to the freedom of theatrical liberalism, and the late 1920s and 1930s witnessed an explosion of Jewish-created popular performance styles, which celebrated changeability itself. The ethnic comedians of vaudeville, who could adopt a character with the change of a hat, a nose, a feather, or colored face paint were a central feature of high-class Broadway revues of the 1920s and '30s such as the *Ziegfeld Follies* and the *George White Scandals*. In a flash, Eddie Cantor transformed himself from Jewish neurastheniac to Greek cook, to black errand boy, to Indian chief and back again in the play and film *Whoopee* (1928). Fanny Brice was well known for her ability to do "imitations." Willie Howard, in the smash hit Gershwin musical *Girl Crazy,* miraculously transformed himself from Jewish taxi driver, to a woman, to a variety of famous performers (Maurice Chevalier, Al Jolson, etc.) to a western sheriff, to an Indian chief.[63] In Betty Boop (created by the Fleischer Brothers) and Looney Tunes (created by a team of mostly Jewish Warner Brothers artists including Mel Blanc) cartoons, characters regularly changed shape, size, character, gender, costume, and performance style in order to outwit pursuers or seduce lovers. In "A Hare Grows in Manhattan," one of a number of stories of Bugs Bunny's early years, Bugs spends the entire cartoon escaping a pack of enormous dogs on the Lower East Side by putting on various costumes, voices, accents, and characters. Likewise, in explaining the origin of his iconic line, "What's up, Doc?," in yet another animated bio-pic, Bugs Bunny shows how he turned the trope of transformation and escape (from Elmer Fudd) into theatrical gold. Superheroes Superman and Batman, invented by Jewish comic book artists in the 1930s, similarly based their success on their ability to change identity, thereby eluding and ultimately triumphing over their enemies.

Jews were not, of course, alone in turning to the theater as an alternate model for constructing identity in the early twentieth century. Indeed, we see similar impulses among black and Irish Americans, both of whom had a stake in retaining control over their own identity-formation and who used self-fashioning as a way of resisting racialized identity definitions imposed by an unsympathetic majority. This qualification also applies, to a certain extent, to gay men, although the dynamic of self-fashioning is somewhat different as many gay writers and directors were also members of the other groups. During the early and mid-twentieth century, however, it is in Jewish-created American performance that the freedom inherent in self-fashioning is thematized most directly and persistently. There are some clear historical reasons for this. By the early twentieth century, Irish Americans were largely seen as white and were therefore increasingly less concerned with their particular racial position in American society. For African Americans, on the other hand, theatrical self-fashioning offered only limited freedoms, due to the visibility of their difference. Jews could play blacks, but it was much more difficult for blacks to play Jews. Jews occupied a racial space that was in flux and therefore subject to the manipulations of self-invention.[64]

A brilliant argument for the liberating possibilities of theatricality, Ernst Lubitsch's 1942 film *To Be or Not to Be*, tells of the escape of a Polish theater company from the Nazis immediately following the Nazi invasion. The mixed company of Jewish and non-Jewish actors uses every theatrical technique at their disposal to escape the worst threat to Jewish freedom in the modern age while also skewering the intensely anti-theatrical philosophy of the Nazis themselves. The film opens with the startling image of Adolf Hitler walking the streets of Warsaw, only to be revealed, a few minutes later, as a member of the Polish theater company dressed in costume for a production about Nazis, which is about to open on the stage. Before the actor has a chance to play Hitler, the Nazis invade Warsaw, the production is cancelled, and the theater is closed. The actors become involved with a member of the Polish Underground, and use all of their talents to save the Resistance from destruction. In the process, the lead actor (of both the theater company and the film), Joseph Tura, played by the real-life Jewish actor Jack Benny (born Benjamin Kubelsky) impersonates a Nazi SS officer and then a Nazi spy. In the first scene, Tura, dressed in the costume for the cancelled play, momentarily fools the Nazi spy Siletski by playing the role of Colonel Ehrhardt. Tura's broad impersonation ("So they call me Concentration Camp Ehrhardt!") seems dangerously unconvincing until we meet the real Colonel Ehrhardt, who turns out to be as vulgar and oafish as Tura imagined him to be. Tura's ability to so successfully "play" a Nazi clearly undermines Nazi power and raises questions about the purity of Nazi ideology. In the second scene, Tura, now dressed as the recently murdered spy Siletski, enters Nazi headquarters for a meeting with Ehrhardt, only to discover in the waiting room the *real* body of Siletski. In a tight spot, Tura thinks fast and, pulling a fake beard from his pocket, replaces the dead Siletski's real beard with the fake one. When Ehrhardt enters, Tura insists that he is the *real* Siletski, and demonstrates his point by revealing that the dead Siletski is wearing a fake beard. The Nazis are, at this point, totally confused, and Tura goes free. The Nazis' inability to distinguish between reality and performance once again undermines their power, turning them into the straight men for yet another Jewish joke. It also raises questions about Nazi racial ideology—if they can't distinguish the real Siletski from the fake one, how can they possibly distinguish a Jew from an Aryan?

In the final climactic (and complicated) escape scene, the Jewish actor Greenberg recites Shylock's speech from *The Merchant of Venice* ("Hath not a Jew eyes?") before an audience of real and fake Nazis, thereby protecting the members of the resistance in Warsaw and enabling the escape of the entire theater company to England. Filmed in 1941, this final suc-cessful performance is both poignant and powerful. On the one hand, the scene is clearly a fantasy; by 1941 Lubitsch must have known that such a performance would have been unlikely to be rewarded with freedom. On the other hand, the scene expresses Lubitsch's firm belief in the power of theatricality to protect the performer from the entrapment of essential identity and to insure freedom from oppression. In the liberal utopia of *To Be or Not to Be*, even a Jew playing a Jew *in front of Adolf Hitler himself* can escape if he gives a good enough performance. Hitler insisted that biology was destiny; Lubitsch protested that freedom means the right to play whatever role you choose. This kind of utopian vision still seemed possible in 1941 when the extent of Hitler's Final Solution was still largely unknown. Only a year later, this film could never have been made and, as we shall see, in the wake of revelations about the concentration camps, Jewish directors and writers began to seriously question their faith in the powers of theatricality to guarantee freedom.

Just as theatrical liberalism gave Jewish actors the tools to escape Hitler, it also gave American women the tools to escape the sexist con-finement of marriage. In countless comedies of the 1930s, women char-acters are forced to choose between their acting careers and marriage. They decide in favor of the theater every time. These actresses at first yearn to leave the stage for a simple, "normal" life with a husband and children, but they quickly come to realize the risks inherent in this trad-eoff. Marriage would force them not just to leave the stage but to leave behind the freedom to play multiple roles and the right to fashion multi-ple selves, which the stage makes possible. For these women characters, as for their Jewish creators, the freedom theatrical performance offers is priceless. In *Twentieth Century*, for example, the star, Lily, boards a train for New York with a young society gentleman with whom she has been having an affair. She plays at being heartbroken at his departure. As the train pulls out of the station, however, her beau informs her that he is not getting off the train, that he is accompanying her to New York. She panics. George Smith is not only a bore, he does not understand the incredible power and freedom that self-fashioning has given to Lily. She will not give it up. In a fit of anger, he cries "stop acting!" But that is just what she refuses to do. Similarly, in the Ferber and Kaufman play *Stage Door* (1936), Louise, one of the beloved members of the Footlights

Joseph Tura (Jack Benny) pulls Siletski's beard while the Nazi soldiers look on in *To Be or Not to Be.*

Club (an actresses' rooming house) that forms the setting for the play, departs to be married in St. Louis. Her choice is presented as the result of failed talent rather than romantic desire:

> LOUISE: I guess I wasn't *very* swell or I wouldn't be getting mar—[*Catches herself.*]—that is, any girl would be glad to give up the stage to marry a wonderful boy like Bob—. . . Well, if any of you ever come out that way with a show, why it's only a hundred miles from Milwaukee. Don't forget I'll be Mrs. Robert Hendershot by that time, and Wisconsin's perfectly beautiful in the autumn— . . . [*It's no use. She cannot convince even herself, much less the rather embarrassed young people around her.*][65]

When a letter arrives from Louise in the second act, describing married life ("The luncheon was lovely. Everything pink," etc.), the girls are horrified. "Well, I'll never complain again," one actress declares. "This makes my eighteen a week on the radio look pretty wonderful."[66] And indeed, by the third act, Louise is back in New York, happily going on auditions again, eating cheap boardinghouse food, and cherishing her right to act.

Edna Ferber and George S. Kaufman's play *The Royal Family,* (very) loosely based on one of early twentieth-century America's most famous theatrical families, the Barrymores (here called the Cavendishes), likewise centers on the struggles of two female members of the Cavendish clan (Julie and her daughter Gwen) to find romantic love and domestic happiness without sacrificing the freedom the theater insures. The young Gwen wants to marry Perry, a solid Connecticut businessman, but Perry does not understand the world of the stage. He loves Gwen, but he can't imagine life married to an actress:

> PERRY: I'd do anything in the world for you, Gwen. I'd die for you! But I can't be one of those husbands. Hanging around dressing rooms! . . . What am I going to do every night. See the show!
> GWEN: But you wouldn't want me to be one of those wives, would you? Bridge and household and babies!
> PERRY: Well, why not! What's the matter with that![67]

Gwen and Perry do manage to come to an agreement but the arrangement does not last. Gwen's turn as happy wife and doting mother is extremely short-lived.

Julie likewise is tempted by Gil Marshall, an old flame who left years ago and returned home a millionaire. Upon their reunion, he tells Julie that he left her so that she could go ahead and become an actress. And now, he asks, "How about it? Are you happy?" Julie, flustered and exhausted by the swirl of events in her family responds, "Happy! I don't know." But Gil does: "You've had too long to think. It's settled," he insists (ibid.). Gil is ready to take over as long as Julie submits to his static image of her, set up as a lady of luxury "in a country house somewhere." She and Gil plan to be married when her show closes and he completes his world travels. Gil returns in act 3, but he is a little bit too enthusiastic that Julie's play is finally closing:

> GIL: When you finally wired that the end was in sight—that the play was actually closing—do you know what I did? I gave everybody on the place a holiday with double pay. . . .
> JULIE: I'm very—honoured. (ibid., 98)

He then goes on to extol the delights of the "substantial" people he works with: "And you'll meet real people. None of your. . . . Solid! Substantial! The kind that make a country what it is" (ibid., 98). It slowly dawns on Julie that Gil knows nothing of who she is and has no appreciation for her talents. Most importantly, he cannot wait to get her away from the freedom of the stage and trap her into a single identity: as his wife. Julie pulls away from him and gratefully accepts an offer to perform in yet another play. The trap that marriage represents for Julie, Gwen, Louise, or Lily is contrasted with the marvelous freedom of performing on the stage, and marriage—at least the sort of marriage that involves giving up the stage and agreeing to a singular version of the self ("Mrs. Robert Hendershot")—falls short. These plays can be read allegorically as a story about Jewish resistance to essentialization. Standing in for Jewish women *and* men (and adding to a long history of feminization of Jewish men), these actresses refuse to commit themselves to relationships that will shut down their freedom to self-fashion and allow others to define them.

Rights vs. Obligations

By insisting on *actor* as the most liberating of all identities—an identity free of identity—theatrical liberalism created a secular, universal rhetoric that protected Jews' newly acquired and deeply treasured civil rights. At the same time, this kind of rights-based freedom, the individual right to self-fashion, is deeply rooted in Enlightenment liberalism and liberal Protestantism, and differs in important ways from Jewish jurisprudence. Throughout these works of theatrical liberalism, the rhetoric of rights— the right to be oneself, to self-fashion, to take advantage of opportunities and advance to fame and fortune free of interference—is in constant tension with another legal rhetoric, emerging from a different legal culture, the system of *obligation* or what in Hebrew is called a *mitzvah*.[68] In the genre-defining backstage musical film *Gold Diggers of 1933*, produced by Warner Brothers and directed by Mervyn LeRoy, the plot turns on a climactic moment when a show may *not* be able to go on.[69] Barney, the producer (Ned Sparks), is stuck without a leading man and is trying to convince Brad (Dick Powell)—investor, songwriter, and love interest in the film—to take his place. Brad, who has hidden the fact that he comes from a deeply anti-theatrical Boston Brahmin family, is resistant to appearing on stage because he doesn't want his older brother to discover that he has been involved in the theater. The girls in the company, however, think he won't perform because he is hiding from the police:

> BARNEY: [*Forcefully*] You've got to go on in his place!
> BRAD: [*Positively*] I can't do that, Barney. [*All cluster around Brad*]
> BARNEY: What do you mean you can't? The curtain is ready to go up. There's a show going on. Your songs are in it, your girl is in it, your money is in it—you've got to go out and do it.
> BRAD: [*Shaking his head*] There's a reason why—
> BARNEY: There is *no* reason—There can't *be* any reason [*Brad shrugs.*] All right—what is your reason?[70]

Trixie, the straight-talking showgirl (Aline MacMahon), steps in to give Barney a hand, backed up by Polly (Ruby Keeler), another performer and Brad's girlfriend:

> TRIXIE: Listen, I don't care even if you have to go to jail after the performance. You ought to forget about yourself and do it anyway. Do you know what this means—if the show doesn't go on? It means that all those girls in this show—all those poor kids who threw up jobs—and who'll never get other jobs in these times—all those kids been living on nothing—starving themselves these five weeks we've been rehearsing—hoping for this show to go on—and be a success— They're depending on you! You can't let them down—you can't—if you do—God knows what will happen to those girls—They'll have to do things I wouldn't want on *my* conscience. And it'll be on *yours*— You can go out and sing Gordon's part and put this show over—and if you don't—I don't care what the reason is—
> [*Brad looks at Trixie, then at Polly, wavering in his decision.*]
> POLLY: [*Catching his arm*] She's right, Brad, *I* don't care what the reason is.

Finally, Brad is won over:

> BRAD: [*Thoughtfully*] I hadn't thought about it that way. [*He pauses. All look at him hopefully. With sudden decision.*] Yes, of course, I'll do it!
> [*There is a general gasp of delight*] (ibid.)

Brad has every *right* to refuse to go on the stage. But the language by which he is convinced is not that of rights but of obligation. Barney could have given Brad a fiery speech about his right to live up to his potential, to be his own person, to resist the anti-theatrical prejudice of his brother that keeps him from doing what he loves. Instead, he insists that Brad is *obliged* to take on the role. Trixie goes on to argue that the entire company is depending upon him and if he doesn't perform, everyone will suffer. (She also reinforces the notion of the theater as a moral site that keeps sin at bay—if the girls can't act, they will become prostitutes.) But what obliges him? Why is it incumbent upon Brad to save the show? The theatrical community has a complicated relationship to a system of individual rights. Theater is fundamentally a collective practice, and the ultimate source of authority in the theater is the collective itself. In other words, without a number of participants each fulfilling a set of prescribed obligations—producer, director, actors, designers, technicians, house staff, and of course audience—the show cannot proceed, and the entire theatrical system would cease to function. In the unwritten but universally acknowledged laws of the theater, all members of the company are obligated to do what they can to make sure that *the show goes on.*

Although the self-fashioning at the center of theatrical liberalism draws its authority from the American liberal ideology of individual rights, the freedom to shape the self in these plays and movies is embedded within and circumscribed by a set of communitarian obligations that more closely resemble Jewish *mitzvot* (commandments). In twentieth-century America, while the individual freedom to perform (and, if one is very talented and lucky, to become a star) is central to the ethos of theatrical liberalism, this freedom is possible only within a system of obligations imposed by the covenant of The Theater, and shared by each member of a theatrical community. When someone in a 1930s play or movie insists to his or her co-star that "the show must go on," the conversation is over. There is no alternative. Members of a theatrical community are responsible to each other, to the audience, to the producers, but even more importantly to the higher calling of the theater, to guarantee that the show goes on night after night and that it is the best show it can be.

Robert M. Cover makes clear in his work in comparative jurisprudence that the liberal rhetoric of rights and the Jewish rhetoric of obligations are based in two different collective myths. "The story behind the term 'rights,'" he argues,

> is the story of the social contract. The myth postulates free and independent if highly vulnerable beings who voluntarily trade a portion of their autonomy for a measure of collective security. . . . The first and fundamental unit is the individual, and "rights" locate him as an individual separate and apart from every other individual.[71]

Collective solutions are certainly possible (and, at times, desirable) under the social contract, but even these collective solutions "arrive at their destination by way of a theory that derives the authority of the collective from the individual." The myth of Judaism, on the other hand, is the myth of Sinai, "a collective—indeed, a corporate—experience" (which likewise allows for individual autonomy, but ultimately derives its legal authority from the collective acceptance of the law). Social movements in the United States organize around civil rights, Cover argues, while in Judaism, the kinds of entitlements that rights legislation protects have little meaning without an accompanying obligation. In other words, U.S. law determines what protections an individual is entitled to. Jewish law determines who is obligated to act in particular situations and what they are obligated to do.[72] Cover is interested in his own hybrid position as a Jewish American lawyer, and so he illustrates how both systems have devices in place to address injustice, but, depending on the situation, one system might be more effective than the other in addressing these problems. For example, in the struggle over women's roles in Judaism, feminists tend to argue for women's *right* to lead prayer or be called to the Torah. But for traditional Jews, this argument from rights is unpersuasive. They argue that women are not obliged under the law to do these things and so the only persuasive way to change the system would be to reinterpret the obligation to include women (a difficult, but not impossible task). On the other hand, while American law may guarantee children the "right" to an education, this "right. . . is not even an intelligible principle unless we know to whom it is addressed. Taken alone it only speaks to a need" (ibid., 9). How to turn need into reality? Of course, the American system makes this happen through a complicated structure of taxation and legislation, but when failures in education occur, no particular person or group is held responsible. Jewish law, on the other hand, never discusses the rights of the child; rather, it addresses those upon whom the obligation to educate is incumbent. The specific obligations of parents, teachers, communities, and homeowners is clearly spelled out in the law and universal (male) schooling among Jews has been a reality for at least two millenia.

Cover makes a strong case for the centrality of obligation to the definition of a Jew: "to be one who acts out of obligation is the closest thing there is to a Jewish definition of completion as a person within the community."[73] Indeed, when Jewish children reach maturity, they do not come into their majority rights; rather they become bar or bat mitzvah, literally son or daughter of the commandments/obligations. This explicitly Jewish version of coming-of-age is echoed in *The Royal Family,* as the daughter Gwen prepares to take on her first major role on the professional stage. Her uncle Dean congratulates her:

> Quite an event! Quite an event in the theatre! . . . About to enter into your great inheritance! To come before the public as the descendant of a distinguished family! It is not a trust to be taken lightly, my dear. Remember that not only will all of us be watching you, but your gifted ancestors as well.[74]

Dean does not describe her debut in the more familiar terms of American coming-of-age, as the moment when she is free to pursue her own path, to make her way in the world. Rather, Gwen's theatrical debut is described here like a bat mitzvah, the moment when she will take her place in her family's history and accept the mantle and obligations of the community.

The notion of "doing a mitzvah" is an extraordinarily resilient one among Jews, even Jews who are, in all other respects, resolutely secular. The theater, especially in the works under discussion here, is uniquely positioned to balance these notions of *obligation* and *rights.* To be a performer is to assert one's right to self-fashion; to perform as well as one can is a means of fulfilling one's obligation to the theatrical community. Cover ends his article with an attempt to synthesize the two legal systems, arguing that believing in the moral value of certain rights is only part of the project of correcting injustice; one is also obligated to make every effort to realize those rights. The theater offered a similar synthesis to secular Jews, albeit a synthesis that required belief not in a transcendent God who issued a set of commandments but in a community of believers and a set of traditions.

The drama of *The Jazz Singer* is an exploration of the conflict a Jewish immigrant faces when trying to reconcile these two differing legal systems. The play sets up a conflict between individual rights (the right to be whatever Jakie wants to be) and obligations (the duty to honor his parents and to observe Jewish tradition). Does he have the right to reject his parents and the traditions of his people to become a jazz singer, to self-fashion? His non-Jewish girlfriend Mary insists he does: "I want to see you live your own life. If the thing you want most is to be a black-face minstrel, then don't let *anything* stand in your way—not your parents—me—anything."[75] Jakie stares into the mirror at his painted face, ready for his upcoming performance, and instead he sees a vision of his father chanting in the synagogue. "The songs of Israel are tearing at my heart!" he cries. Jakie is torn apart trying to figure out to which system—individual rights or communal obligation—he owes his loyalty. As we have seen, he ultimately chooses to honor the obligations of his Jewish community. The play leaves the ending ambiguous, unsure how (or if) the Jewish system of obligation can survive in the American theater. The film, on the other hand, which spoke to a broader audience, insisted on a synthesis of the two, placing Jakie squarely on the stage at the end. Somehow, *The Jazz Singer* film argues, by pursuing a career as a performer, Jakie has found a way to assert his newfound rights *and* also meet his incumbent obligations.

One of the distinguishing features of the *mitzvot* is that only Jews are obligated to practice most of them; most *mitzvot* must be fulfilled within a Jewish family or Jewish community. The borders of that community are extremely well-protected by Jewish law, and among the worst sins in traditional Judaism therefore is exogamy. When children marry non-Jews, parents are instructed to mourn for them as if they were dead. As Jews acculturated to American society, intermarriage became a more common and more acceptable choice, and marriage between Christian and Jew formed the centerpiece of numerous plots of American plays, novels, films, and television shows.[76] The struggle in these stories is between the rhetoric of obligation and a rights-based argument, which insists on the primacy of romantic love and free choice in marriage. *The Royal Family* provides a fascinating obligation-based counterargument to this standard plot. The play does not deal directly with Jews, Christians, or intermarriage, but it does set up two distinct value systems, the "normal" world of businessmen, Connecticut lunches, rising early and meeting people of substance, and the theatrical world of high-strung characters, personal eccentricity, family loyalty, and devotion to art. In the first instance, individual rights are paramount; in the second, unexpectedly, communal obligation determines appropriate behavior.[77] To be more specific, in the first, the individual rights of the *men* are paramount—their rights as husbands to define women as their wives and to curtail their life choices. In the second, the *women's* obligations counterintuitively insure their freedom, specifically the freedom to play any role they choose. The liberal subject is figured as *male* here, and the freedoms promised by liberal individualism apply only to men. For women, the more liberating choice is, ironically, the world of communal obligation: the theater.

The men are represented here as interlopers who will take the women away from family, tradition, heritage, and true spiritual fulfillment. If the women intermarry with them, they will not only lose their freedom but will also sacrifice the opportunity to bequeath that freedom, and its accompanying heritage, rituals, and traditions to the next generation. The stark contrast between these two options is, needless to say, far more simplistic and monolithic than the reality of Jewish and liberal Protestant approaches to communal obligation and individual rights. It reflects a particular American Jewish response to liberal individualism, dramatized and heightened for the stage. Nonetheless, the structure of this choice sets up the theatrical life as a sort of stand-in for Jewish life in more ways than one.

In *The Royal Family*, both potential suitors, Gil and Perry, are represented as outsiders. They do not share the family's faith, they do not understand the pull of theatricality, they do not appreciate the obligations family members have to the theater, and they believe that their "normal" lives are clearly preferable to the Cavendishes' unusual lifestyle. Fanny, the grande dame of the family and fierce protector of their theatrical heritage, firmly disapproves of Julie's choice of Gil, despite his enormous bank account, but she didn't mind Julie's first husband. He was a loafer, she says, but at least he was an actor.[78] Furthermore, the "Jews" here are women, or at least figured as women (the male members of the Cavendish family do not face the same challenges to their freedom), once again referencing the well-established feminization of Jewish men in late nineteenth- and twentieth-century American culture, and raising questions about who exactly constitutes a Jewish liberal subject.[79]

Gwen's first scene with her fiancé Perry points out their nearly irreconcilable differences. Gwen is supposed to go to a lunch prepared by Perry's mother in Connecticut, but it conflicts with a play reading she needs to attend. The reading is an incontrovertible obligation. In their argument, it becomes clear that Perry simply cannot understand the obligations of the theatrical life:

> GWEN: I can't go with you, Perry. I've got to go to Wolfe's office to hear the play read. There's no way out of it. I've got to do it. . . .
> PERRY: You're joking.
> GWEN: But, Perry, I'm not! I know it sounds silly—
> PERRY: Silly! It's cuckoo! I never heard anything so ridiculous in my life. You can't mean you're breaking this date just to go and hear somebody read a play . . .
> GWEN: Now, Perry, please try to understand this. It's part of my job, and it's important.
> PERRY: Important to hear some idiot read a play that you've read again and again!
> GWEN: But it's more than that—it's a ceremony! (*Royal Family*, 37)

Perry, living in a totally different cosmos from Gwen, cannot see the importance of these theatrical rituals; they seem to him utterly pointless. We can see here how theatrical rituals are rendered sacred. These rituals have intrinsic meaning for Gwen; she intuitively understands the importance of the ceremony, although she cannot explain it effectively or rationally to Perry. She might as well tell him that she cannot go out with him for ice cream because she ate meat two hours earlier, or that after the birth of their first son, he will need to be circumcised. When Gwen and Perry discuss their differences, the conversation often sounds like countless similar arguments in films and plays of the 1920s over Jewish-Christian intermarriage: "We'll be living in two different worlds!" Perry complains. "But those things adjust themselves. Lots of other people have got around it," Gwen responds (ibid., 38–39).

In a fury, Gwen decides she will give up the stage and convert completely to Perry's way of life. She will not allow her family's commitment to arcane traditions to ruin her life:

> GWEN: If you think I'm going to give him up for a miserable little stage
>   career just because we've always done it . . . You're not going to
>   ruin my life! . . . I'm going to marry Perry Stewart and be a regular
>   person! And nothing you can say is going to stop me! (ibid., *Royal
>   Family,* 42)

Gwen wants to be a "regular person"; she wants to assimilate, to reject the peculiar obligations her family and her heritage demand, and just melt into the comfortable embrace of a real, normal, non-theatrical American man. She makes an argument for the universal over the particular that echoes numerous Jewish sons' and daughters' of the stage, page, and screen arguing with their immigrant parents: "I'm sick of being a Cavendish! I want to be a human being!" (ibid., 42).

Her mother, Julie, and Fanny, her grandmother, impress upon Gwen the importance of the theatrical gifts she has inherited, insisting that even if she decides to marry Perry, she not give up her distinctive way of life. Julie offers an American Jewish solution to her problem:

> JULIE: Marry him if you love him, Gwen, but don't give up everything
>   to do it! The day might come when you'd hate him for it. . . . Oh, I
>   know! There's love. But you can be the most fortunate person in the
>   world, Gwen. You can have both. But for God's sake don't make the
>   mistake of giving up one for the other. (ibid., 61)

To "have both" is to combine individual freedom with a life of obligation. The mother and grandmother launch into a passionate defence of the theater, describing what they've given up to remain faithful to it ("I've missed parties and dinners and rides and walks!"), and how it sustains them in their darkest moments: "You've got to leave, and go down to a stuffy dressing room and smear paint on your face and go out on the stage and speak a lot of fool lines, and you love it! You couldn't live without it!" (ibid., 62).

Gil and Perry, both fine upstanding businessmen, want traditional wives, and they fail to understand the rituals, faith, and values of the Cavendish family. The play turns the standard American Jewish intermarriage plot on its head. In conventional intermarriage stories of the time, of which the long-running play *Abie's Irish Rose* (1922) was the best known, a young Jewish man succeeds in winning the hand of a non-Jewish girl, usually of a higher social class. The couple faces opposition from both families, which is resolved through the extraordinary force of romantic love (or the power of grandchildren to sway the sentimental hearts of their grandparents). The parents are portrayed as backwards and old-fashioned, the children are romantic and sympathetic. In *The Royal Family*, however, the audience's sympathy lies squarely with the unconventional, theatrical (and arguably old-fashioned) Cavendishes. The upper-class, blueblood life of wealth, privilege, and respectability offered by the men is seen as an ironically individualist trap, and the happy ending occurs when both women reject their men in favor of meeting their theatrical and familial obligations, and performing in another play. By the end of the play, the entire Cavendish family is planning an enormous extravaganza, in which all of the members of the family, the baby included, will perform. The non-Cavendish men are completely marginalized (The stage directions read, "*They stand a little apart from the group, hands in pockets, thoughtful.*") and eventually they depart to do "business," and the women gratefully return to their family's, and the theater's, warm embrace.

Conclusion

Nearly thirty years after penning "God Bless America," Irving Berlin wrote a rousing anthem that neatly expressed all of the values of theatrical liberalism. Introduced in the musical *Annie Get Your Gun* in 1946, "There's No Business Like Show Business" is sung by a couple of theater producers aiming to convert the backwoods Annie Oakley into the world, and worldview, of the theater. Here we see the America upon which Berlin asked that God rain blessings. "What's show business?" Annie asks. Her producers respond with a rousing celebration of theatrical liberalism. They describe the many roles available: "The cowboys, the wrestlers, the tumblers, the clowns, the roustabouts who move the show at dawn." They note that this is an actively self-fashioned world: "the costumes, the scenery, the makeup, the props," a world in which acting takes precedence over truth: "There's no people like show people / They smile when they are low." A world which is meritocratic, with success dependent on good acting:

> Yesterday they told you you would not go far,
> That night you open and there you are,
> Next day on your dressing room they've hung a star.
> Let's go on with the show!

The rewards of good acting? "*Ev'rything* about it is appealing." The commitment to acting:

> You get word before the show has started
> That your fav'rite uncle died at dawn.
> Top of that your Pa and Ma have parted,
> You're brokenhearted, but you go on.

And even in a capitalist culture, the obligation to the theater comes first:

> Even with a turkey that you know will fold,
> You may be stranded out in the cold,
> Still you wouldn't change it for a sack of gold
> Let's go on with the show.[80]

For Berlin, for the characters in *Annie Get Your Gun,* and for the writers, performers, and producers of the works of theatrical liberalism, the theater *is* "show business." It is a commercial practice, which is squarely situated within the liberal free market; the success of a show depends upon its popular commercial appeal. And yet, the practitioners of "show business" nonetheless have an ambivalent relationship to profit. In refusing to exchange one's commitment to the stage for a "sack of gold," Berlin's devotees of "show business" revise Max Weber's Protestant work ethic in a manner typical of theatrical liberalism. To stick with the theater, even when it does not generate a profit, does not make rational sense in the world of business. While success in the theater certainly depends on talent and dedication, for Annie and her colleagues, "show business" is not exactly a "calling" in the Weberian sense—a God-given vocation through which she can generate profit.[81] Rather, it is an entire worldview. Individual plays may run forever or fold overnight, but the theater itself is not up for sale. To trade the theater for a sack of gold would be to place oneself outside of the theatrical liberal system altogether. Insisting on a vision of America which is theatrical at its core, Irving Berlin's "show business" argues that to be American is to be a theatrical liberal and vice versa. In turning the "wicked stage" into a site for American virtue, theatrical liberalism transformed assimilationist American ideology from an either/or choice between religious Judaism and secular liberalism into a remarkable synthesis of the two, a new American ethos for the twentieth century.

In the period following emancipation in Europe, Jews were often negatively identified as actors, as ciphers, chameleons, rootless cosmopolitans, always working to fit in, trying a bit too hard. Jews were, according to this model, deeply *in*authentic, a people willing to exchange internal consistency for artifice in order to reap the superficial rewards of assimilation and acceptance. But Kern, Hammerstein, Hart, Ferber, Kaufman, Berlin, Raphaelson, Lubitsch, and many others turned this anti-theatricality on its head. In *The Royal Family*, Gil claims that he will take Julie away from imitation and introduce her to real men, men of substance. But as the Cavendish family draws together at the end, with all of their eccentricities, superstitions, arcane rituals, and devotion to performance, they are nonetheless undeniably *real*, tied to something larger than themselves, loyal to one another and to their heritage, and determined to persist in the face of the forces of "normalcy" that aim to convert and entrap them at every turn. As the grandmother Fanny says, "[W]e're held together by something more than tables and chairs" (*Royal Family*, 85). Like *Trouble in Paradise, To Be or Not To Be, Show Boat*, and countless others (as well as in Levinas's reading of Jacob), these plays and movies ultimately reposition theatricality *as* authenticity. Acting is not a jettisoning of substance but rather an assertion of a kind of freedom that entails, for Jewish writers of this period, an ecstatic celebration of the most substantial version of reality they can imagine. For an eager generation of American Jews, this new Jewish secularism promised a heady, never-before-achieved combination of individual freedom, communal mission, spiritual sustenance, and action that regulated and sustained itself without recourse to divine revelation or divine judgement, promised full acceptance into American society, and at the same time resisted total assimilation. Theatrical liberalism is a Jewish secularism that retains many of the forms, behaviors, and values of a religious civilization, while effectively distancing itself from the specifically Jewish rituals and practices that would impede acculturation. While theatrical liberalism shares many features of Protestant American secularism (language, dress, calendar, diet, devotion to individual freedom, and civil rights, to name a few), even casual observers sense a difference. For better or worse, references to "New York culture," "East Coast liberals," "Broadway and Hollywood," mark a vaguely defined "sensibility," which is American yet somehow different from that of Protestant America. The relatively peaceful co-existence of these alike yet different sensibilities within the borders of a single national culture is a testament to the flexibility of both American liberalism and Judaism.

And yet there is a nagging insufficiency here. Is the transition from Judaism to theatrical liberalism perhaps too easy, too smooth? After all, the actions, the obligations, the national mission, the spiritual heart of Judaism are contained in the Torah, which is not simply a shared literary text, play, or screenplay, but divine revelation. Is it possible that the theater could provide to its initiates the kind of sustenance that God provided to religious Jews? Julie, in *The Royal Family*, believes that it can: "Earthquakes, and cyclones, and fire and flood, and somehow you still give the show. I know it says in the contract that you stop for acts of God, but I can't remember that I ever did" (ibid., 61). In Julie's world, and in theatrical liberalism, people acting takes precedence over acts of God. But it is difficult to sustain a belief system with no clear source of authority at its core. Torah, divinely revealed, had shaped Jewish life for millennia; theatrical liberalism needed to remain connected to that heritage to nurture a truly sustainable and revolutionary American Jewish secularism. This connection, which demanded not the re-establishment of religion but a new understanding of the relationship between the religious and the secular, began with theatrical liberalism, but it would be decades before Jews could openly embrace and assert this liberalism as a type of *Jewish* secularism. The path toward this goal involved a significant detour in the direction of humanism and authenticity.

3

Theatrical Liberalism under Attack

In acting take Nature as your model—but never fall into the
error of attempting to present Nature in the stead of art. The
speech of the stage should seem to be the speech of Nature.
I say "should seem to be" because it is one of the paradoxes
of acting that it cannot seem to be and never has seemed to
be the speech of Nature when actually it is so. . . . Everything
about a stage representation is radically artificial.
—David Belasco (1921)[1]

The extraordinary thing about acting is that life itself is actually used to create artistic results . . . since the actor is also a
human being, he does not pretend to use reality. He can literally use everything that exists. The actor uses thought—not
thought transcribed into color and line as the painter does,
but actual, real thought. The actor uses real sensation and
real behavior. That actual reality is the material of our craft.
—Lee Strasberg (1947)[2]

In the first half of the twentieth century, theatrical liberalism became
a central defining ethos of American popular culture. Plays and films
such as *The Jazz Singer, Show Boat, Annie Get Your Gun, Babes in Arms,
The Royal Family, Stage Door,* and *To Be or Not to Be* promoted the theater as a spiritually elevating pursuit. The theatrical community in these
musicals served as a model of a meritocratic society in which what an
actor did was more important than who an actor was or what he or
she believed. Theatricality promised the anti-essentialist freedom to
self-fashion, and members of the theatrical community not only strove
for love, fame, and financial success, but they also accepted the serious
obligations that went along with being part of a theatrical community.

But as the Nazis marched across Europe, the Depression continued at home, and America teetered on the brink of war, Jewish writers and composers began to question the efficacy of theatrical liberalism for a new and darker world.

Much has been said about the dramatic defection of many Jewish writers, artists and intellectuals from radical left-wing causes in the 1930s and their conversion to liberal anticommunism in the 1940s and 1950s.[3] Less acknowledged, but equally widespread, was the move by Jewish creators of popular culture of the same time period away from the optimistic premises of theatrical liberalism and toward a more pessimistic and deterministic worldview. The plays we consider in this chapter question whether we actually have the freedom to fashion our own selves, at times violently condemning an earlier generation's investment in self-fashioning as naïve and misguided. Some question the location of truth itself, adopting a more Protestant approach by suggesting that external action is a kind of illusion, and the authentic core of the self is found not in what one does but in who one *really is*. Others retain a theatrical worldview but see that theatricality as morally and spiritually empty, a vehicle for a selfish individualism, devoid of communal connection, much less obligation. All of these plays test the values of theatrical liberalism by critiquing its most identifiable genres: romantic comedy and backstage drama. Each of the three plays we examine in depth–*Pal Joey* (1940), *Death of a Salesman* (1949), and *West Side Story* (1957)–attempts to rewrite the backstage musical to reflect deep disillusionment with the very ideals that genre was invented to express.

The reasons for this disenchantment are closely related to the traumatic historical events of the time. In the summer of 1939, Russia revealed that it had signed a non-aggression pact with Germany, dashing the hopes of the antifascist Left in the United States and Europe, and shaking to its core the faith of the many American Jews in the socialist and communist movements. That same summer, the Jewish refugee crisis burst into public consciousness when the German ship, the *St. Louis*, laden with nearly one thousand Jews who were escaping Nazi Germany, was turned away from Cuba and then the United States and sent back to Europe, where most of its passengers fell victim to the Nazis. In late 1939 and 1940 Poland, Finland, Denmark, Norway, Holland, Belgium, and France fell to the Nazis, and Britain braced for the inevitable onslaught. At home, the decade-long Depression was lifting but only because the world was once again at war, and America was beginning the process of rapid industrialization necessary to supply the British army with the equipment they needed to fight Hitler. Congress passed a bill in mid-1940 calling for the first peacetime draft in American history. (Indeed, partway through the run of *Pal Joey,* lead actor Gene Kelly was called up by the U.S. Navy.) Americans were deeply divided about the war, and tension between isolationism and intervention shaped the 1940 presidential campaign, in which Franklin D. Roosevelt broke with tradition to run for a third term. Unlike the triumphant 1936 referendum on the New Deal (which was celebrated by the Rodgers and Hart musical *I'd Rather be Right,* in 1937), the 1940 election turned out to be a hard-fought campaign.

Jews were particularly anxious, not only for their brethren abroad—and enough was known by 1940 to know that Jews in Nazi-occupied territories had been stripped of civil rights and were dying in large numbers—but also at home where anti-Semitism had reached its peak. Groups such as the Christian Front gained support from outspoken and popular anti-Semites like Charles Lindbergh in their insistence that Jews were leading the country to war. Old nativist prejudice combined with the economic anxiety of ten years of depression meant that Congress refused to budge on the strict immigration quotas that limited the possibility of Jewish escape from occupied countries. Despite the strong efforts of the American Jewish community, the American people were not willing to risk their own economic security in order to open their doors to more refugees from Europe.[4] In the years before America entered the war, writers and directors such as Richard Rodgers, Lorenz Hart, and Ernst Lubitsch had created plays and movies that celebrated the triumph of theatrical liberalism over European fascism. Reflecting in his memoir *Musical Stages* on the development of the musical *I'd Rather Be Right* in 1937, for example, Rodgers evokes the close connection he drew between the values connected with theatrical liberalism and anti-fascism:

> [C]reating such a musical comedy at this time was in itself an affirmation of the freedom we had always enjoyed and had long taken for granted. Hitler, who had come to power in Germany the same year Roosevelt first

took office, had already instituted repressive measures against non-Ary-ans and "enemies of the state." Abolition of all forms of dissent was also part of Mussolini's Fascist regime in Italy and of the aggressive military leaders in Japan. Spain was in the midst of a civil war led by Franco, with the blessing and backing of Hitler and Mussolini. In one country after another, one saw the extinction of human life and liberty. Suddenly all those who had been moaning about what had happened to us during the Depression were beginning to realize that ours was one of the few nations on earth where people weren't afraid of their leaders. We could talk against them, we could vote them out of office—and we could even put them up on a Broadway stage as the butt of ridicule in a song-and-dance show.[5]

By the early 1940s, though, it no longer seemed to matter how well Jews in Europe played their parts as Germans, French, Romanians, Poles—they were being killed regardless. And it didn't matter how much they were willing to embrace American ideology—they were not going to be allowed in. Hitler and Mussolini put on shows as impres-sive as anything on Broadway—indeed, their lines of soldiers goose-stepping in unison bore a strong resemblance to the chorus lines of the Broadway musical, as Mel Brooks showed thirty years later in *The Producers* but that theatricality celebrated not freedom but unity, not integration but exclusion. American Jews likewise had worked hard for generations to perform their American identities, had achieved much, and yet seemed to be falling behind in their struggle for integration into the wider American community and were subject instead to increasing stigmatization as Jews.

With the end of the war in 1945, American Jews (and Jewish sol-diers in particular), buoyed by economic expansion, the opportuni-ties offered by the GI bill, and a new public ethos of religious toler-ance, began to express renewed optimism about the possibilities of assimilation into American culture. Official wartime cultural materials preached an ethos of obligation to the nation, and World War II mov-ies made during and immediately following the war tended to feature a sort of rainbow platoon in which soldiers from a variety of ethnic and religious backgrounds supported one another in the theater of war.[6] But it quickly became clear that this assimilation differed greatly from the self-fashioning of pre-war culture. The range of role models for Jews and others eager to be accepted into post-war culture were highly circumscribed. Discourses of belonging in the 1940s and 1950s fought prejudice and exclusion by preaching universalism, insisting that ethnic and religious difference was inconsequential and that all (white) Americans held similar beliefs and shared universal values.[7] This version of universal humanism became popular among Jews following World War II, when many of its basic tenets were accepted as a reaction against Nazism. In addition, as Judaism became increasingly accepted as one of the three "major faiths" of America, Jewishness was increasingly dismissed as merely a superficial difference: Jews go to different churches but are basically the same kind of people as all other Americans. The term Judeo-Christian likewise became increasingly popular as a way of describing American religious values, especially in contrast to fascism and communism, neatly subsuming Catholicism and Judaism into what was often a restatement of liberal Protestant values with allowances for a few cosmetic differences.[8]

The fragility of this universalism in providing Jews with a secure American identity was highlighted by the hysteria of the early Cold War, and especially the Red Scare of the late 1940s and early 1950s, in which Jewish artists, writers, and entertainers suddenly found themselves the subject of an intensive effort to root out communists and subversives in the American entertainment industries. The creation of the House Un-American Activities Committee (HUAC) to investigate alleged subversive domestic activities, the development of a studio-authorized blacklist, which ended the careers of countless writers, actors, and directors considered to be communists or "fellow-travelers," led to a culture of fear in the world of Hollywood, television, and Broadway. Anyone who had participated in a demonstration or signed a petition in the 1930s—and thousands had—could suddenly find themselves hauled before a congressional committee, questioned about their political activities, and asked to name the names of friends and associates who might also be suspect. Jewish writers, performers, and directors found themselves suddenly accused of being "un-American."

The Jewish-created popular culture of the 1940s and 1950s reflected the uncertainties, anxieties, and desires of this unstable historical moment. The war and its aftermath left writers questioning the very values that had initially made theatrical liberalism so seductive—the power of action, the freedom to self-fashion, the duty to a specific community of fellow believers. Jewish-created popular entertainment questioned the basic premises of theatrical liberalism by pushing the boundaries of, and sometimes rejecting completely, the distinctly American genres and performance styles that had emerged in the 1920s and 1930s. In *Pal Joey* (1940), the backstage musical became a modernist meditation on the failures of communal obligation and the pitfalls of relentless self-fashioning. *Death of a Salesman* (1949), one of the most popular American plays of all time, transformed the vaudevillian comic energy of self-transformation of an earlier era into a dangerous psychological delusion. The rise in popularity of psychoanalysis, psychological realism, and Method acting raised questions about the privileging of external action over internal motivation in earlier performance modes. The late 1950s musical *West Side Story* pushes this argument even farther, featuring a character literally named "Action" who serves as a catalyst for the tragic events of the play. At the same time, *West Side Story* blurs the line between romantic comedy and tragedy, searching for a popular form that can adequately express disappointment with theatrical liberalism, while still affirming many of its most powerful motivating features.

* * *

Theatrical liberalism offered secular Jews, and many other Americans, a way to express their yearning for purpose, meaning, and community without marginalizing themselves within particular religious or ethnic groups. Theatrical liberalism also allowed secular Jews to sidestep difficult questions about faith and about the relationship between religious practice and political citizenship by situating the world of the theater as an alternative locus for eternal truths, a way of ordering the world, a sense of heritage and community, and a code of ethics. But for many American intellectuals of the time, the very possibility of eternal truths—religious, political, aesthetic—was subject to doubt. Modernist writers had already been questioning the possibility of fixed truths for nearly two decades when Rodgers and Hart's paean to theatrical liberalism, *Babes in Arms*, was produced. They peered into the intellectual and spiritual abyss, the horrifying heart of darkness, and wondered how, in the absence of faith in God and all of the fixed truths such faith made possible, people could make meaning of their lives. William Faulkner and Willa Cather mourned the lost innocence of the pre-modernist world, while F. Scott Fitzgerald offered ambivalent tribute to those who invented their own pasts and their own truths, masters of self-fashioning like Jay Gatsby.

But Jewish writers and composers, especially those working in the popular sphere, largely resisted the underlying despair of modernism through the 1920s and 1930s, choosing instead to devote their secular faith to the optimistic set of truths promised by American liberalism and expressed in the theater. By the late 1930s and early 1940s, however, historical pressures led to the hollowing out of many of the ideals of the immigrant generation and their children. A number of Jewish writers, many of whom had made their reputations defining and celebrating theatrical liberalism, began to echo their modernist contemporaries, articulating probing concerns about the secular Judaism embodied in theatrical liberalism. Are there any limits to the freedom promised by theatricality? What is the relationship between acting and belief? What holds a theatrical community—or any community—together? In the absence of a clear, authoritative source of truth, what, if anything, compels us to take on communal obligations? What if the audience, or the other performers, choose not to adopt those obligations? Just as modernist poets and novelists experimented with form in order to raise questions about truth, so modernist writers of plays and movies used the heavily formulaic nature of their genres to shock audiences into questioning the assumptions of theatrical liberalism upon which these popular forms relied. Richard Rodgers and Lorenz Hart's 1940 musical *Pal Joey* offers an example of this highly commercial and theatrical engagement with modernist concerns. *Pal Joey* uses the popular genre Rodgers and Hart helped to create—the backstage musical—in order to raise questions about the viability of the values of theatrical liberalism in an era plagued by fascism, Nazism, and war.

Throughout their long theatrical partnership, Rodgers and Hart invented much of the standard musical comedy format while also poking fun at it. Their love stories, and Hart's lyrics in particular, were always more self-consciously about theatricality than those of their contemporaries Irving Berlin, George and Ira Gershwin, or Jerome Kern and Oscar Hammerstein.[9] "Falling in Love with Love," from *The Boys From Syracuse* (1938), for example, offers a cynical counterpoint to more sentimental standards of the time like Kern and Hammerstein's "Make Believe" from *Show Boat*:

> Falling in love with love is falling for make believe.
> Falling in love with love is playing the fool;
> Caring too much is such a juvenile fancy.
> Learning to trust is just for children in school.[10]

Whereas most works of theatrical liberalism tend to support the power of external acting to shape internal emotions (to "make" belief), Hart's lyrics warn against the seductive powers inherent in the ability to "make believe." It is okay, indeed unavoidable, to fall in love but not to lose sight of the fact that "love" is a theatrical construct; to fall in love with the *idea* of love, as Magnolia does in *Show Boat,* is to assume that playing at love will create "true" love. For Hart, the relationship between acting and reality is a deeply complex and often dangerous one; those who actually "make believe" not only allow their performance to shape reality but are also in danger of forgetting that this reality is "made" and therefore can be unmade: they risk "playing the fool." The edgy nature of Hart's lyrics work in tension with Rodgers's lush music to create songs that sound and act like love songs almost in spite of themselves.[11]

With *Pal Joey* Rodgers and Hart extended this critique of theatrical liberalism from an individual song to an entire play. *Pal Joey* deconstructed the very form Rodgers and Hart had been instrumental in creating, and threw open to question the moral and spiritual purpose behind the theatrical energy of so many 1930s plays and films.[12] One of Rodgers and Hart's last plays as a team, *Pal Joey* is loosely based on a series of short stories by John O'Hara published in the *New Yorker,* which consist of letters from a second-rate nightclub performer to his far more successful bandleader friend. The play tells the story of Joey Evans, a handsome but none-too-smart singer who dreams of bigger and better things. In the first act, he manages to charm and seduce a number of attractive women through the use of various theatrical devices. His conquests include a naïve shopgirl, Linda English ("I Could Write a Book"), a few of the dancers at the nightclub at which he performs ("You Mustn't Kick it Around"), and, finally, a rich society lady, Vera Simpson ("Bewitched, Bothered, and Bewildered"), who agrees to finance Joey's career in return for his attentions. Assured of fame and riches, Joey is ecstatic as he imagines his future in an extended dream ballet, which ends the act. In the second act, the nightclub is about to open and Joey seems to be at the top of his game. When he tries to use his old theatrical tricks on the reporter assigned to cover the opening, however, things begin to fall apart. Melba, the reporter, reveals Joey's inadequacies as a performer ("Zip"), and only moments later a gangster cons Joey into signing away his paycheck, revealing Joey to be not only a bad actor but a bad spectator as well—a dupe who can't distinguish performance from reality. Emasculated and beaten, Joey can no longer charm Vera, who unceremoniously dumps him with the help of Linda ("Take Him"). Out of a job, and about to leave town, Joey runs into Linda once more. She offers him another chance but only if he is willing to give up the theater and embrace domestic respectability by taking a job with a trucking company. Joey refuses. He seems dimly aware that theatricality has gotten him nowhere but still stubbornly resists being locked into the stable identity Linda demands. Linda departs, and the play ends with Joey alone, on the road to the next town to try to sell himself anew.

In refusing a neat romantic and comic resolution—the ending offers neither the promise of marriage nor the hope of a better world to come—*Pal Joey* forces an examination of the basic assumptions of theatrical liberalism. Exposing the nightclub stage as a place exclusively designed to make money by pandering to men's basest sexual impulses, the play raises questions about the viability of theatricality as a fulfilling spiritual alternative to religion. By refusing to allow the romantic love plot to run its usual course, the play also raises questions about the relationship between external action and internal faith. In this play, neither love songs nor sex necessarily lead to love, and virtuoso performances do not necessarily make one a star. Like many works of theatrical liberalism, *Pal Joey* highlights the close relationship between theatricality and self-fashioning, but it also raises crucial questions about the limits of self-fashioning as a means of achieving freedom. While the play showcases virtuosic examples of the liberating potential of theatricality, at the same time it insists that this liberation exists only *as* theatricality (which is not necessarily translated into tangible measures of romantic, spiritual, or financial success). The end of *Pal Joey* in particular makes blatantly clear that the unstable theatrical self is the *only* reward guaranteed by theatrical liberalism. This instability, while liberating, offers no comfort to those searching for the kind of strong theatrical community showcased in works such as *The Royal Family* and *Stage Door*. Likewise, in *Pal Joey*, the language of obligation nearly disappears. The theater becomes a space dedicated solely to personal fulfillment. Since the characters are not willing to be bound by a common set of rules and values, theatricality ceases to function as a mode of community building. With characters more than willing to unmask each other, the practice of performance becomes a competitive con game of persuasion and seduction. The result: all of the central characters, despite varying levels of performance virtuosity, end up both free *and* lonely.

The tired banter that structures the first few scenes of the play reveals a very different theatrical world than that of *The Jazz Singer, Show Boat, Gold Diggers of 1933,* or *The Royal Family.* In the nightclub that forms the central location of the first act, Joey must force the girls to rehearse. There is no discussion of the glory of the theater, no ambition to improve the show, no young eager types dreaming of becoming stars, just hard work, day in, day out:

> JOEY: Go ahead, keep on rehearsing.
> GLADYS: Keep on rehearsing, that's what he thinks.
> SANDRA: My feet hurt.
> WAGNER: What does he think this is, the Follies?
> KYLE: This is a hell of a way to make a living.
> FRANCINE: Rehearse all day and work all night . . .
> SANDRA: I used to get by just showing my shape. Now I have to dance my
> fanny off for fifty bucks a week.[13]

The nightclub numbers these girls are rehearsing are parodies of 1930s musical numbers—over the top, tacky, and terrible. And the entire company knows it. Conventional 1930s backstage musicals built toward a grand theatrical number, which celebrated the success of the show the characters had been working so hard to perfect throughout the story. In *Pal Joey,* the theatrical "finale" happens earlier, in the middle of act 2.

But it is only a rehearsal; we never see the final product, and the show as a whole turns out to be a failure. Within a few scenes, Joey is out of a job. The theater in *Pal Joey* has been stripped of its spiritual pretensions and reduced to a dreary commercial enterprise.

Pal Joey undermines the standard backstage musical formula, partially by raising questions about the relationship between external action and internal truths. In so many of the works discussed earlier, acting has transformative power; it brings about a new reality. In *Show Boat*, when Magnolia and Ravenal sing of love, they end up falling in love; when Lily Garland screams properly in *Twentieth Century*, she becomes a star. In *Pal Joey,* however, acting rarely brings about change. Rodgers and Hart use musical comedy conventions—that a soaring love song must indicate true love, for example—to undermine audience expectations and to raise questions about the power of acting to shape thoughts, feelings, or future behavior. Early in the first act, the ingénue, Linda, stands in front of a pet shop window, staring lovingly at one of the puppies. Joey enters, sizes her up, and then puts on a sentimental dog-loving act in order to impress her. It works. Joey seals the deal with a love song:

> If they asked me I could write a book
> About the way you walk and whisper and look.
> I could write a preface on how we met
> So the world would never forget.
> And the simple secret of the plot
> Is just to tell them that I love you a lot;
> Then the world discovers as my book ends
> How to make two lovers of friends. (ibid., 26)

This song, with its soaring refrain, immediately shapes our expectations about the relationship between Joey and Linda. The comforting familiarity of the show tune, with its foxtrot rhythm (which, as Mark Grant notes, is the "default show-tune rhythm" of the period) quickly works its magic.[14] How could someone who sings so beautifully not really be in love? Or at least not really *want* to be in love? Hart's lyrics make a point of avoiding the self-conscious pyrotechnics that deconstruct so many of the other songs in the play. Linda sings in the second verse: "It was never my endeavor / To be too clever and smart. / Now

I suddenly feel / A longing to write in my heart" (*Pal Joey*, 26). Linda's "heart" is simple and straightforward, a space of sincere emotion and naïve faith. There are hints in the song, however, that despite what the music, with its sentimental strings and cut-time foxtrot beat, seems to be indicating, we should not take the song at face value as the beginning of a relationship that will necessarily culminate in a happy ending.[15] Joey tells Linda that she "inspires him" to sketch out a standard romantic love plot, with a simple secret that is of course no secret at all ("I love you a lot"). But he does not *actually* write that book, only indicates that "if they asked him," he "could." Who is "they"? It is, of course, anyone with a stake in the success of this (or any) musical comedy: the directors, producers, critics, audiences. The plot of Joey's proposed book is the plot that audiences are expecting, indeed hoping for. This conditional voice in the song, however, serves as a warning. Joey does not actually write the book he proposes. But in focusing on the act of writing, the song draws our attention to the fact that this plot is (or could be) self-consciously constructed ("I *could* write a book") in order to remind us, at the beginning of the musical, that it can also therefore be deconstructed.[16] In most musicals, a pair joined together in a song with the particular rhythm, tempo, and key (C major) of "I Could Write a Book" are destined to end up in love, no matter how many obstacles (mistaken identities, jealousies, and the like) they have to overcome. In *Pal Joey*, however, the action—singing a love song—does not lead to the expected change in feeling. Linda is seduced by Joey's performance, but Joey remains largely unmoved. His acting has no apparent impact on his own thoughts and emotions.

Just as a romantic song does not lead to a happy ending for Joey and Linda, likewise sex does not lead to love between Joey and Vera. Vera is acutely aware of the theatrical nature of her encounter with Joey, and hence of its temporary and unstable quality. She sees Joey as physically appealing but hopelessly lacking in self-consciousness: "He's a fool and don't I know it— / But a fool can have his charms," she sings in her signature song, "Bewitched" (*Pal Joey*, 57). Vera knows that the theatrical game Joey plays will not deliver on its promise of a happy ending; indeed, she has little interest in that version of happiness (she is *already* rich and married). This blithe disregard for psychological consequences, for the relationship between external action and internal feeling, allows her to play roles and have affairs with little risk to her emotional well-being. Indeed, the temporary and unstable quality of love affairs are what make them exciting for Vera: "I'm wild again! Beguiled again! A simpering, whimpering child again! Bewitched, bothered and bewildered am I!"(*Pal Joey*, 58). Vera self-consciously scripts roles for herself (she is "like a babe in arms," "like sweet seventeen a lot," etc.), and plays them with relish. When she decides to seduce Joey, she makes a number of phone calls to break other dates, playing a different role in each conversation (sick Vera, faithful-wife Vera). Yet this type of acting leads not to faith, understanding, or love but simply to more acting. "Lost my heart, but what of it?" Vera asks. The performance of romance is endlessly repeatable, endlessly changing. Hearts will be lost, regained, and lost again in a predictable cycle that denies any link between acting and "reality."

Perhaps the most surprising "acting" link that is broken in *Pal Joey* is the link between performance virtuosity and commercial success. Although Joey is ostensibly a second-rate performer, as played by the young Gene Kelly in the Broadway opening, he sang and danced beautifully. A character with such theatrical talents would, in any standard narrative of theatrical liberalism, ultimately become a star by the end of the show. In the first scene in the play, the club manager lists for Joey the qualities expected of the master of ceremonies, a list that could have been taken directly from an early twentieth-century success manual: "He has to have a lot of self-confidence. He has to be able to get up and tell a story. He has to be sure of himself in case he gets heckled" (*Pal Joey*, 5). Joey can (and does) clearly follow these directions on stage, but somehow the directions no longer insure success. It turns out that while Joey can sing and dance, his acting skills fail to convince. Joey's attempts to con the women around him seem outdated, cheesy, and transparent; as the play proceeds, his performances become increasingly pathetic and unsuccessful. He is unmasked by one woman after another as stupid, unself-conscious, and phony, and ultimately they all give him up. No matter how beautifully he can sing and dance, Joey will never become a success in the world of *Pal Joey* because he lacks the self-consciousness to effectively adapt to changed theatrical circumstances.

In backstage musicals of the 1920s and 1930s, central characters are often torn between the lure of the footlights and more stable or "respectable" choices. Numerous Warner Brothers film musicals of the period turn on just this dramatic conflict. In *Pal Joey*, no one makes a choice. The theater is life itself, a life consumed by trying to find the right show to please a fickle and self-involved audience. Good performers get more money, more sex, and more power. Bad performers get fired. And performers who lack self-consciousness, like Joey, end up on the road to the next gig. *Pal Joey* argues that the worldview of theatrical liberalism cannot provide the spiritual nourishment, community support, and rich heritage it seemed to promise in earlier Rodgers and Hart plays; at the same time, the play laments the loss involved in this realization. This is no morality tale, however, for morality involves choice. Although the play insists that theatricality defines modern life, it does not condemn this fact as immoral. Theatricality is not moral or immoral; it simply is. Indeed, it is *all* there is; recognition of this existential fact is both inevitable and frightening.

As if in response to the existential and social vicissitudes of an amoral, theatrical universe, the play becomes a relentless search for the "heart of the matter," a search that will of course prove fruitless but that must be conducted nonetheless. Time and again, *Pal Joey* makes use of the standard romantic metaphor of the heart, only to reveal the heart itself as an unstable symbol; like an actor, the heart has no fixed identity beyond the roles it plays. Throughout the play, one song after another asks, "what is a heart?" How many roles can this word-actor play before it ceases to mean anything? If we cannot understand or fix the meaning of "heart," what does that say about the possibility of real human feelings, of communication, of love itself? What lies at the "heart" of the matter? Is there anything there?

Consider the first song in the play, sung by Joey at a rehearsal for his first night in a third-rate club, "You Mustn't Kick It Around":

> If my heart gets in your hair
> You mustn't kick it around.
> If you're bored with this affair
> You mustn't kick it around.
> Even though I'm mild and meek
> When we have a brawl,
> If I turn the other cheek
> You mustn't kick it at all. (*Pal Joey*, 14)

The word "heart" becomes an actor in this song, changing costumes and roles in order to dramatize the instability of both language and love. "Heart" is at first used symbolically, meaning, "my sincere emotions, my real feelings for you." But with love "getting in your hair" the figurative language acquires a new role (or two). The image is simultaneously of a cut-out valentine heart tangled in a woman's hair, and of a real human lover whose attentions are annoying his lady. In the next phrase, the "heart" changes costumes again: "you mustn't kick it around." Now we have the image of something clearly three-dimensional, a ball, perhaps, that can be thrown and kicked. By the end of the refrain, the heart is playing at least three roles simultaneously: that of the love, the lover, and the lover's body parts—the heart, but also the cheek, which in turn could refer to either the face or the buttocks. The symbolic relationship between "heart" and romantic love is rendered dizzyingly complex, and any stable meaning of the word "heart" becomes as elusive as the material body of a quick-change artist.

In another nightclub number, "The Flower Garden of My Heart," the "heart" performs even more dazzling theatrical and linguistic stunts through a profusion of similes, metonymies, and mixed metaphors. The song begins with a send-up of the common Depression-era refrain that one doesn't need riches if one only has love:

> I haven't got a great big yacht,
> But I'm contented with my lot.
> I've got one thing
> Much more beautiful and grand.

The singer then invites the listener to wander in a much grander "showplace," the "lovely spot out yonder" that is his own heart. The lover's symbolic heart here—his love for his lady—gains sufficient earthy materiality to grow a flower garden:

> In the flower garden of my heart
> I've got violets blue as your eyes,
> I've got dainty narcissus
> As sweet as my missus
> And lilies as pure as the skies.

> In the flower garden of my heart
> I've got roses as red as your mouth.
> Just to keep our love holy
> I've got gladioli
> And sun flowers fresh from the South. (*Pal Joey,* 77)

In this heart/garden grow flowers that in turn serve a metonymic function, standing in for parts of his lady's body or aspects of her virtue (violets = eyes; roses = mouth, lilies = purity, etc.), images that apparently reside in this lover's heart. The dance number that follows involves a burlesque parody of "flowery" Victorian language. Each of the flowers is made to stand for a national or regional identity (sunflower = South, heather = Scotland, rose = America, etc.), which is then embodied by a different showgirl in an exaggerated costume. The symbolic romantic language of the flowers is also rendered ridiculous by the cheap sexuality of the showgirls; the woman who sings of youthful purity, for example, has a deep raspy voice and wears a skimpy, revealing costume.

The refrain of the song repeats three times, and in each case ends with increasingly baroque imagery:

> (1) But you are the artist and love is the art
> (2) But you are the archer and I am the dart
> (3) But you are the pastry and I am the tart!

The entire garden, apparently, is fashioned by the lady herself, whom the singer calls "the artist" and whose artistry is theatrical. She plays many roles: she is not only the artist and the subject of the song but also the embodiment of the flowers that grow in this garden. This artist could also possibly be the listener, the audience. We have, after all, also been invited to wander in this "lovely spot out yonder." As the song progresses, it gets increasingly kaleidoscopic; this proliferation of heart-language leads to dizzying levels of theatrical and verbal virtuosity that at times force the listener to strain to make sense of the performance. How can the lady be the archer if she is also the flowers? How can the lover be the dart if the heart is in his own body? And what in the world does it mean to be the pastry or the tart in a flower garden? This abundance of possible meanings, possible roles, possible symbolic functions for the "heart" renders it impossible to imagine that the "heart" could ever be tied to a singular symbolic truth. The song becomes a meditation on the liberating potential of theatrical representation, while at the same time serving as a warning against mistaking performance for stable truth.

The final nightclub song, "Plant You Now, Dig You Later," transforms the flowery romantic imagery of "The Flower Garden of My Heart," into the much less ethereal vegetable patch waiting to be harvested:

> Bye-bye, my hep-chick,
> Solid and true.
> I'll keep in step-chick,
> Till I come digging for you.
> So, little potater
> Stay right where you are,
> Plant you now, dig you later
> Means au revoir! (*Pal Joey*, 98)

Now a potato rather than a lily or a rose, the lover's heart is described here as "solid and true" (and what is more solid than a potato?). The singer asks the lover, or the love itself, to "stay right where you are," to wait, to remain solid, true, unchanging. But the singer is on the run: the accented rhyming phrases in the song are "on the lam," "scram," "on my way," "not going to stay." The music is a driving jazz beat, and the accompanying dance number has often been performed by a chorus dressed as escaped convicts frantically running from the law.[17] The song immediately follows, and comments on, a scene in which the gangster successfully cons Joey out of his salary, using—not surprisingly—theatrical techniques. The plea here for a stable truth, one that remains where it was planted, is made within the context of a song about mobility, indeed about escaping from the very law (of language? of the theater?) that threatens to pin down and imprison the performer like a potato planted in the earth. The song acknowledges the loss involved in accepting the instability of the theatrical world ("My regret couldn't be greater / at having to scram") but offers no alternative to this reality.

The extraordinary instability of the "heart," is represented in the play as both liberating and deeply disturbing. If the heart can perform so many roles, so, of course, can we. When a reporter, Melba, shows up at the club to interview Joey for a puff piece, Joey tries to con her with various outlandish stories about his youth. She has heard it all and is far from convinced. To cut Joey down to size, Melba demonstrates her superior performance abilities in a song about her best interview, with the stripper Gypsy Rose Lee.[18] According to Melba, Gypsy actually thought great thoughts while stripping off her clothes—"Zip! I was reading Schopenhauer last night. / Zip! And I think that Schopenhauer was right" (*Pal Joey*, 87). As Melba, a connoisseur of artifice, sings, she herself begins to imitate Gypsy's act, removing her glasses and articles of her own sensible clothing to reveal . . . another costume underneath. On the one hand, the song purports to tell us about the "real" Gypsy Rose Lee, not the stripper but the intellectual woman. On the other, the song insists, in fine modernist fashion, that no matter how many layers of costume you peel away, no matter how much flesh you reveal, the theatrical strip never reveals a "real" person underneath. And the representation of Gypsy's thoughts, as performed by a reporter devoted to making the facts fit the story, are not likely to get us any closer to a real, stable person than does the revelation of her flesh.

To have the freedom to be who you want, to perform the self you want to be and to change your identity as easily as you change a costume, a name, or an accent is extraordinarily liberating—indeed it forms a core element of theatrical liberalism—and was especially attractive in a time and place when so many people felt trapped by fixed racial identities. At the same time, this kind of freedom is potentially terrifying. If a word can signify so many things, how can we ever come to agree on its meaning? If simply donning a sequined dress turns a dowdy reporter into a famous celebrity, what does it mean to have an identity? If we can be whoever we want to be, are we all simply a parade of surfaces, without authenticity or depth? In a world of theater and artifice, who are we *really*? *Pal Joey* refuses to answer these questions. Whether onstage or off, when Joey or Melba or Vera sings, they are always performing versions of themselves; there is no single, real Joey or Melba or Vera. In one of the final songs of the play, the two women who have loved Joey decide to give him up. "Take him," Linda sings to Vera, "but don't ever take him to heart" (*Pal Joey,* 118). Enjoy him for the moment; appreciate the surface he presents to you. But don't fall into the trap of believing that what you see is what he is.

Although it contained some of the most beautiful songs written for the musical stage and featured the remarkable talents of Gene Kelly and Vivienne Segal, the play's unsentimental narrative and sharp cynicism led to mixed reviews when it opened on Broadway in 1940.[19] Among the most famous and most telling of the responses was Brooks Atkinson's *New York Times* review, which began by commenting, "If it is possible to make an entertaining musical comedy out of an odious story, *Pal Joey* is it" and ended the review asking "Although it is expertly done, can you draw sweet water from a foul well?"[20] Atkinson, and many in the 1940 audience, whose expectations were dashed by *Pal Joey*'s refusal to adhere to the familiar values of theatrical liberalism, were disturbed by the "foul well" represented onstage. While Atkinson does not specify exactly what he means by this, he does make it clear that the fact that the characters (and especially Joey) are so selfish and self-absorbed makes it difficult to enjoy the theatrical virtuosity through which they express that rampant individualism.

One of the core virtues of theatrical liberalism is the privileging of communal obligation over individual rights. In *Pal Joey,* the language of obligation disappears, wholly replaced by the language of individualism. Almost no one looks outside himself, and the theater is a space not of communal cooperation but of hopelessly self-absorbed competition. The only person who still speaks the language of obligation is Linda, the one character in the play who has nothing to do with the theater.

In the final scene, after Joey has been dumped by everyone else, Linda makes one last attempt to save Joey from himself. She invites him to her sister's house for dinner so he can meet her brother-in-law who is in the trucking business. Perversely, the one person who reaches out to Joey offers him the very trap refused by the actresses in *Stage Door, The Royal Family,* and *Twentieth Century.* According to Linda, Joey can be redeemed only if he gives up his theatrical career and gets a steady job. Linda's offer seems to be the best possible option Joey has. Where else is he to go? But this kind of self-sacrifice neither Joey nor *Pal Joey* is willing to make. The option offered by Linda—earnestness—is revealed to be a pose of the worst sort, largely because Linda does not recognize it as a pose.[21] Linda offers the promise of respectability, of a "real" life outside the world of the theater, and this is far more dangerous than the theatricality Joey, Vera, and the others practice because of its claim of stability. With her dream of domestic wedded bliss, Linda implies that Joey could just stop pretending, stop acting, and become himself. If Joey and the audience come to learn anything by the end of the play, it is that he and they have no self beyond the versions of a self he is always inventing. But this realization involves the rejection of any possibility of communal coherence. This freedom to perpetually reinvent the self prevents Joey from being imprisoned in a single identity (as a truck driver, for example) but includes no insurance that this freedom will ultimately reward him with love, real human connection, community, or faith. By shifting the balance from communal theatrical obligation back toward the language of individual rights, *Pal Joey* posits that theatrical liberalism cannot overcome a basic paradox of American liberalism, which promises the freedom to pursue happiness but not necessarily the means or the right to achieve it.

One of the saddest songs in the play was not used in the Broadway opening. It served as an act 1 closer when the show was on the road in Philadelphia and was cut before the play opened in New York. But recent directors of *Pal Joey* have recognized the power of the song to express Joey's enduring faith in American individualist ideals in the face of all evidence to the contrary, and so have reinstated it as Joey's farewell. Sung at the end of the play, "Talking to My Pal" is a tragic indictment of theatrical liberalism:[22]

> I'm independent.
> I'm a descendant
> Of quite a family of heels.
> I'm never lonely.
> I and I only
> Know how my pal Joey feels.
> Who else would pay for my meals?
> I'm talking to my pal,
> Myself, my closest friend.
> And that's the only pal
> On whom I can depend.

Instead of a joyous communal finale, this play ends with the image of a lonely performer off to try to make another sale of the only thing he has to sell—himself. As this defiant paean to self-reliance ends, the music segues back into a final reprise of "I Could Write a Book." Theatrical liberalism is not dead yet. Joey is off to peddle his theatrical skills somewhere else, in the hopes that maybe this time he will finally achieve his dreams. In a 2002 Philadelphia production, Joey sang these final lines, with suitcase in hand, walking on a moving sidewalk to nowhere. The image evoked nothing so much as the opening tableau for *Death of a Salesman*, an image of Joey walking out of this musical and into that famous critique of the myth of theatrical liberalism and self-reliance. Give Joey a few more years at this game and he, too, will be lamenting a world that eats him up and throws away the peel.

* * *

In *Pal Joey*, theatricality is a fact of life. The play calls into question whether theatrical liberalism can deliver on its promises, but it offers no viable substitute. Indeed, alternatives that posit non-theatrical choices, that offer the actor the opportunity to stop performing, are seen as at best misguided and at worst a threat to the freedom theatrical liberalism makes possible. Theatrical liberalism may not deliver on all of its promises (Joey's performance does not necessarily insure his success or happiness), but the alternatives—authenticity, stability—are seen ironically as false, and potentially dangerous, choices. If theatricality is inevitable, to believe in authenticity is to believe a lie, the very same lie that, in the guise of racial science, was killing people around the world in the 1940s. The best choice for Rodgers and Hart's characters is to be self-conscious, smart, and talented in the theatrical game that is life. As second- and third-generation Jews became increasingly comfortable in Protestant America in the 1940s and '50s, however, this theatrical worldview underwent yet another revision. Theatrical liberalism was repeatedly challenged by the notion that knowledge of the "authentic" interior self was a truer and more reliable (not to mention more Christian) route to salvation and success.

It was Arthur Miller's *Death of a Salesman*, more than any other work of American popular culture, that etched a narrative of post-war disillusionment into public consciousness, spawning a host of imitators and influencing a generation of popular writers.[23] Arthur Miller's work questioned the apparently redemptive power of theatrical liberalism, reformulating the impetus to perform at the heart of theatrical liberalism as a lie. His anti-theatrical plays critiqued those who retained faith in illusion and dreams, lived "phony" double lives, or were duped by con men. Miller was certainly not the first to focus on the theatricality of con-men and salesmen; such characters have a rich history in American literature and culture. With the rising popularity at the turn of the century of Horatio Alger's rags-to-riches tales featuring self-made heroes who effectively cultivated the skills of the confidence man—the arts of social manipulation, of personality, of selling the self—the salesman quickly became the respectable version of the confidence man in American society. Not coincidentally, increased emphasis on this theatrical mode of achieving success accompanied the rise of theatrical liberalism on stage and screen, and peaked in 1937 with the almost simultaneous production of Rodgers and Hart's paean to theatrical liberalism, *Babes in Arms*, on Broadway and the publication of Dale Carnegie's *How to Win Friends and Influence People*, an enormously popular advice manual in which the skills and behaviors of the salesman, con man, and actor were conflated into a single theatrical model for American success. If there is a central hero (or more often, anti-hero) of Miller's post-war Jewish culture, it is the salesman; however, in this case, he is usually a failed salesman. Failed actors and would-be con men also made frequent appearances, and in some cases a character could be all three at once.

Despite the intense critique of "phoniness" in all of Miller's plays, his work, as well as that of other important popular Jewish artists of the period, did not ultimately reject the theatrical liberalism it purported to despise. *All My Sons* (1947), *Death of a Salesman* (1949), and *The Crucible* (1953), as well as Saul Bellow's *Seize the Day* (1956), Arthur Laurents, Stephen Sondheim, and Jule Styne's *Gypsy* (1959), and many others questioned the foundations of theatrical liberalism, often overtly rejecting its performance-based ethos. At the same time they made use of the very theatricality they condemned in order to communicate with an audience still deeply committed to theatrical liberalism. Despite Miller's overt commitment to naturalism, and the play's clear rejection of Willy Loman's "delusions" about himself and about American dreams, *Death of a Salesman* proves itself to be much more closely linked to self-consciously theatrical popular culture than either Miller or most of his champions would care to acknowledge.

The popularity of *Death of a Salesman* is unmatched in the history of American realism. Within a year of the Broadway opening, productions had been mounted in Great Britain, Denmark, Sweden, Switzerland, Argentina, Italy, France, Austria, Greece, Germany, and Israel. The play has seen three successful Broadway revivals since its opening in 1949, as well as major professional and amateur productions around the world. According to the theater historian Brenda Murphy, since its premiere in 1949, "there has never been a time when *Death of a Salesman* was not being performed somewhere in the world."[24] It won the Pulitzer Prize and the Tony Award when it initially appeared, and won additional Tony awards for two of its revivals. Likewise, the critical celebration of *Death of a Salesman* established Arthur Miller as America's pre-eminent playwright.[25] The play is standard reading on American high school and college curricula and is widely considered universally applicable.[26] Miller has been lauded as the only playwright able to produce a serious tragic drama about American life.[27] As Stella Adler points out to her acting students in her memoir *The Art of Acting*, "*Death of a Salesman* is as near as you will get [in American theater] to playing Hamlet."[28] Furthermore, the impact of *Death of a Salesman* on works of the 1950s and beyond is immense. Numerous Jewish-authored works from the late 1950s in particular are deeply indebted to *Salesman*. Philip Roth's salesman Leo Patimkin in "Goodbye Columbus" bears a striking resemblance to Willy Loman. Mordecai Richler has his young salesman Duddy see a Broadway production of Miller's play in *The Apprenticeship of Duddy Kravitz* in order to express his deep resistance to Miller's work. Saul Bellow uses Willy Loman as the model for Tommy Wilhelm (a failed actor turned failed salesman) in his novella *Seize the Day*. And Arthur Laurents is clearly referencing *Salesman* in *Gypsy*, the musical tale of a dominating, deluded, and highly theatrical stage mother and her two alienated daughters. As in *Salesman*, *Gypsy* ends with an onstage representation of the main character's nervous breakdown, which counterintuitively becomes the theatrical high point of the show.

Death of a Salesman has long been considered a crypto-Jewish text and its popularity has led to an ongoing sense of wonder (or pride, or anxiety) that a "Jewish" play, written by and about members of a group which has never constituted more than 3 percent of the American population, could become so central to American culture and so popular with audiences across the globe. Since its opening in 1949, critics and scholars have attempted to describe the language of the play as Yiddish-inflected, to expose the Loman family as assimilated Jews, to read Willy as an example of a stock shtetl character (a *luftmensch* or schlemiel) or the leftist critique of capitalism in the play as a "typical" expression of Jewish socialist values.[29] While many of these arguments are persuasive—the Jewishness of the Loman family is certainly plausible, and Miller himself acknowledges that he modeled his characters on members of his own extended family—none accounts for the popularity of the play with such broad audiences. Both the Jewishness and the popularity of *Death of a Salesman* are rooted in an American debate (in which Jews vigorously participated) over the definition of character and the accommodation of difference in a dramatically altered Cold War universe. In his plays and other writings, Miller expressed a firm belief in the popular American universalism of the day—that skin color, cultural background, or religious affiliation were merely superficial distinctions, which served to mask the fundamental *sameness* of all humanity. Underpinned by an embrace of the notion of America as a "Judeo-Christian" country, universalism also flattened out the differences between the three accepted American faiths—Protestantism, Catholicism, and Judaism—by making all three look a bit more like liberal Protestantism. One of the key features of the work of those Jewish writers and artists who embraced Judeo-Christianity was an increasing rejection of "surface" presentations of the self in favor of deep psychological truth. This version of identity assumes that the truth of a person is determined not by how he or she looks or acts but by who he or she *is* inside. And as we are all human, we all share basic values, dreams, impulses, and desires. Anything which serves to mask or alter our fundamental humanity is therefore to be treated with suspicion.[30]

Arthur Miller became America's most celebrated playwright with three important plays, *All My Sons* (1947), *Death of a Salesman* (1949), and *The Crucible* (1953), all of which are devoted to the demystification and unmasking of hypocrisy, artifice, illusion, and faith in false gods. Redemption for Miller's central characters lies in *dis*illusionment, the rejection of artifice, and the embrace of something that can best be labeled authentic humanity. The plays are decidedly anti-theatrical in the sense that Jonas Barish (a contemporary of Miller's) in *The Antitheatrical Prejudice* traces back to Plato: they rail against the immorality of artifice and illusion that form the very backbone of the theater itself. The self-conscious theatrical liberalism that guided many in his father's generation in their quest to join the middle and upper classes of American society in Miller's work threatens to be the source of the son's—and the whole society's—undoing. In the wake of the Depression and with the failure of his father's business among many others, Miller condemns those who live within a world of illusion (especially about socioeconomic mobility), those who manipulate illusion to ensnare others, those who lie, and especially those who lie to themselves. In each play, Miller creates dramatically rich central characters—Joe Keller, Willy Loman, Abigail Williams—whom he then critiques for the very theatricality that makes them so powerful on the stage. The better these characters perform, the more immoral they are judged to be. This anti-theatricality appears early in *All My Sons* (1947) with Joe Keller's convincing performance of innocence before a jury and later in front of his neighbors. Likewise, Abigail Williams in *The Crucible* is a brilliant actress, but the more successful her performance is, the more manipulative, selfish, and immoral she appears. *Death of a Salesman* rejects the theatricality of the title character even more categorically. Willy's theatricality, which takes the form of a nervous breakdown, is crippling and his belief in the powers of theatricality only serve to pass on that neurosis to his sons. Audience members are meant to feel pity for a man so wholly deluded by theatricality, but they are certainly not to be deluded by theatricality themselves. We see no liberating possibility for theatricality in any of these plays. Far from being a beacon of freedom and anti-essentialism, theatricality here bears the morally damning mark of insincerity.

Miller understood his mission of demystification in explicitly religious terms, arguing that his "personal ambition as a playwright [was welded to his] hopes for the salvation of the Republic." As a writer, he saw himself as a "mediator between the Jews and America, and among Americans themselves as well."[31] By the middle of the McCarthy era, Miller was shouldering the burden of demystifying the illusions of theatrical liberalism not only for American Jews but for Americans in general. Rejecting the notion of performed identity altogether, Miller's plays instead encourage audiences to discover their own "authentic" humanity and, in doing so, to see the larger, universal human motivations behind their actions and desires. Miller hoped to show Jews that they did not need theatricality, the "performance" of Americanness, in order to be accepted into American society, to be well liked. In fact, like Willy Loman, Jews are bound to be disappointed, or ostracized, if they continue to follow this particular strategy of self-making, to remain, as Miller said fifty years later, "on the sidewalk side of the glass looking in at a well-lighted place."[32] Instead, Miller aimed to show all Americans that Jews, like other Americans, are simply human beings, and as such are *already* part of a group that shares "common emotions and ideas."[33] Performance of identity becomes unnecessary, indeed counterproductive, in this universalist vision.

Arthur Miller's plays subject theatrical liberalism to a rough beating; yet it is remarkable how well it survives the onslaught. Even in the work of an author determined, as Miller wrote in 1957, "to be as untheatrical as possible," who wrote plays about the problems of artifice and illusion, it is theatrical liberalism that ultimately accounts for his extraordinary success. But theatrical liberalism is obscured in this play by an insistent anti-theatricality. The overt content of *Death of a Salesman* violently rejects illusion. The American dream of material success is presented in this play as a con, a cruel deception that destroys the common man. Willy's faith in this illusory dream leads to his own downfall and damages his family irreparably. In his book *Timebends*, Miller explicitly connects salesmen and actors: "In a sense, these men lived like artists, like actors whose product is first of all themselves, forever imagining triumphs in a world that either ignores them or denies their presence altogether" (*Timebends*, 127). As a salesman, Willy too is an actor and is rejected by his son Biff (and the play) as inauthentic. Likewise, Willy's imaginative life, his ability to speak to people who are not there, to bring the past to life, to invent and reinvent scenes of conflict and joy on the stage defines Willy not as an artistic genius (as might have been the case in a different play or at a different historical moment), but as mentally unbalanced and literally sick.

The dramaturgical features of *Death of a Salesman* on the other hand, in its dramatic structure, its performance style, its form, ironically reinforce the very aspects of theatrical liberalism the play purports to critique. When asked about his theatrical influences, Miller was always careful to trace a path that led from his early interest in classical Greek drama, Ibsen, and the plays of Clifford Odets and the Group Theater directly to the psychological realism of *Salesman*. Realism, after all, carried a certain high-art and morally serious cache that was deemed utterly lacking in the more popular commercial theater of the time. By the mid-twentieth-century, dramatic realism had become the gold standard by which "serious" plays on Broadway were judged.[34] Even musicals of the 1940s, beginning with *Oklahoma!* were praised or criticized on the basis of their realist pretensions: those musicals that effectively "integrated" song and story within a realist structure were considered mature works of art; those that didn't tended to be dismissed as commercial fluff. The overarching goal of dramatic realism was to create a believable world into which audiences could enter both intellectually and emotionally, forgetting that they were in the theater for the two or three hours of the play, in order to sympathize more fully with the characters on the stage. Actors in the realist theater worked hard to create a sense of a complete world on the stage, and avoided at all cost the habits of performers in more self-consciously theatrical genres, such as exaggerating gestures, vocal styles, or emotions, breaking character, referring self-consciously to the audience beyond the footlights. Kirk Williams describes the project of the late nineteenth-century naturalists from whom Miller borrowed many of his own ideas:

> Their explicit objective was to completely remove the barrier separating theater from life, to create an illusion so powerful that it would render the theatrical medium absolutely transparent. One must experience theater as one experiences life itself . . . seeing in the events onstage "a slice of life as if one is peering through a window." The point is to replace theatrical artifice with "a near-perfect reality, in other words, to drive the 'Theater' gradually from the theater."[35]

Miller himself writes about the importance of this naturalist strategy in his own work. In the Introduction to his *Collected Plays* in 1957, Miller writes of *All My Sons*:

> My intention in this play was to be as untheatrical as possible. To that end any metaphor, any image, any figure of speech, however creditable

to me, was removed if it even slightly brought to consciousness the hand of a writer. So far as was possible nothing was to be permitted to interfere with its artlessness.[36]

Like the naturalists, Miller is especially concerned here with the removal of obvious metaphors and with self-conscious artifice, with anything that suggests a world outside of the play. Farther on in the essay, Miller comments that "the strategy [with *Death of a Salesman*], as with *All My Sons,* was to appear entirely unstrategic . . . to hold back nothing, at any moment, which life would have revealed, even at the cost of suspense and climax."[37] Miller's goal is to reproduce on stage, as exactly as possible, the inner workings of the human mind. To achieve this psychological realism, it was necessary to reject everything that smacked of what Miller calls "theatrics": "It began to seem to me that what I had written until then, as well as almost all the plays I had ever seen, had been written for a theatrical performance, when they should have been written as a kind of testimony whose relevance far surpassed theatrics."[38] For Miller, there is something higher that lies outside of or above the theater—*testimony*—and artlessness is the route to creating this more moral art form. As did Bertolt Brecht, Miller wants his audience to respond to the ethical problems in his play like a jury at a trial, but he aims to reach that goal not through the alienating effects of Brecht's self-conscious epic theater but through the all-encompassing illusion of psychological realism.

Embedded within this rhetoric of realism are two fundamental contradictions that complicate the attack on theatrical liberalism. First, Miller's stated goal is not to make theater into life but simply to make theater seem like life.[39] His goal is to reduce self-conscious theatricality, what he calls "theatrics" in his plays, to keep the theatricality obscured in order to create a "natural" scene on the stage but not necessarily to erase theatricality altogether. This desire to "naturalize" the theatrical is exactly what theatrical liberalism resists. The freedom promised by theatrical self-fashioning depends upon a society that assumes artifice to be a key feature of identity construction. As we will see, Willy Loman responds to this threat to his freedom with a violent defense of theatrical liberalism.

Second, the goal of Miller's naturalism—to create a more perfect illusion—seems to contradict his depiction of Willy's dire psychological state. In taking dreams for realities, Willy does what the audience members are supposed to do, but Willy suffers tragically from this delusion. Audiences have delighted in this play *because* it allows them to take Willy for the kind of real person he fatally mistakes his brother Ben to be. If, as reasonable characters like Biff and Charlie see, Willy's illusions destroyed him, by extension spectators would be better off if they openly accepted the unreality and artificiality of Willy Loman. Illusion thus represents, in *Death of a Salesman*, both the moral problem and the theatrical strategy for solving that problem.

The newly developed Method acting style in which this "unstrategic" and "inartistic" play was performed embodied these same contradictions. As Steven Vineberg observes in his history of Method Acting, this acting style "sees as the actor's essential task the reproduction of recognizable reality—verisimilitude—on stage (or screen) based on an acute observation of the world . . . [which] clearly links the Method to American naturalism, which has the same aim."[40] Popularized largely by Jews raised in the Yiddish theater—Lee Strasberg, Stella Adler, Sanford Meisner—Konstantin Stanislavski's Method became the gold standard for "authentic" acting in the second half of the twentieth century on both stage and screen.[41] With its focus on individual personality, and its emphasis on psychological verisimilitude and genuine emotion, it grew in popularity in response to, and in conjunction with, the rise of realism and the rejection of overtly self-conscious theatricality on the American stage. For example, Morris Carnovsky, a Yiddish theater actor and founding member of the Group Theater denounces the "showmanship" of the American stage of the early twentieth century, and instead celebrates the Stanislavski-influenced acting style of the Group, which allowed him to discover "his true Self," "a wholeness" or "integrity," in the art of acting.[42] Lee Strasberg, another of the founding members of the Group Theater and one of the most important teachers of the Method in the 1940s and '50s at the Actors' Studio, draws the connections between "life" and "acting" even closer in "The Actor and Himself":

The extraordinary thing about acting is that life itself is actually used to create artistic results. In every other art the means only pretend to deal with reality. Music can often capture something more deeply than any other way, but it only tells you something about reality. Painting tells something *about* the painter, *about* the thing painted, and *about* the combination of the two. But since the actor is also a human being, he does not pretend to use reality. He can literally use everything that exists.[43]

For Miller, the goal of the theater is to use this "actual reality" Strasberg celebrates to drive the theater from the theater. When Miller describes the first time he sees actor Lee J. Cobb (born Leo Jacob) perform Willy, he writes "And the theater vanished. The stage vanished." At the same time, Miller's description of Cobb's performance reinforces the very essence of the freedom that theatrical liberalism promises, indeed even sacralizes it: "a Godlike creation was taking place; a new human being being formed before all our eyes, born for the first time on this earth." He describes Cobb's Willy Loman as a character "made real by an act of will . . . a man was here transcending the limits of his body and his own history. . . . Through the complete concentration of his mind he had even altered the stance of his body, which now was strangely not the body of Lee Cobb, but of a sixty-year-old salesman."[44] The mechanics of the process, the "theatrics" may be obscured, but Cobb's extreme version of self-fashioning dramatizes not the rejection of theatrical liberalism, but its ultimate fulfillment.[45] Cobb has succeeded where many Jews feared failure—in convincing his spectators that he is what he performs. This is not a "natural" process (Cobb must become Loman through hard work and an act of will), but a highly artificial process that is deemed successful because it "looks" natural.

Despite Miller's insistence on his realist and high-culture goals, his description of theatergoing in his childhood and teenage years in his memoir reveals a fascination with the more self-consciously theatrical popular culture that complicates the straightforward path from the Group Theater to psychological realism that Miller continually reasserts elsewhere. In *Timebends,* Miller describes how, at his first play, a melodrama about a cannibal about to blow up a ship with a bomb, he felt intense anxiety: "What anguish! The bomb would go off any minute, and I kept clawing at my mother's arm, at the same time glancing at the theatre's walls to make sure that the whole thing was not really real."[46] Miller recognizes here the power of the theatrical event to "distract and delude" and is relieved that he can comfort himself by looking away from the stage at the "real" walls of the theater in order to remember that what he is watching is artifice. Miller also remembers, with trepidation, his hopes that the audience could traverse the fourth wall on the stage and shape the action of the play by shouting instructions to the actors. "People were yelling, 'He's in the barrel,'" "But," Miller remembers, "the passengers were deaf" (ibid., 58).

This experience is soon followed up by regular and enthusiastic attendance at the local vaudeville theater. Instead of synagogue, Miller remembers attending "the vaudeville show on Saturdays, always the most anticipated day of the week, the opening acts—the mildly amazing Chinese acrobat families with their spinning plates and flying children, fairly boring after you had seen them twenty times" (ibid., 59). Vaudeville was clearly the shaping theatrical influence of Miller's childhood. Miller remembers fondly the great performers he saw week after week:

> These included jokers and singers like Eddie Cantor and George Burns and Al Jolson and George Jessel, the black tap dancers Buck and Bubbles and Bill "Bojangles" Robinson, and the headline acts like Clayton, Jackson, and Durante, whom my father all but revered. (ibid., 59)

The deliberate connection Miller makes between his father and the popular theater offers insight into the theatrical nature of the father figure of Willy Loman. He says that his father was "a connoisseur, having seen these performers so often during his days on the road that he could tell me how their routines had changed." The "road" is conflated with the experience of vaudeville here as it is, in symbolic ways, for Willy. As a teenager, Miller attempted to make a career as a singer of popular show tunes and actually auditioned for a radio show in the Brill Building in Manhattan, crooning a Lorenz Hart ballad. The career choice obviously did not work out, but the fact that he considered it indicates his own familiarity with, and affection for, the songs and performance styles of the popular musical theater of the 1930s (ibid., 109).

Knowing of Miller's repeated exposure to and early love of vaudeville and musical comedy—the very forms in which theatrical liberalism was best expressed—we can map a journey through *Death of a Salesman* that unearths the places where theatrical liberalism asserts itself.[47]

One key feature of the popular musical theater and vaudeville to which Miller refers is the episodic nature of the performance, the clear division between story and song in musicals, the rapid movement between different performance modes in vaudeville. This episodic structure prevents audiences from forgetting that they are in a theater and demands self-consciousness on the part of both actors and spectators. In the brief pauses between acts or numbers, audiences are expected to respond directly to the performers, preferably through applause and cheering for encores. We see vestiges of this self-consciously theatrical episodic structure in *Death of a Salesman* in the constant shifting between the present and past, the real and the remembered. In a musical, when a character's emotions reach a peak and the character can no longer express those feelings in a scene, the character breaks into song. Instead of breaking into song in *Death of a Salesman,* Willy goes into a memory.[48] As is appropriate for the star, Willy gets all of the good "songs," and his family serves as the supporting chorus.[49] Memory scenes, like musical numbers, are generally introduced by instrumental music and a change in lighting. In *Salesman* in the first memory scene, the stage directions indicate that "the apartment houses are fading out, and the entire house and surroundings become covered with leaves. . . . Music insinuates itself as the leaves appear."[50] In the introduction to the second memory scene, "music is heard as behind a scrim" (ibid., 24). The memory that introduces Willy's successful brother Ben begins when "Ben's music is heard" (ibid., 30). And so on. This use of music introduces a shift in theatrical mode, and evokes an earlier melodramatic style; each of the characters from Willy's past (Ben, the Woman, his father, and Willy himself) have their own musical theme, which cues the audience to particular emotional and moral responses.

Another crucial feature of the vaudeville and musical stage that Miller highlights in his description of the cannibal and the bomb is the unstable relationship between the audience and the players. To "break" the fourth wall—the invisible, imagined wall that divides the stage from the audience—is to commit an unforgivable breach of the rules of dramatic realism. In popular theater of the early twentieth century, in contrast, especially in vaudeville, the melodrama of the Yiddish theater, and the musical theater, the fourth wall was highly permeable. Audiences frequently communicated with the players on stage, applauding and shouting for encores in the middle of the show, shouting out directions to the actors, throwing flowers, and sometimes even "stopping the show" with cheers, applause, and standing ovations. Actors showed an awareness of the audience as well, making self-conscious asides directed at the audience, hamming up jokes to get a few more laughs, performing songs downstage center in full frontal position even if the songs were ostensibly directed at other characters in the play, going out of character to bow after musical numbers, even taking requests from the audience.[51] Even the ostensibly realist theater of Clifford Odets and the Group reputedly broke the fourth wall at the end of the political piece *Waiting for Lefty,* when the actors on stage (including Elia Kazan, the director of *Death of a Salesman)* exhorted the audience to "strike!" and the audience responded by shouting "Strike! Strike!" While Arthur Miller aimed to abolish the theatrics that draw attention to the constructedness of the theatrical event, these other theatrical forms depend for their success on a knowing playfulness regarding the respective roles of the audience and the players.

In *Death of a Salesman,* there is an extreme concern in the play with walls and the way in which walls are to be treated by the actors. As the curtain rises, we see the Lomans' small house, surrounded on three sides by apartment buildings which loom over it, shutting out the light and enclosing the house as if in a trap. The opening stage directions then describe the manner in which the walls of the house itself map the movement between realism and self-conscious theatricality: "Whenever the action is in the present the actors observe the imaginary wall lines, entering the house only through the door at the left. But in the scenes of the past these boundaries are broken, and characters enter or leave a room by stepping "through" a wall on to the forestage"(Miller, *Salesman,* 1).[52] Willy's first scene highlights the importance of walls (and windows) as a metaphor for theatricality. Willy has returned home because he keeps driving off the road. He describes his experience to his wife Linda: "I was driving along, you understand? And I was fine. I was even observing the scenery. You can imagine, me looking at scenery, on the road every week of my life" (Miller, *Salesman,* 3). Willy is surprised at his interest in scenery. He has been a traveling salesman for years. He's played this scene a million times. Why take a sudden interest in the scenery? Something about the scenery, or the way Willy looks at it, must have changed. And a change in the scenery signals an important shift in both the theater in which Willy performs and in the life he leads. Willy continues, "I opened the windshield and just let the warm air bathe over me. And then all of a sudden I'm goin' off the road! I'm tellin' ya, I absolutely forgot I was driving" (Miller, *Salesman*, 3). Willy opens the windshield and loses control of the car. Something in the act of opening the windshield is dangerous, even violent. "I might've killed somebody," he continues. We learn a few pages later why the opening of the windshield nearly leads to disaster:

> LINDA: And Willy—if it's warm Sunday we'll drive in the country. And we'll open the windshield, and take lunch.
> WILLY: No, the windshields don't open on the new cars.
> LINDA: But you opened it today.
> WILLY: Me? I didn't. [*He stops*] Now isn't that peculiar! Isn't that a remarkable—[*He breaks off in amazement and fright as the flute is heard distinctly*] . . . I was thinking of the Chevy. Nineteen twenty-eight . . . when I had that red Chevy—That funny? I coulda sworn I was driving that Chevy today. (Miller, *Salesman*, 7–8)

To open the windshield is, for Willy, to experience freedom, the joy of literal, temporal, and metaphorical mobility (the warm breezes "bathing over" him, the memory of the past, the dream of a better life). To be unable to open that windshield is to be trapped within the car, within the present and within a self-representation that offers no hope of escape. The windshield, the clear glass through which one observes the scenery, seems a fine metaphor for the fourth wall on the stage. According to the play, Willy's failure lies largely in his inability to acknowledge that the windshield is sealed shut, his inability to recognize theatrical mobility as an outdated dream, and to accept the inevitability of dramatic realism . . . of walls that stay where they belong, of hard truths that shine like diamonds in the jungle.

Willy Loman is the most overtly theatrical performer in the play, able to not only sustain his own over-the-top performance style in the face of incredible odds but to continually wrest the play from its realist moorings and engage the audience in flights of fancy reminiscent of the self-consciously theatrical forms in which he clearly feels more comfortable. It is Willy who always has a story, who is always performing, who manages to conjure whole scenes of the past out of thin air, complete with music, lighting, performers and sets. In this, Willy bears more than a passing resemblance to another traveling salesman (albeit a happier one) who had been performing for sell-out crowds on Broadway for the six years before *Death of a Salesman* opened (and reappeared on Broadway in the 1951 revival). This popular salesman, the peddler Ali Hakim in the Rodgers and Hammerstein musical *Oklahoma!*, established a place for himself in the musical and on the American frontier by creating dream visions for Laurey, the leading lady, through the use of his "Elixir of Egypt" and for the villain Jud through pornographic postcards.[53] Willy's memory scenes, in which the actors play younger versions of the characters in the realist scenes, briefly recapture the power of the uplifting musical number to reimagine and reinvent the self, as D. A. Miller describes it, "sending the whole world packing." While Willy breaks the fourth wall between the audience and the actors only once in the play (and then only obliquely), he continually threatens its stability in the memory scenes, which take place on the apron downstage, outside of the realist set and closest to the audience. Willy moves back and forth between the two stages—his mind and the world—continually traversing the walls that should (according to the play at least) keep a more sane man contained.

Willy's despair is rooted in the fear that as a theatrical character, if he runs out of stories, he will cease to exist. "The gist of it is that I haven't got a story left in my head," he tells his sons Biff and Happy when he meets them in a restaurant. Biff wants to "hold on to the facts tonight," and Willy refuses (Miller, *Salesman*, 83). Willy simply cannot perform in the style demanded by the play. When he turns to his memories for guidance, he loses himself in them, and in doing so he encourages the very artifice that the realist theater is supposed to dispel. According to the play, Willy's flaw is that he imagines he can return to a time when the windshield still opened. Even worse, he still believes that the open windshield is the gateway to freedom and opportunity. Willy perpetually returns to 1928, when car windshields still opened, when the fourth wall was still permeable, vaudeville was still a hit, when he still imagined he could connect with an audience, sell a dream, and reinvent himself at will. The fact that most of Willy's memories are of the last year of vaudeville's popularity before it was eroded by "talking pictures," further anchors Willy's performance in the theatrical style of an earlier era. He is trapped by this faith in outmoded performance styles and genres. He believes in the power of a charming face, a strong voice, and a persuasive narrative. He believes in comedy. But Willy is incapable of achieving anything tangible with these theatrical hallucinations because the play insists on undercutting their power, on making them the product of insanity rather than brilliance. In *Death of a Salesman*, the breaking of theatrical walls, the following of musical dreams, the opening of windshields, can only represent a destructive concession to the illusory myth of American freedom and opportunity.

Willy Loman is in a struggle to the death with Arthur Miller. Miller wants to banish self-conscious theatrics; Willy himself is artful and brilliantly theatrical. Willy does not submit easily to the play's rejection of theatricality. In fact, his refusal to submit is an example of the very quality that Miller claims defines tragedy. In "Tragedy and the Common Man," Arthur Miller aims to justify his own work as tragedy despite the fact that it features a common salesman as opposed to a king. The modern tragic flaw, he argues, is the central character's "inherent unwillingness to remain passive in the face of what he conceives to be a challenge to his dignity, his image of his rightful status."[54] In this case, Willy's "rightful status" is his self-conscious theatricality, and his tragic flaw is, ironically, his faith in the power of theatrical liberalism. Audiences love and sympathize with him not because he is deluded and certainly not because he is common. Audiences connect with Willy because he is theatrical. He is the one character who believes that it is important to be well liked, and while that appears to get him and his sons nowhere in the world of the play, it goes a long way in the theater. Willy resists the play's insistence that the windshield is locked shut; he continually breaks through those walls, at the price of losing everything. Willy refuses to submit to the vision of hard, real authenticity that the play proposes and in doing so, he taps into the audience's own need to have faith in the promises of theatrical liberalism, *even if* those promises prove to be illusory. Willy is the one character who dares to acknowledge the audience, and when he does so the audience weeps for him. In the penultimate scene in the play, just before Willy's suicide, Willy sings his final "song," in the guise of a conversation with his ghostly brother Ben. Willy has realized that his son, Biff, still loves him, and with this knowledge he can die happily. The ghost of Ben convinces him to pass on his faith in theatricality by killing himself and bequeathing the insurance money to Biff. Willy speaks to Biff, and to himself, as he gears up for his final act. And as he does so, he makes it clear that he has been an actor all along:

> WILLY: Now when you kick off, boy, I want a seventy-yard boot, and get right down the field under the ball, and when you hit, hit low and hit hard, because it's important, boy. [*He swings around and faces the audience*] There's all kinds of important people in the stands, and the first thing you know . . . [*Suddenly realizing he is alone*] Ben! Ben, where do I . . . ? (*Salesman*, 108, my emphasis)

Willy begins by reprising the pep talk he gave to Biff before the Ebbets Field game, although it quickly becomes clear that the pep talk is directed at himself. Then suddenly, as if emboldened by his choice to resist the play's rejection of an older more self-conscious theatricality, he breaks out of his interiority, faces the audience full front for the first time, and acknowledges them directly. "There's all kinds of important people in the stands." Willy has, for a moment, escaped the bounds of the play, but his brief revelation that there *are* actually people out there, watching him, is quickly repressed. The text immediately shuts down Willy's impulse and he "suddenly realiz[es] he is alone." But that moment of theatrical self-consciousness emboldens him to perform his final act. Willy opens the windshield for the last time, and drives off the stage forever, taking the last vestiges of theatrical liberalism with him.

Or so it seems. At his funeral, just before the curtain comes down, Linda comments that at long last the mortgage is paid off and laments that Willy is not there to share in this milestone: "I made the last payment on the house today. Today, dear. And there'll be nobody home. [*A sob rises in her throat*] We're free and clear. [*Sobbing more fully, released*] We're free. [BIFF *comes slowly toward her.*] We're free. . . . We're free. . ." (*Salesman*, 112). This "freedom" Linda evokes is generally taken as an ironic comment on the steep price Americans must pay, with their bodies and souls, for the freedom to pursue material success. Or as an acknowledgment that now that Willy is gone, the family—especially

Biff, who has just asserted that he "knows who he is"—is finally free of the illusory dream Willy insisted on. On the one hand, the play insists that Willy's freedom was circumscribed by a corporate culture, which does not allow him (or Biff or Happy) to "be himself" (Biff says, "He had the wrong dreams"). On the other hand, this "being oneself" is ultimately revealed by the play as far more limiting. In peculiarly heightened language that seems to have absorbed some of the self-conscious theatricality Willy no longer can provide, his friend Charley offers his thoughts on "being oneself": "Nobody dast blame this man . . . for a salesman, there is no rock bottom to the life" (*Salesman*, 111). Charley seems to understand what the family does not—that Willy's refusal to be fixed into one, solid, "rock bottom," image of self *is* the most accurate definition of who Willy was.

Just after the family exits the stage, there are two final, and contradictory, stage directions: "*Only the music of the flute is left on the darkening stage as over the house the hard towers of the apartment buildings rise into sharp focus*" (*Salesman*, 112). The play ends with the battle for theatrical dominance raging on between the realism of those "hard towers" and the theatricality of the melodic flute of Willy's memory scenes. But the theatrical experience itself has one more scene to play. Willy does return to the stage, of course, in the curtain call. And as the audience roars with appreciation—for the actor's remarkable performance or for Willy's tenacity or both?—Willy finally gets what he wanted all along. He is, without question, "well-liked." People do not flock to *Death of a Salesman* to learn about how corrupt, debased, and deluded their own ideals are. People rarely do. Rather, *Death of a Salesman* is popular because it tells a familiarly American narrative, albeit in an indirect, resistant manner. The play celebrates the life and mourns the death of a dreamer who fights against a system that threatens to take away his dreams, to deny him his basic freedom to self-fashion (even if he is deluded about how effectively he can make use of that freedom). This play is a work of American popular culture turned inside out. In attempting to repress or reject theatrical liberalism, *Death of a Salesman* becomes a celebration of the very thing it denies. Theatrical liberalism may not have saved the Loman family, but it did wonders for *Death of a Salesman*.

* * *

When *West Side Story* opened on Broadway in 1957, it caused a sensation in the world of musical theater. Americans had seen Shakespeare adapted for the Broadway stage before. Cole Porter's *Kiss Me, Kate* (based on *The Taming of the Shrew)* and Rodgers and Hart's *The Boys from Syracuse* (based on *The Comedy of Errors*) were both enormously popular musical adaptations of the Bard's work. But both of these were comedies. *West Side Story* was something different—a musical based on one of Shakespeare's tragedies. Drawing on the conventions of musical comedy and of Shakespearean tragedy, *West Side Story* tests the boundaries of both genres, ultimately inhabiting a hybrid form ideally suited to express the tensions and concerns of 1950s American liberal culture, which included not only debates about universalism and assimilation but also the complexities of Cold War hysteria, a rising teenager culture and accompanying concerns about juvenile delinquency, the increasingly urgent fight for black civil rights, and a creeping consciousness about the horrors of the Holocaust.

West Side Story's generic instability emerges from a fundamental contradiction between the musical's ideological roots in early twentieth-century theatrical liberalism and the concerns of the historical moment in which the play appeared, when the basic values of theatrical liberalism were increasingly under attack. While it may come as no surprise that *West Side Story* privileges distinctively American values in its adaptation of Shakespeare's play, what is surprising is the way in which the play wrestles with the basic thematic and formal values of theatrical liberalism. *West Side Story* is deeply indebted to the Broadway musical comedy, yet resists the kind of happy ending audience members in the 1950s might have expected. The play takes its cues more from the post-war musicals of the 1940s and '50s, which privileged realism and treated the highly self-conscious theatricality of the earlier comedies with ambivalence.

By the 1950s, as we have seen, new ideas about acting, theater, and the sources of the self had begun to reshape Broadway. With the success of *Death of a Salesman* and *A Streetcar Named Desire,* Method acting became the gold standard for stellar performances, an acting technique that insisted that authentic feeling must come first. Once an actor has figured out how to "feel" the part, then he or she can begin to perform it. There were problems, of course, with this radical shift in dramaturgical fashion, the most obvious being that in works like *Death of a Salesman,* it led to an ironically anti-theatrical attitude toward performance. The best performances were considered to be those that came from the most authentic place, which were, in effect, the least theatrical. The push for realism in American drama of the 1950s is well known, but how to translate this anti-theatrical embrace of authenticity to a musical? While critics praised the heightened realism of the "integrated" musicals of the time, they also tacitly acknowledged that musicals are inherently theatrical. Musicals represent extremes of emotion in highly unrealistic ways: through song and dance. In *West Side Story,* musical numbers not only further the action and develop character (the simple definition of the integrated musical), but they also explore the relative power of interior psychological states and external theatrical "action," raise questions about the authenticity of theatrical self-fashioning, and interject comedy into tragic source material. In this innovative use of the musical form, *West Side Story* managed to simultaneously embrace realist authenticity while making a political statement that relied on the tenets of theatrical liberalism for its explanatory power.

Created by Leonard Bernstein (music), Arthur Laurents (book), Jerome Robbins (direction and choreography), and Stephen Sondheim (lyricist), *West Side Story* closely follows the plot of Shakespeare's *Romeo and Juliet,* with some notable differences.[55] Originally intending to create a drama of Jewish/Catholic rivalry on New York's East Side, the writers eventually chose to focus on the more timely problem of juvenile delinquency, gang violence, and tensions between Puerto Rican immigrants and "white" Americans on Manhattan's West Side. Many of the characters map neatly onto Shakespeare's script: Romeo becomes Tony, a Polish American, and Juliet becomes Maria, a newly arrived Puerto Rican immigrant. Tony's best friend, and the leader of the Jets street gang, is Riff, who, like Mercutio, is cut down by Bernardo, Maria's brother (closely modeled on Juliet's cousin Tybalt) and a member of the rival gang, the Sharks. Like Romeo and Juliet at the masked ball, Tony and Maria meet at a (settlement house) dance and fall in love at first sight. With the soaring musical number "Tonight," Bernstein and Sondheim effect a remarkable transformation of the balcony scene in musical theater terms. A rumble between the rival gangs at the end of the first act leaves both Riff and Bernardo dead, and Tony in hiding at the drugstore where he works, protected by Doc, adapted from Shakespeare's Friar Lawrence into a hapless shopowner ("I have no mind," Doc says at one point, "I am the village idiot"). In lieu of a sleeping potion in the original play, Maria sends her friend Anita (Bernardo's lover) to the drugstore to give Tony a message, but Anita is attacked and nearly gang-raped by the Jets. In retaliation, instead of giving Maria's message to Tony, she tells them all that Maria is dead. Maria's false death becomes not just a plot device but a passionately impulsive response on Anita's part to the racial and sexual mistreatment she has suffered at the hands of the Jets. In making this choice, Laurents further entrenches the fate of the two lovers in the racial prejudice that infects the entire world of *West Side Story*. Tony, hearing Anita's "news," runs out into the street offering himself up to the Sharks. He sees Maria approaching, and realizes he has been misled, but at the same moment, Chino (a member of the Sharks who, like Paris in *Romeo and Juliet*, was intended to marry Maria), emerges from the shadows and shoots him. In the penultimate tableau, Maria cradles Tony's dying body in her arms, like a modern pieta, just before grabbing the gun from Chino and threatening to shoot all of them and then herself. In a turn away from Shakespeare's script, Maria's despair gives way to a resigned determination as she—instead of the prince, or in this case the police—insists that the gang members join together to carry Tony's body off the stage.

While the writers clearly took great pains to remain faithful to the spirit of *Romeo and Juliet*, *West Side Story* is, like any adaptation, a product of its time and place.[56] The ethos of 1950s America is evident not only in the modern dress and setting of the play but also in many of its key formal and thematic choices. Perhaps most obviously, the two gangs are not "two households both alike in dignity" as the Chorus describes the Montagues and Capulets in the Prologue to *Romeo and Juliet*. While all the characters in *West Side Story* are poor and struggling to survive on the city streets, the Jets have a clear edge in gaining the sympathy of both the police and the audience. The Jets, of course, are perceived by the Sharks to be privileged because they were born in America. The authority structure represented by Lt. Shrank and Officer Krupke supports this perception. While neither of them is fond of the Jet boys, Shrank in particular claims to be on their side. Calling the Jets "regular Americans" and the

Sharks "gold-teeth," Shrank insists, "I'm for *you*. I want this beat cleaned up and you can do it for me. I'll even lend a hand if it gets rough."[57] The liberal American audience member is clearly meant to recognize Shrank's racism and to be repulsed by it. In refusing Shrank's offer of help, the Jets manage to maintain the moral high ground. Although they fight the Sharks on a daily basis, they are not so low as to become stool pigeons for the police. Indeed, the fact that they refrain from almost all racist language is remarkable, considering the level of otherwise unjustified hatred they express for the Sharks.

The Jets are indeed privileged, not only because they are "American" but also because, unlike the Sharks, they are a group of well-developed characters with songs, dances, and psychological motivations for their actions. Both groups are eager to fight, but the structure of the musical ensures that the audience's sympathy lies with the Jets. The play opens with a remarkable dance number, the famous Robbins's kicks, jumps, and finger-snapping, performed by the Jets with joyous energy, peaking in a glorious moment of virtuoso unison dancing, immortalized in the advertisements for the Hollywood film. The Sharks, who interrupt this dance with a fight, ultimately wounding one of the younger, more innocent members of the Jets, have no comparable number. The opening stage directions plotting out the action of the dance likewise offer detailed descriptions of each Jet boy:

> Their leader is Riff: glowing, driving, intelligent, slightly whacky [*sic*]. His lieutenant is Diesel: big, slow, steady, nice. The youngest member of the gang is Baby John: awed at everything, including that he is a Jet, trying to act the big man. His buddy is A-rab: an explosive little ferret who enjoys everything and understands the seriousness of nothing. The most aggressive is Action: a catlike ball of fury. We will get to know these boys better later, as well as Snowboy: a bespectacled self-styled expert. (ibid., 137)

We will not, on the other hand, get to know the Sharks better later. On the contrary, aside from a brief description of Bernardo, which lacks any of the mitigating qualities given to the Jet boys ("handsome, proud, fluid, a chip on his sardonic shoulder"), the stage directions give us no details about the Sharks except that they are numerous and that they choose to gang up on little A-rab, who is innocently pretending to be an airplane, viciously branding him by piercing his ear. The Jets have multiple scenes in which they discuss their plans, concerns, and friendships. They also have three important ensemble numbers in the play, "The Jet Song," "Cool," and "Gee, Officer Krupke," all of which work further to develop character, to establish sympathy, and, of course, to entertain. The Sharks have barely any dialogue and no songs at all. Unlike the Puerto Rican girls, the Sharks are apparently too foreign to sing in the Broadway style and therefore remain uneasy outsiders to the main performance action. Even in their one scene that establishes their own turf, which precedes the Puerto Rican girls' song "America," Bernardo (the only Shark to have a real speaking part) reveals his discomfort with American conventions ("back home, women know their place," he says to Chino). For a musical ostensibly about the pitfalls of prejudice, then, the theatrical scales are surprisingly skewed in favor of the "white" boys.

American ideas about romantic love—and the ways in which romantic love stories shape generic conventions—likewise determine key aspects of the adaptation. In *Romeo and Juliet,* Romeo is a lover from the beginning. In love with Rosalind, he moons about, depressed that she will not return his love. A teenage romantic, he cannot imagine that anyone or anything will change his heart—until he sees Juliet of course. ("Did my heart love till now? Forswear it sight, For I ne'er saw true beauty till this night" [act 1, sc. 5, 49–50]). And because Juliet returns his affections, Romeo's fate is sealed. In this way, *Romeo and Juliet* bears a resemblance to many of Shakespeare's comedies, most notably *A Midsummer Night's Dream,* in which romantic love is represented as a temporary and blinding affliction. Romeo and Juliet are as much in love with the drama of love as with each other. This implicit critique of the drama of romantic love was a staple of many Broadway musical comedies of an earlier generation. In Rodgers and Hart's hat-tip to Shakespeare, *The Boys From Syracuse* (1938), romantic love is repeatedly treated with suspicion and world-weary sophistication. Two of the most successful songs in that show deliberately reference the dangers of getting caught up in the drama of romance. "Falling in Love with Love," laments: "falling in love with love / Is falling for make-believe. Falling in love with love / Is playing the fool." And "This Can't be Love" draws a direct comparison between the love represented in *Romeo and Juliet,* the kind of love that makes one sick or dead, and the more self-aware kind of romance privileged by the comic characters in the play:

> In Verona, my late cousin Romeo
> Was three times as stupid as my Dromio.
> For he fell in love
> And then he died of it.
> Poor half-wit!
> This can't be love
> Because I feel so well—
> No sobs, no sorrows, no sighs.
> This can't be love,
> I get no dizzy spell,
> My head is not in the skies.[58]

The familial relationship Lorenz Hart assumes between Dromio and Romeo extends to many features of the play, but ultimately, unlike *The Boys from Syracuse*, *Romeo and Juliet* is not a comedy. The lovers' fascination with romance leads to death, and the reconciliation at the end of the play is effected not by romantic love but by the parents' grief and the prince's forbearance.

The ability of *West Side Story*, on the other hand, earnestly to champion romantic love, even romantic love thwarted by violence, to insist that romantic love is *the* redemptive force that can break down the barriers of prejudice, lies at the heart of what makes this version of *Romeo and Juliet* so distinctly an American musical of the 1950s. The play begins with Tony not in love like Romeo but disenchanted with gangs and fighting. Tony is, it seems, growing up and has lost his taste for the kind of performance necessary to be a Jet. "Now go play nice with the Jets," he tells Riff. He has taken on a responsible job and imagines a bright future for himself, convinced that "something's coming," as he sings in his opening song. That something, it turns out, is Maria. There is no irony in their first meeting at the dance at the gym and certainly no skepticism about the "drama of romance." The lights dim to a single spotlight, the dance music fades out, and a dreamy quality overtakes the entire stage. Their love is immediate, passionate, and true. Unlike the skepticism with which Romeo's friends treat his various love affairs,

Tony and Maria's constancy and judgment are never in doubt. The love scene is broken off suddenly, when Bernardo pulls Maria away, but Tony is unfazed and moments later breaks into the soaring aria "Maria," suggesting (more sincerely than Joey in *Pal Joey*'s "I Could Write a Book") that anyone who can sing like that must be really in love. The authority of romantic love in this musical is such that the lovers are fully capable of marrying themselves. No friar, no church is needed. In the bridal shop, a couple of scenes later, Tony and Maria kneel next to mannequins (standing in for their parents), pledge their vows, and are married.[59] By the end of the play, the power of romantic love reigns supreme. Although Tony dies, Maria's love lives on and effects the reconciliation between the gangs that no other authority could achieve—not the police, parents, war councils or death itself.[60]

Free choice in romantic love is a moral touchstone for the play, an American assertion of the democratic power of individuals to choose their own partners and fashion their futures free of interference from parents and inherited conditions like race, religion, or social class. But this active embrace of self-fashioning conflicts in *West Side Story* with deep concerns about the power of performative action to shape reality. This concern first becomes apparent in the bridal shop scene with Maria and Tony that culminates in the song "One Hand, One Heart." Using the dress dummies that surround them in the bridal shop, Tony and Maria pretend that they are meeting each other's parents, asking for permission to marry, and receiving it. They then don costumes—Maria a bridal veil and Tony a top hat—and set up a theatrical wedding scene for themselves. The two appoint dummies to serve as maid of honor and best man, then they kneel solemnly before the audience, which serves as the priest. Engaging in the paradigmatic performative speech act, as described by J. L. Austin in his famous lectures at Harvard in 1955, two years before the opening of *West Side Story*, Tony and Maria recite their wedding vows, exchange rings, kiss, and sing of their love in "One Hand, One Heart." They use speech that Austin calls performative; it doesn't just state facts, it actually brings about change. In musically and choreographically consenting to be married, within the context of a proper wedding ceremony, they actually become married. Their speech is action; their acting changes their reality. The stage directions indicate that the actors should demonstrate awareness of this transition from "acting" to "reality": "They look at each other—and the playacting vanishes." And a bit later, "They look at each other, and at the reality of their 'game'" (Houghton, *West Side Story*, 185). Tony and Maria have performed a wedding ceremony, and this action has changed their internal sense of themselves. From this point on, they believe they are married.

Austin stresses repeatedly, however, that for language to be performative, the circumstances of the situation must be correct. Language can be performative only when spoken by someone with the authority to bring about change. Do Tony and Maria have the authority to marry themselves, with only the audience and a few dress dummies as witnesses? Does anyone in this scene have the authority to speak the words, "I now pronounce you man and wife"? In their song, Tony and Maria appeal to some unnamed higher authority to "Make of our hands one hand / Make of our hearts one heart." The song is structured like a prayer, but to whom are they praying? God is not mentioned. Rather, the pair appeals directly to the audience. The stage directions read: "Slowly, seriously, they turn front, and together kneel as before an altar" (Houghton, 184). An altar to what? In the worldview of theatrical liberalism, the theater itself is a sacred space. Authority, in this sacred universe, lies with the audience, and with the formal conventions of the stage. No one literally speaks the words that confirm the marriage, but they are symbolically indicated by the audience, which has been invested with the authority belonging to the friar—and the church—in Shakespeare's version. When the audience applauds at the end of "One Hand, One Heart," it has given its consent to this marriage. The sound of applause pronounces the young couple man and wife.[61]

Elsewhere in *West Side Story,* however, the power of action to shape reality is a source of anxiety, a power that needs to be questioned, analyzed, and controlled. Action is not only the motivating force behind theatrical liberalism, he is also a character in the play. Action, a member of the Jets, is the boy eager to fight, to perform, to act. Always preferring action over talk, he is characterized by lines such as, "I say go, go!" (Houghton, *West Side Story*, 142) and "In, out, let's get cracking!" (ibid., 144). Riff spends a great deal of energy trying to calm Action down, to keep him under control. In the very first scene, Action is ready to rumble and Riff replies, "Cool, Action boy" (ibid., 142). When Riff enters the drugstore before the "war council," he again needs to pacify Action,

Tony (Richard Beymer) and Maria (Natalie Wood) marry themselves in *West Side Story*.

"Unwind, Action" (ibid., 171), and a few pages later, physically holding him back, he insists, "Easy, Action, save your steam for the rumble" (ibid., 173). And when Action can barely control himself before the big fight, Riff lectures him on the nuances of different kinds of acting:

> ACTION: I swear the next creep who calls me hoodlum—
> RIFF: *You'll laugh!* Yeah. Now you all better dig this and dig it the most. No matter who or what is eatin' at you, you show it, buddy boys, and *you are dead.* You are cuttin' a hole in yourselves for them to stick in a red-hot umbrella and open it. Wide. You wanna live? You play it cool. (ibid., 173)

Riff then moves into the number "Cool," a musical response to Action's impulsive energy, in which he tutors the boys in a form of acting, which involves self-control and the performance of a believable, cool "front." The number is fraught with tension and ambivalence. Action is one of the most dangerous characters in the play. His need to express his deepest emotions, to act on his uncontrolled violent impulses, represents both the dark force that drives the tragic denouement of the play and the aesthetic impulse, in 1950s drama and literature, to probe the depths of the soul and reveal the honest "truth" of a character.[62] Riff also counsels the boys to "act," but he means something quite different by it. Riff speaks the language of theatrical liberalism. For Riff, external performance is the best way to shape reality, not the other way around. The boys should *not* show their anger; according to Riff, rather, they should laugh. Riff is concerned that the impulsive expression of authentic feelings will get the boys killed. Laughing (i.e., acting) will save them. Riff resists Action's instinctive energy, his desire to feel first and act second, and favors instead a performance style which depends on the exterior presentation of self as a means of shaping both the plot of the boys' lives and the ways in which they respond to provocation.[63] "Take it slow, and daddy-o, you can live it up and die in bed," Riff sings.

Alas, Riff does not die in bed. Instead he falls victim to the impulsive action of another character, Tony, and is killed in the rumble. The style of acting Riff preaches suffers along with him. Following the rumble, early in act 2, the boys regroup to try to figure out how to act now that Riff is gone. Acting/Action is the subject of one of the most theatrical and rousing numbers in the show, and a welcome bit of comic relief in an otherwise unrelenting second act. Action and Snowboy meet up with the other boys on the street after a brief encounter in the station house. The boys want to know how they got off so easily. Snowboy replies, "Cops believe everything they read in the papers," and Action adds, "To them we ain't human, we're cruddy juvenile delinquents. So that's what we give 'em" (Houghton, *West Side Story*, 205). Action argues here for performance, for "putting on a front" and giving the audience—in this case the police—what they want and expect. But in performing for the cops, the boys are also compromising themselves, presenting themselves as if they "ain't human." Performance is both necessary and suspect. The gang then launches into a song, "Gee, Officer Krupke," in which one boy after another plays the role of an expert trying to figure out who or what Action really is. First, Action appeals to "Officer Krupke" (played by Snowboy), insisting that he has been shaped by his family and therefore is not responsible for his behavior:

ACTION: Dear kindly Sergeant Krupke,
　　　　You gotta understand—
　　　　It's just our bringin' upke
　　　　That gets us out of hand,

> Our mothers all are junkies,
> Our fathers all are drunks.
> ALL: Golly Moses—natcherly we're punks! (ibid., 206)

In this verse, Action's bad behavior is a response to his environment but doesn't represent his true "good" self. He is just *acting* that way:

> Gee, Officer Krupke, we're very upset;
> We never had the love that every child oughta get.
> We ain't no delinquents,
> We're misunderstood.
> Deep down inside us there is good!

So is Action bad, as his behavior would suggest, or good, as he insists? Is there a difference between who he is and how he acts? What makes Action act badly and who is responsible for him? The song becomes a theatrical tour de force, with Action shunted from judge to psychoanalyst, to social worker, with the other boys taking on roles as needed in quick-change vaudevillian style. It ends with a crowd-pleasing, chorus-line style refrain, topped off by a final curse at Krupke. The boys satirize each of the experts they encounter, experts eager to find out what motivates Action and the other boys, making it clear that they have little sympathy for those who think they can explain them with a simple unifying diagnosis:

> DIESEL [as judge]: The trouble is he's crazy.
> A-RAB [as psychiatrist]: The trouble is he drinks.
> BABY JOHN [as social worker]: The trouble is he's lazy.
> DIESEL [as judge]: The trouble is he stinks.
> A-RAB [as psychiatrist]: The trouble is he's growing.
> BABY JOHN [as social worker]: The trouble is he's grown!
> ALL: Krupke, we got troubles of our own! (ibid., 208)

The more the experts probe, the more ridiculous and contradictory their responses ("growing? Grown?").[64] These boys fault the adults around them for making judgments based on surfaces, for jumping to conclusions about them based on their behavior. The truth about them, and about Action in particular, lies deep inside him. Action perceives his encounters with the world of adults as an exhausting process of being explained, pinned down, flattened into one stereotypical character trait or behavior pattern after another. What Action seems to need is the very thing denied him by the poverty of the city streets, by the institutional structures designed to keep him out of jail, and also by the cult of authenticity that has him in its grip: the freedom to shape his own life.

The song "Gee, Officer Krupke" is both uplifting and horrifying. In its form, it represents the freeing power of theatricality in a liberal society. As the boys perform multiple roles and see Action in multiple ways, they demonstrate the very social mobility promised by theatrical liberalism. At the same time, the boys sing this song in the wake of the death of their good friend and leader in a pointless fight over racial prejudice, the very boy who counseled them on appropriate acting styles, on the ways to "act cool" in order to cheat death. The placement of this song in the second act raises questions about the efficacy of this kind of acting to prevent real violence and about the possibilities for theatrical freedom, for personal agency, in a world so circumscribed by poverty, prejudice, and the pursuit of authenticity.

Action and the boys evoke theatrical liberalism's celebration of quick-change performance but with an ironic twist. They seem to be arguing for broad freedom to self-fashion, but this is a freedom that they reserve for themselves, insisting in the second act that the Puerto Rican Anita cannot escape her racial self, that she is "too dark to pass," and that Anybodys, the tomboy who wants to be a member of the Jets, should stop acting like a boy and wear a dress. Tony and Maria also reject the possibilities of self-fashioning, instead succumbing to the romantic mysteries of the heart and the authentic self. When Anita bursts into Maria's room in act 2, just missing Tony who has escaped out the window, she berates Maria for having anything to do with him: "a boy like that, who'd kill your brother / forget that boy and find another / one of your own kind, stick to your own kind!" (Houghton, *West Side Story*, 212). Maria responds with the language of the immutable interior self, the heart:

> I hear your words
> And in my head
> I know they're smart,

Action (Tony Mordente) being analyzed in "Gee, Officer Krupke" from *West Side Story*.

> But my heart, Anita,
> But my heart! (ibid., 213)

Not only is she incapable of changing herself and her feelings, she is destined to be in love with Tony no matter what he does:

> I have a love, and it's all that I have.
> Right or wrong, what else can I do?
> I love him; I'm his,
> And everything he is
> I am, too. (ibid., 213)

For Maria, and for Anita too, who eventually concedes that Maria is right, agency is not the issue. Only the truth revealed by romantic love matters. Maria has no control over who she is, what she feels, or how she acts. Her heart has taken over—a space deep inside, which works of its own accord—and she willingly trades the freedom to perform her own self for the assurance of a fixed, true, and authentic love.

Convinced that Maria is dead, Tony, crazed by grief, rejects the possibility of disguise, escape, or acting "cool" and instead acts on impulse, racing into the street and daring Chino to come and get him. Suddenly, the tomboy Anybodys emerges from the shadows and attempts to bring him to his senses:

ANYBODYS: [*A whisper from the dark*] Tony . . .

TONY: [*Swings around*] Who's that?

ANYBODYS: [*Darting on*] Me: Anybodys.

TONY: Get outa here. HEY, CHINO, COME GET ME, DAMN YOU!

ANYBODYS: What're you doin', Tony?

TONY: I said get outa here! CHINO!

ANYBODYS: Look, maybe if you and me just—(ibid., 222)

Like Action, Anybodys is aptly named. A girl who wishes she were a boy, she represents the core of theatrical liberalism's promise: the freedom to become anybody at all. Anybodys brags, "I'm very big with shadows, ya know. I can slip in and out of 'em like wind through a fence" (ibid., 210). Echoing Shakespeare's Puck ("If we shadows have offended"), Anybodys is as changeable as the fairies in *A Midsummer Night's Dream* and the actors on Shakespeare's stage. She lurks in the wings, ready to emerge on cue and play her part. At this crucial moment in the play, she offers Tony a safe haven, encouraging him to retreat to the shadows, to make use of the magic of the theater to effect his escape. But Tony sees no hope in the solution Anybodys offers. He rejects not only her offer of assistance, but also her entire ethos of self-fashioning:

TONY: [*Savagely*] It's not playing any more! Can't any of you get that?

ANYBODYS: But the gang—

TONY: You're a girl: *be a girl!* (ibid., 222)

Insisting that Anybodys must be who she is biologically destined to be, Tony crushes both her fantasy and his own, as he rushes into the light, only to be confronted by another character from the shadows, Maria. She offers a radically different philosophy. "I didn't believe hard enough," Tony laments. "Loving is enough," she insists as Tony lies dying in her arms. And in the final tableau, Maria's faith in the power of romantic love triumphs as she brings together Sharks and Jets in a funeral procession, "the same procession they made in the dream ballet," making real the utopian vision of love and harmony Tony and Maria had dreamed of the night before.

In Raymond Williams's *Modern Tragedy*, published only a few years after the successful opening of *West Side Story,* he argues that liberal tragedy of the twentieth century differs markedly from the Greek model. Our modern tragedy, he asserts, is rooted in the psychological struggles of a lone individual, a heroic figure who battles against society, ultimately becoming a tragic victim as he recognizes the limitations of his individual strength. We pity this hero, a victim of the false promises of liberal individualism.[65] This may describe the liberal tragedy of Ibsen or O'Neill, but it does not fully take into account the peculiarly American theatrical liberalism of *West Side Story*. Tony does not easily fit Williams's model of the liberal tragic hero. He seems to aspire to individual happiness; he tells Doc of his dream that he and Maria will start a new life together in the country. But when this dream is expressed in the haunting song "Somewhere," he and Maria sing of a place for *us,* and as they are joined, in song and dance, by the entire chorus of street kids, this "us" is clearly meant to be larger than the two of them.[66]

Tony's death certainly limits his ability to achieve individual happiness. But Tony dies *not* because he rages against society. He dies because he has given up that fight. Anybodys, and the theatrical liberalism she represents, offers him a way out and he rejects it: "I didn't believe hard enough," he laments as he dies. In what? In the eternal possibilities of romantic love, of course, but also in the eternal optimism of theatrical liberalism, the ideology that made that love possible. Theatrical liberalism ultimately privileges obligations to the theatrical community, even at the expense of individual rights. While the love story between Tony and Maria is of course central to the play, *West Side Story* is not a story of a lone individual or even of a couple. It is the story of a community. The central characters are not really the lovers but the gangs, two groups of American kids who battle over a bit of sidewalk, who struggle to create "a place for us." They dream not of overcoming theatrical liberalism but of achieving it. If the play ended with Maria acting on her threat to shoot all of them and then herself (because "now she has learned to hate too"), this would be liberal tragedy. But the final tableau, in which she drops the gun and instead brings the warring gangs together to mourn their failure restores hope in the audience. As the curtain falls, the promise of theatrical liberalism lives on.

4

The Theatricality of Everyday Life

All the world is not, of course, a stage, but the crucial ways in
which it isn't are not easy to specify.
—Erving Goffman, *The Presentation of Self in Everyday Life*
(1959)

Toward the end of Mel Brooks's 1974 parody of the Hollywood Western, *Blazing Saddles,* a fight in a Wild West town literally bursts out of
its set. Walls come tumbling down as the camera pulls back to reveal
that the frontier town is actually a stage set on a Warner Brothers back-
lot in contemporary Los Angeles. Cowboys break through one set into
another, disturbing a rehearsal for a lavish musical comedy number
(replete with fountains, top hats, and tuxedoes) and then tumbling into
the studio commissary, where they initiate an enormous pie fight. A
tour group caught in the mayhem emerges covered in whipped cream
as the bad guy and the sheriff confront one another in front of the very
theater in which the film *Blazing Saddles* is about to be screened. The
sheriff shoots the evil railroad man Hedley Lamarr (who falls dead
on his own footprinted "star" on the sidewalk) and then goes in to see
the movie with his cowboy sidekick. *Blazing Saddles* announces in no
uncertain terms that by 1974, the boundary between theatricality and
reality, between onstage and off, had been blurred beyond recognition.

In the short period between the opening of *West Side Story* and *Blazing Saddles,* theatrical liberalism underwent yet another transformation, which began in the later 1950s and early 1960s with Jewish writers
and intellectuals expressing increasing interest in the theatrical nature of
identity. While many still explored these concerns within the boundaries of popular entertainment, social scientists also began to examine the
ways in which a theatrical understanding of reality might spill out beyond
the walls of a theater and inform the behavior of people in everyday life.

Mirroring the disintegrating walls of the Hollywood Western set in *Blazing Saddles,* theatrical liberalism in this transitional period became ever more closely connected in public discourse to the shaping of identity on the street, in social life, and in narratives of the Jewish past. The close connection between theatricality and social behavior was central to Erving Goffman's groundbreaking and popular study *The Presentation of Self in Everyday Life* (1959).[1] Goffman took the theater as a metaphor for social interaction and encouraged his readers to think of all human behavior in theatrical terms. The question of performance in daily life in turn shaped numerous aspects of popular entertainment in this period. Sid Caesar's early TV variety program *Your Show of Shows* reveled in the details of self-presentation in sketches such as "The German General"; Alan Jay Lerner and Frederick Loewe's successful adaptation of Shaw's *Pygmalion* for American audiences, the musical play and film *My Fair Lady* (1956, 1964), conducted a more serious investigation of the ethics of self-fashioning (and fashioning selves) by theatrical means. With the rise of a new ethnic consciousness by the mid-1960s, and increasing visibility of Jewishness in the public sphere, questions also arose about the relationship between performance and ethnic pride. Many Jewish writers, performers and directors became interested in the American Jewish past—both Eastern European and early twentieth-century American theatricality—as a source of contemporary ethnic identity. The popular culture of the 1920s and 1930s, the heyday of theatrical liberalism, became an accepted part of Jewish history, a touchstone for expressions of Jewish identity in the 1960s and beyond. Rather than privileging the transformative theatricality of so many works of theatrical liberalism from the early twentieth century, however, these new works of ethnic pride often celebrated a more authentic expression of Jewishness, reifying the very theatricality depicted in the works into an essential aspect of Jewish identity. The overtly Jewish plays and movies *Fiddler on the Roof* (1964, 1972) and *Funny Girl* (1964, 1968), for example, provided Jews and Americans with a history not only of Jewish immigration to America but also of the Jewish investment in popular entertainment. This focus on the performance of authentic Jewishness led to questions about the apparently secular nature of theatrical liberalism and set the stage for far more radical experiments in theatricality, authenticity, and religious practice in the later 1960s and 1970s.

* * *

One of the first, and most important, of the mid-century Jewish intellectuals to use theatrical terms to describe social interaction was Erving Goffman, whose book is considered one of the founding texts of performance studies. Goffman introduced the term "dramaturgy" into the field of sociology and used the terminology of the theatrical stage—performer, role, audience, frontstage, backstage—as metaphors to explain how we "stage manage" the images we convey to those around us. Goffman takes the features of theatrical liberalism and applies them to the performance of everyday life. Like his theatrical peers, he views performance as sacred ritual. "To the degree that a performance highlights the common official values of the society in which it occurs," he writes, "we may look upon it . . . as a ceremony—as an expressive rejuvenation and reaffirmation of the moral values of the community. . . The world, in truth, is a wedding"(ibid., 35–36). Similarly, he describes social groups as teams, casts of characters obliged to insure the success of a scene. Team members depend upon one another, a bond which Goffman calls "dramaturgical loyalty" and which he describes in terms similar to those expressed in early twentieth-century musicals such as *Gold Diggers of 1933*. "It is apparent that if a team is to sustain the line it has taken, the teammates must act as if they have accepted certain moral obligations. They must not betray the secrets of the team when between performances—whether from self-interest, principle, or lack of discretion" (ibid., 212). This is the reason, for example, for excluding children from a conversation involving gossip about the neighbors: they cannot be depended upon to maintain discretion (team loyalty) the next time one encounters those neighbors. Like the director Oscar Jaffe in *Twentieth Century*, or the theologian Abraham Joshua Heschel, Goffman also believes in the power of behavior and action to determine reality; his work involves precise attention to the details of social interaction. For Goffman, everyone is at once an actor and a spectator, always playing a social role while simultaneously observing the roles played by others. Goffman sees social interaction as "impression management," meaning the work that individuals do to consciously or unconsciously shape the impressions they give others. Impression management is closely aligned with the way an actor builds a character, and just as there are good and bad performances, there are more and less effective versions of impression management.

According to Goffman, people develop their social roles in theatrical ways, through the judicious use of "front" and "back" stage regions. The front is "that part of the individual's performance which regularly functions in a general and fixed fashion to define the situation for those who observe the performance" (ibid., 22) and, like in the theater, includes *setting* (furniture, décor, physical layout) and *personal front* (appearance, manners, speech, and gesture). The backstage, alternately, is "a place, relative to a given performance, where the impression fostered by the performance is knowingly contradicted as a matter of course. . . . Here the performer can relax; he can drop his front, forgo speaking his lines, and step out of character" (ibid., 112). The difference between theater and real life, however, is that in real life, the location of the front and back stage is constantly shifting. When a hostess is in the dining room for a dinner party, for example, she is in the front stage, and when she retires to the kitchen, she is backstage. But in the kitchen she may encounter a cook, a maid, a child, or a spouse. Her role will shift (from "hostess" to "mother" for example) and she will once again be in the front stage, albeit playing a different role in a different show. Indeed, it quickly becomes clear that one is only truly "backstage" when one is alone, and perhaps not even then. According to Goffman, therefore, all performances are relative, and the walls between front and backstage are, like those of the movie set in *Blazing Saddles,* easily breached.

As social performers, we are constantly shifting roles, and our belief in the roles we play also shifts depending on the context. Goffman describes a continuum of belief on the part of the performer from sincere to cynical. The sincere performer is completely taken in by his own act, sincerely convinced that the impression of reality that he stages is "real" reality. This is, by far, the most common type of acting; in other words, we generally believe that the parts we play are who we "really are"; we do not think of ourselves as "acting" in our day-to-day life. The cynical performer, on the other hand, is a self-conscious actor who knows that he is playing a role and has no belief in his own act as reality. An extreme example of this type of performance is the confidence man, whose crime, according to Goffman, is "not that he takes money from his victims but that he robs all of us of the belief that middle-class manners and appearance can be sustained only by middle class people" (ibid., 18, n. 1). But one can also perform cynically with good intentions, for example, the doctor who prescribes a placebo to a needy patient or the woman who dyes her hair in order to feel and look younger.

In blurring the boundary between theater and life, Goffman raises questions about the nature of reality and the ways in which a self or a society is constructed, and forces his readers to reconsider the limitations of the freedom to self-fashion in a liberal society. "In our own Anglo-American culture," Goffman notes, we have two ways of viewing behavior: "the real, sincere, or honest performance; and the false one that thorough fabricators assemble for us" (ibid., 70). We know that performances by actors on the stage are false, and we hope to be able to similarly "see through" the kinds of false performances we might encounter in real life—by confidence men, parvenus, flatterers, or imposters. We assume that these kinds of performances are "painstakingly pasted together, one false item on another, since there is no reality to which the items of behavior could be a direct response." What we don't consider is that "real" performances are as constructed as "false" ones. "We tend to see real performances as something not purposely put together at all, being an unintentional product of the individual's unself-conscious response to the facts in his situation" (ibid., 70). By insisting that identity is constructed via behavior, Goffman destabilizes any essential or fixed conception of social roles: "[W]hile persons usually are what they appear to be, such appearances could still have been managed. There is, then, a statistical relation between appearances and reality, not an intrinsic or necessary one"(ibid., 71).

The idea that identity is constructed and performed is commonplace today, but it was a radical proposition in the mid-twentieth century, especially in a society deeply concerned with authenticity and suspicious of theatricality. In the fifteen years between the end of World War II and the beginning of the 1960s, the material realities of life changed dramatically for most American Jews. By the early 1960s, the freedom of socioeconomic mobility promised by theatrical liberalism was a reality for a majority of American Jews. Despite lingering barriers to social and educational advancement in the upper echelons of American society, by the end of the 1960s, Jews had achieved a level of professional accomplishment unparalleled by any other recent immigrant group in the United States, and Goffman explicitly uses his theory to support this mobility: "A status, a position, a social place is not a material thing, to be possessed and then displayed; it is a pattern of appropriate conduct, coherent, embellished, and well articulated. Performed with ease or clumsiness, awareness or not, guile or good faith, it is none the less something that must be enacted and portrayed, something that must be realized" (ibid., 75). If we accept that social life is constructed like a performance on the stage, then it naturally follows that social roles are not innate possessions of a privileged few but instead are ways of behaving, and can therefore be inhabited by anyone able to play the role effectively. For Goffman, and for the generation of performance theorists who followed in his footsteps, reality and identity are produced in the very same way that a theatrical performance is produced. "A correctly staged and performed scene leads the audience to impute a self to a performed character, but this imputation—this self—is a *product* of a scene that comes off, and is not a *cause* of it" (ibid., 252). Our freedom to invent ourselves is fundamentally dependent therefore on a theatrical understanding of society.

Scholars of performance studies have tended to look to the avant-garde and experimental theater of the mid- to late-twentieth century to explore the relationship between performance and identity.[2] Popular entertainment of the late 1950s, '60s, and '70s engaged with these same issues, often in much more influential ways, exploring the limits of theatricality through comedy. Countless comic works of the period focus on the self-conscious imitation of manners, language, and genre with the express purpose of drawing attention to the subtle differences between originals and copies. The new television variety shows of the late 1950s, many of which were created, produced, and performed by Jewish writers and actors who began their careers either in vaudeville or on the Borscht-belt circuit, reveled in parodies of Hollywood films, Broadway shows, famous singers, political figures, and upwardly mobile ethnic characters of all sorts.[3]

One of the most successful of these programs was Sid Caesar's *Your Show of Shows*, which aired live every Saturday night for five seasons on NBC in the 1950s. A precursor to *Saturday Night Live* and countless other variety shows, the series offered its viewers the equivalent of a brand-new Broadway revue each week.[4] One particularly hilarious sketch, which engages directly with Goffman's ideas of the dramaturgical structure of social life, opens with the comedian Howard Morris, dressed as a valet, shining a pair of shoes while humming and mumbling in a gibberish "German." Sid Caesar enters, in a bathrobe, and Morris proceeds to dress him in the uniform of a Hollywood-style "German general." The entire encounter appears to take place "backstage" and revolves around the careful construction of the general's "front." The valet helps him on with his coat, sash, and beret, clips his collar, shines his buttons, polishes his medals, tidies his epaulets, and presents him with his sword. Both characters speak a comic pseudo-German heavily peppered with Yiddish and German-sounding English. As the general finishes dressing, for example, he looks at himself in the mirror and asks, "Mirror, mirror auf dem vall, who is de schlickest one of all?" The scene draws much of its humor from the constantly shifting location of backstage and frontstage. When it opens, the valet is alone backstage in relation to the general, who is still in his room. But he is frontstage in relation to the audience. When the general enters, the two characters are performing for one another, and also for the dual television audiences in the studio and at home. They inhabit multiple frontstages. At the same time, the general is preparing for a grand entrance, and so his dressing room is also backstage.

Their comic use of language creates yet more backstage/frontstage splits. The pseudo-German they speak is the frontstage language of performance while their slips into English give the audience a glimpse backstage, a view of the actors behind the roles. The use of Yiddish complicates this further. Those members of the audience who can distinguish German from Yiddish (in other words, the Jewish spectators, for the most part) recognize that the actors themselves are slipping between a frontstage presentation of themselves as assimilated Americans and a backstage "reality" in which they are actually Yiddish-speaking ethnic Jews.[5] As the scene draws to a close, the boundaries between frontstage and backstage shift yet again. Now fully dressed, the general leaves his dressing room and enters a ballroom full of elegant ladies and gentlemen. He smiles and nods as he passes through, playing the role of the distinguished general to the hilt. But then he steps through the revolving door to the sidewalk. A couple emerges from the door, whispers something to him, at which point he steps forward, blows a

"Mirror mirror auf dem vall . . . " (Sid Caesar and Howard Morris in "The German General").

whistle, and shouts "taxi!" The "General," it turns out, is actually a door-man. Simultaneously skewering the pretensions of the upwardly mobile (as well as the puffed-up stiffness of Hollywood Germans) while reveal-ing how easily all of us are fooled by well-performed "fronts," "The Ger-man General" beautifully illustrates Goffman's argument that all social behavior is a performance. We watch precise action, costume, gesture, language, and teamwork *create* the General for the audience, and then watch how comic slips, which rend the fragile boundaries between back and frontstages, redefine that careful construction. The General and the doorman are one and the same; all that changes is the setting.

One of the most successful Broadway musicals of the late 1950s, adapted into an equally successful Hollywood film in 1964, *My Fair Lady* offers another compelling argument for the relationship between theater and social life, and delves into the ethical problems inherent in the dramaturgical understanding of social roles that Goffman details in his work. Written by Alan Jay Lerner with music by Frederick Loewe,

My Fair Lady was adapted for the Broadway musical stage from George Bernard Shaw's 1912 play *Pygmalion*.[6] The play tells the story of Eliza Doolittle, a common flower girl in 1912 London, who is taught to speak and act like a "lady" by Henry Higgins, a specialist in vocal dialects. Although based quite closely on Shaw's original, *My Fair Lady* nonetheless is a distinctly American show. It is both a backstage musical and a work of theatrical liberalism, one which, like Goffman's book, raises questions about the freedom promised by self-fashioning (and fashioning selves). The first act takes place largely backstage, in a series of rehearsals for a grand performance. Eliza approaches Higgins for speech lessons, so that she might acquire a better job. Higgins enthusiastically embraces the idea, betting his friend Colonel Pickering that he can turn Eliza into a lady. Higgins acts as theater director, in a style much like Oscar Jaffe's in *Twentieth Century* (or like Svengali's), relentlessly drilling Eliza in correct pronunciation, teaching her how to speak and move like a member of his own class, and forcing her to rehearse late into the night until she has mastered the details of socially appropriate behavior. Higgins and Pickering costume Eliza lavishly and choose the ideal setting in which to launch her performance: the Embassy Ball. At the end of act 1, Eliza emerges onto the frontstage and performs brilliantly, convincing all of the guests (including a rival speech expert) that she is, indeed, a lady of high birth and simultaneously illustrating Goffman's point that selves are made, not born.[7] Higgins's democratic impulse, and Eliza's upward striving are both apparently rewarded. His high society peers are forced (albeit unconsciously) to accept a lower-class woman as their equal; Eliza achieves the stardom, with its promise of wealth and position, which she so desired.

At this point, however, the play shifts from the standard backstage musical format. Eliza receives few of the rewards of a brilliant performance. Not only do Higgins and Pickering fail to congratulate her, they barely even notice her, taking all of the credit for the performance themselves. They choose not to accept the obligations of the theater; for them, the show is over while for Eliza it has just begun:

HIGGINS: Now you are free and can do what you like.
ELIZA: What am I fit for? What have you left me fit for? Where am I to go? What am I to do? What's to become of me?[8]

Furious, Eliza departs in a huff, but she quickly realizes she has nowhere to go. She cannot go back to the flower market; nor does she fit in the salons of high society. Self-fashioning might insure freedom, but Eliza has only been partially involved in her own self-creation. Far from feeling free to reinvent herself at will, Eliza is limited to a single role— society lady—and unsure how to make use of its power. Like the women in 1930s plays and films who leave the stage to get married, Eliza is trapped by the very self Higgins has created for her. Higgins suggests, "You might marry, you know." And Eliza, fully aware of the limited field available to her, rejects his suggestion: "I sold flowers. I didn't sell myself. Now you've made a lady of me, I'm not fit to sell anything else" (Lerner, 190).

Our sympathy for Eliza is shaped by the part of her that Higgins does not control—her extraordinary singing voice. In her introductory song "Wouldn't It Be Loverly?," her joyous solo upon first dancing with Higgins, "I Could Have Danced All Night," and her insistence to her would-be paramour Freddy that she is tired of words, "Show Me," Eliza demonstrates, to the delight of audiences everywhere, that she has a spark of something inside her that cannot be shaped by Higgins and that needs no refining. Her singing voice, as distinct from her speech, is, from the beginning of the play, authentic and spontaneous. When she leaves Higgins, she remarks: "You have my voice on your gramophone. When you feel lonely without me you can turn it on" (ibid., 211). Finally coming to realize that the recordings of Eliza's speech—which he shaped—lack that spark of authentic selfhood (over which he has no control) that he so admires in Eliza, Higgins replies, "I can't turn your soul on." Throughout the play, Eliza refuses to believe that her manners of speech define her. Although she is the one who first seeks out speech lessons, she is deeply suspicious of Higgins's intentions toward her because she believes that he, unlike her, has no feelings, no internal self ("You ain't got no heart, you ain't"). This lack is further reinforced by the fact that Higgins, unlike Eliza, cannot sing. Eliza's inherent singing ability leads to the suspicion that Higgins—and Goffman—might be (partially) wrong. Perhaps behavior and action alone do *not* determine the self after all; perhaps Eliza possesses some essential spark of selfhood that Higgins cannot reshape.

On the one hand, the play insists that all class and identity is the result of performance. Eliza is accepted as a lady when she can speak and act like a lady. The theatrical understanding of everyday life, which Higgins (and Goffman) both believe in wholeheartedly, seems to promise equality and freedom. Anyone willing to work as hard as Eliza does will earn the material comforts and rewards of class mobility. And yet, the mobility Eliza actually achieves is highly circumscribed. On the other hand, many of the most riveting theatrical moments, the best songs in the show, resist the careful shaping that Higgins insists on, instead seeming to emerge from the characters' souls, from the heart Eliza insists Higgins lacks.[9] The singing Eliza is equally circumscribed in her ability to self-fashion, although the limitation is considered morally valuable: she is unable or unwilling to refashion the core of her being, her soul. *My Fair Lady* promotes a theatrical understanding of identity and social relations, but cautions us against the naïve assumption that performance can correct all of the inequities inherent in liberal democratic society. Like so many works of this era, *My Fair Lady* firmly believes in the values inherent in theatrical liberalism while insisting that deep within us is an authentic self that ultimately cannot be performed away, that defines us and limits us—for better and worse—to be who we are.

* * *

An important piece of that authentic self turned out to be Jewish identity. Assisted by the opportunities created by the G.I. bill, declining levels of anti-Semitism in the wake of revelations about the Holocaust, and a booming economy, the new generation of Jews that came of age in the late 1950s and 1960s had only the mildest sense of being held back by discriminatory prejudice or debilitating poverty.[10] Many young Jews in this period began to drop protective assimilationist gestures (such as name changes) and to emerge into the public sphere *as Jews.* This newfound comfort allowed Jews to begin to view the Old World shtetl and the urban slums of first generation American Jewish immigrants with nostalgia. A new narrative of Jewish identity emerged in the popular culture of the 1960s, one that placed Jewish characters and Jewish history at the center of key works of American popular culture after a nearly thirty-year period of largely limiting Jewish characters on stage and screen to marginal victims and comic sidekicks. It took into account Jewish socioeconomic success in America, and rewrote the past to reflect that success story, in effect reimagining key moments in Jewish modernity and repopulating them with characters who were *already* proto-Americans, and in many cases already familiar with the values of theatrical liberalism.

Fiddler on the Roof, for example, depicts the backstory to American Jewish immigration by reimagining the Eastern European shtetl as the birthplace of American liberal values, and arguing that those Jews who would become successful Americans were those who embraced universal ideals about humanity, equality, and civil rights. *Funny Girl* likewise uses the Jewish comedienne Fanny Brice's accomplishments in popular entertainment as a marker of Jewish ethnic identity. The play and film transform the Lower East Side immigrant experience into an ethnic coming-of-age story, in which Jewish success in popular culture is (rather ironically) conflated with Jewish ethnic pride.[11] The central characters in these plays and movies are overtly Jewish, but their American Jewish selves differ radically from Jewish characters of the 1920s such as Jakie Rabinowitz in *The Jazz Singer*. While these characters are situated in the same historical moment as Jakie and face similar challenges, they have already gone through the internal process of synthesis with which Jakie struggled and are already authentically American. Unlike Jakie's father, Cantor Rabinowitz, Tevye undergoes a journey in *Fiddler on the Roof* toward theatrical liberalism before he ever leaves home, while Fanny Brice is already so Americanized that she no longer needs to undergo the process of self-transformation so familiar to American Jewish immigrants. They succeed as proto-Americans because they *already* possess the liberal values necessary for assimilation and upward mobility. These expressions of Jewish authenticity are rooted in a history of Jewish performance, but they strenuously argue that the era of the performance of identity is over: Jews *are* Americans and therefore no longer need the strategies of theatrical liberalism to *become* Americans.

Adapted from stories by the Yiddish writer Sholem Aleichem, *Fiddler on the Roof* represented a breakthrough in Jewish-created American popular culture. In an oft-repeated show business legend, *Fiddler* nearly didn't get produced because few of the regular core of Broadway backers, most of whom were Jewish, were willing to support it. They were convinced that the show was too Jewish to appeal to a broad audience.[12] They were wrong. *Fiddler on the Roof* went on to become the longest running musical in Broadway history, in its first incarnation running for over three thousand performances in eight years and garnering ten Tony Awards. It was adapted in 1971 into a phenomenally successful Hollywood film. Like many of the works of theatrical liberalism, *Fiddler on the Roof* entered the American canon, while simultaneously becoming remarkably successful around the world.[13] Songs from *Fiddler* became—and remain—standard fare in wedding celebrations (Jewish and non-Jewish); thousands have marched down the aisle to the strains of "Sunrise, Sunset" and danced at parties to the rousing beat of "L'Chaim."[14] In 2008, *Time* magazine reported that *Fiddler on the Roof* was still the seventh most frequently produced musical by high schools, more than thirty-five years after it opened on Broadway. And as Alisa Solomon has persuasively argued, *Fiddler on the Roof* provided Jews, especially those assimilated Jews with little connection to traditional Jewish culture or practice, with a usable past, a history that seemed both distinctive, and universal.[15] As revealed by a controversy over the 2004 Broadway revival, which was directed by and starred non-Jews, American Jews feel deeply connected to *Fiddler on the Roof* and imbue it with the kind of spiritual energy generally reserved for national symbols or religious relics.[16] For American Jews of the later twentieth century, *Fiddler on the Roof* came to stand for Old World Jewish authenticity, and the fact that this authenticity contained important markers of American theatrical liberalism only made the play and film more powerful as a source of identification for assimilated American Jews.

The story of a traditional Old World father, Tevye, desperately trying to keep his family together in the face of the challenges of modernity, *Fiddler on the Roof* spoke to (and continues to speak to) a wide swath of potential audiences, in effect anyone who has had rebellious children, has yearned for independence from a conventional lifestyle, or has overcome obstacles in the name of love. But *Fiddler* offered American Jews in particular personal narratives of identity, which connected them not only to the Old Country but to the Old Theatrical Liberalism of the early twentieth century. *Fiddler* offered a transformed version of theatrical liberalism redeemed from the disillusionment of the post-war period, one which attempted to strike a balance between theatricality, action and obligation on the one side and realism, emotion, and individualism on the other, a balance which proved to be simultaneously as shaky and as successful as that of the eponymous fiddler.

Fiddler on the Roof, like *The Jazz Singer* and *Death of a Salesman,* details the struggle of a patriarch to come to terms with the modern ideas of his children. Tevye is, in many ways, an optimistic rewriting of Willy Loman, and Tevye experiences some of the same tensions between his character and the form of the play that Willy does. While it might be a stretch to call *Fiddler on the Roof* a backstage musical, by featuring a central character who continually breaks the fourth wall and is acutely aware of his audience(s), the show reintroduces theatricality as a redemptive and even sacred mode. Tevye is the heart and soul of the play, serving as the narrator, the central character, and the audience's link to the world of traditional Judaism. And Tevye is an exuberantly theatrical Jewish patriarch, recovering an almost vaudevillian joy in performing from the sobering fate of his predecessor Willy Loman. Like Willy, Tevye is the only meta-theatrical character in the play, the only character who realizes that there is a world outside of the life represented on stage, but in *Fiddler,* this meta-theatricality is a gift that offers Tevye the opportunity to reflect on his own journey toward theatrical liberalism.[17] It was no accident that Jerome Robbins and Harold Prince chose Zero Mostel for the role of Tevye. Just like Pseudolus, the character Mostel had just finished playing in *A Funny Thing Happened on the Way to the Forum,* Tevye speaks to multiple audiences during the course of the play—and often even in the course of a single scene—and, at least in the first act, directs the action of the characters around him. Famous for his pseudo-biblical "sayings," he constantly lectures his family and the villagers of Anatevka, most of whom are reluctant, but amused, audience members. The butcher Lazar Wolf draws attention to Tevye's habit at Tzeitel's wedding, when Tevye rises to thank Lazar for his generous gift of chickens: "Reb Lazar, you are a decent man. In the name of my daughter and her new husband, I accept your gift. There is a famous saying that . . . " Lazar interrupts him: "Reb Tevye, I'm not marrying your daughter. I don't have to listen to your sayings."[18] When faced with the problem of having to convince his wife Golde to cancel their agreement to allow Lazar Wolf to marry Tzeitel, Tevye invokes a standard musical comedy conceit, that of the dream ballet, and stages an elaborate performance for Golde. Pretending he has just awoken from a dreadful nightmare, Tevye describes his dream to Golde, and as he speaks/sings his dream, the characters come to life on the stage. Acutely aware of audience reaction, Tevye looks to Golde for her reaction to each theatrical moment before proceeding to the next. When Golde's grandmother, in the dream, says that Tzeitel will marry the tailor Motel Kemzoil, Golde responds, "A tailor! She must have heard wrong. She meant a butcher" (ibid., 74). Tevye listens to Golde, then runs back to the dream character and responds "You must have heard wrong, Grandma / There's no tailor / You mean a butcher, Grandma." This scene redeems theatricality from the degrading depths it had suffered in *Death of a Salesman*. When Willy Loman conjured such dreams on stage, he was deemed insane. When Tevye does it, the virtuosic performance is so convincing that Golde is thoroughly frightened and immediately insists that Tzeitel must marry Motel.

As the dream scene ends, Tevye silently mouths the words "Thank you" to God and goes to sleep. Tevye speaks regularly with God; he performs an entire musical number, "If I Were a Rich Man," just for God's benefit. As Irving Howe noted disapprovingly in his 1964 review of the play, Tevye uses God as his straight man, but what Howe does not quite see is that far from being disrespectful, this representation of God as part of a vaudeville team is a potentially sacred one, both to Tevye, who has worked hard to perfect this special relationship, and to *Fiddler*'s audiences, who appreciate the intimacy of a God who both participates in and approves of Tevye's informal performance style.[19] Tevye's most important audience, of course, is the audience for this musical itself. Tevye establishes an easy rapport with the audience at the very beginning of the play, effortlessly breaking and re-establishing the fourth wall as he draws the audience into his world with his famous opening line "A fiddler on the roof. Sounds crazy, no?" (*Fiddler*, 2) He sings the song "Tradition" for the audience and returns to it, and to the audience, every time he is confronted by the difficulties of modernity. When Tzeitel tells Tevye she does not want to marry Lazar, that she and Motel actually gave each other a pledge that they would marry, Tevye turns to the audience and sings "They gave each other a pledge, unheard of, absurd. They gave each other a pledge, unthinkable!" (ibid., 67). The audience, in their sympathetic silence (and occasional laughter) gives

Tevye the support he needs to edge into modernity and to slowly accept the values of romantic love that the play embraces.

It becomes clear, however, that Tevye's theatricality is closely linked to a vibrant Jewish tradition and as this tradition becomes untenable in the shtetl, so, too, does the buoyant theatricality of the first act. As the play progresses, Tevye's direct addresses to the audience recede and a darker realism takes over. Early in the second act, events begin to spiral out of Tevye's control, his theatrical gifts lose their power, and he no longer looks to the audience for support or encouragement. When Hodel departs for Siberia, she sings an elegiac goodbye directly to Tevye. When Chava wants to marry the non-Jewish Fyedka, Tevye does not turn to the audience to debate this as he did in confronting the choices of his first two daughters. And when Chava ultimately does marry, Tevye sadly disowns her with a song addressed directly to a younger Chava ("Little Bird"). His final debate is with God, not with the audience. By the time the constable arrives to tell the villagers that they must leave Anatevka, it seems that Tevye's theatrical power has failed. Only in the very last moment of the play is there a glimmer of hope, a hint of the theatrical liberalism that lies ahead for these migrating Jews. The fiddler, who represents both performance and tradition in the play, plays his iconic theme as the villagers depart for distant shores in the final scene. At the last moment, however, the stage directions read: "Tevye stops, turns, beckons to him. The fiddler tucks his violin under his arm and follows the family upstage as the curtain falls" (ibid., 153). He will join Tevye in America where together they will build a new type of Jewish theatrical tradition.

While the ending points ahead to the theatrical liberalism of the early twentieth century, however, *Fiddler on the Roof* as a whole charts a journey in which a tradition and action based community is prepared for their journey to America by slowly transforming this key aspect of theatrical liberalism into a more "American" or at least more Protestant ethos, which privileges internal motivation. The play is ambivalent about this transformation and about the discarding of a key feature of theatrical liberalism—and of Judaism—which it implies. The ambivalence is expressed through two sets of equally sympathetic characters. Tevye and Golde, the Old World parents, live a life in which action precedes motivation. Their daughters, and the men who marry them, follow their hearts; political passion and romantic love initiate the action they take in the world. The play acknowledges that the daughters represent the future (i.e., the present for the audience) but it also treats the action-motivated impulses of Tevye and Golde with nostalgic sympathy. The play opens with an anthem to the action- and obligation-based philosophy at the core of Judaism: "Tradition!" As Tevye tells the audience in his opening monologue, "Here in Anatevka we have traditions for everything—how to eat, how to sleep, how to wear clothes. . . . Because of our traditions, everyone knows who he is and what God expects him to do" (ibid., 2–3). The villagers spill on to the stage singing of their roles in the society, and the actions each is individually obligated to do: "Who must know the way to make a proper home / A quiet home, a kosher home?" (ibid., 3). Each member of the community is a performer: "in our little village of Anatevka you might say every one of us is a fiddler on the roof, trying to scratch out a pleasant, simple tune without breaking his neck." Each of the "special types" among the villagers is likewise identified by the things that they do: the matchmaker, the beggar, the rabbi. Conflicts arise in Anatevka over marriage. The matchmaker makes love happen (if the couple is lucky) by creating pairs that seem well matched ("the way she sees and the way he looks, it's a perfect match!"). But the younger generation is decidedly opposed to this sort of matchmaking. As the girls dream about who Yente might bring for them ("a scholar," "rich," "as handsome as anything"), the oldest sister Tzeitel, in an uncharacteristic meta-theatrical moment, pretends to be Yente and admonishes them:

> You heard he has a temper.
> He'll beat you every night,
> But only when he's sober,
> So you're all right.
> Did you think you'd get a prince?
> Well, I do the best I can.
> With no dowry, no money, no family background
> Be glad you got a man. (ibid., 19)

This game of matchmaking is a dangerous one, Tzeitel implies, one which depends on factors beyond the girls' control: money, family background. With little say in their own futures, these girls could "get stuck for good." The sense that these girls are being sold to the highest bidder is further reinforced when Tevye first meets Lazar. Tevye thinks the butcher wants to buy his milk cow; Lazar is actually speaking about Tevye's daughter. The mix-up is comical but pointed—how much difference was there, in this Old World society, between a daughter and a milk cow? Perchik, who will soon become Hodel's husband, makes his opinion known when he "congratulates" Tzeitel upon hearing that she is contracted to wed the butcher:

> PERCHIK: Congratulations, Tzeitel, for getting a rich man.
> TEVYE: Again with the rich! What's wrong with being rich?
> PERCHIK: It is no reason to marry. Money is the world's curse. (ibid., 61)

Marriages, according to the daughters, and their spouses, must arise from within, from the heart. Money and other practical considerations should never dictate choices in romantic love. This sentiment was, of course, far from radical in 1964. Indeed, it was so accepted as to be considered universally true and morally correct. As we know, the mythology of American romantic comedy is deeply rooted in the triumph of the heart over more material considerations. And just like Maria, who cannot help loving Tony in *West Side Story*, Hodel, as she departs to join Perchik in Siberia, sings "Helpless, now I stand with him / Watching older dreams grow dim" (ibid., 124). Her heart leads the way; she has little or no control over its mysteries.

This privileging of the heart is so commonplace, it seems almost unworthy of notice. But the apparent truths of romantic love are called into question by Tevye and Golde's song in the second act, "Do You Love Me?" "It's a new world," Tevye says to Golde, "Love." And then he asks her, in song:

> TEVYE: Do you love me?
> GOLDE: Do I what?
> TEVYE: Do you love me?

Golde responds with a litany of all the things they have done together:

> For twenty-five years I've lived with him,
> Fought with him, starved with him.

> Twenty-five years my bed is his.
> If that's not love, what is? (ibid., 117)

Golde and Tevye were, of course, brought together by arranged marriage. As the song tells us, they met for the first time on their wedding day. Their parents told them that they would get married first, and later learn to love one another. According to all the rhetoric about romantic love that has preceded this song, which appears far into act 2, this match should never have worked. But the song concludes:

> TEVYE: Then you love me?
> GOLDE: I suppose I do.
> TEVYE: And I suppose I love you, too.
> TEVYE AND GOLDE: It doesn't change a thing,
>   But even so,
>   After twenty-five years,
>   It's nice to know. (ibid., 118)

Apparently, arranged marriages can also sometimes work. For Tevye, acting in the world and in his home has led to marital happiness. The girls, the new generation, believe that the opposite is true. All of these characters are portrayed sympathetically, and yet they profess radically different ideas of how love happens, of the relative power of external action to effect internal change. While the weight of both convention and history are certainly with the daughters (few if any of the American audiences watching the show would have argued for the reinstitution of arranged marriages), the song "Do You Love Me" is deeply affecting. There is something to be said for the prioritizing of action over intention, and *Fiddler* insists on saying it. And while the daughters stride confidently into the future on paths dictated by their hearts, the play is ultimately unsure whether parents or children will have the better life.

While *Fiddler* expresses ambivalence about the role of action, it sidesteps almost completely one of the core features of theatrical liberalism, that of self-fashioning. In *A Funny Thing Happened on the Way to the Forum,* Zero Mostel spent most of his energy as Pseudolus transforming himself and others in order to gain freedom and happiness. In *Fiddler,* however, his Tevye is a stable and almost quintessentially authentic character; even those who rebel against tradition in the play—Hodel, Perchik, Chava—know *exactly* who they are. The shtetl in which they live offers little room for self-transformation. This is, indeed, a defining feature of small town life. The self-transformation promised by *Fiddler* will have to wait until these characters get to the cosmopolitan space of the American city. But will they really be transformed there? Or will they, like Eliza Doolittle, instead achieve the potential and essential selves that already lie dormant within them? This question forms the core of *Funny Girl*, a play about Jewish vaudeville star Fanny Brice. A backstage musical focusing on Brice's rise to stardom and her relationship with the gambler Nicky Arnstein, *Funny Girl* seems the ideal vehicle with which to showcase the transformative possibilities of theatrical liberalism. But while the show is situated squarely in the heart of jazz age theatrical liberalism—telling a story of a Ziegfeld Follies star—it extols instead 1960s attitudes toward self-making and authenticity.

The real Fanny Brice rose to stardom on her remarkable transformative power; she was particularly known for doing imitations. In *Funny Girl*, Brice can only transform herself into a more "true" and authentic version of herself. When she lets herself "be herself"—distinctively Jewish—she is funny and successful; when she tries to "act," she fails. Early on in the movie and play, we learn that Fanny is different from the other girls trying to make it in show business. She is kicked out of a chorus line because she doesn't look like the other girls (she looks Jewish). Fanny quickly shows us why this difference is her greatest asset as she begs her first director, Mr. Keeney, to give her a job. She begins by explaining why she has not yet landed a starring role:

> Suppose all you ever had for breakfast was onion rolls. All of a sudden one morning, in walks a bagel. You'd say, "Ugh, what's that?" Until you tried it! *That's* my trouble. I'm a bagel on a plate full of onion rolls! Nobody recognizes me![20]

But Fanny has no intention of transforming herself into an onion roll in order to get recognized. Rather, she insists on the world appreciating her for who she is: her bagel-ness *is* her talent. As she launches into her first show-stopping number, "I'm the Greatest Star," she touts her many expressions but makes clear that they all emerge from one "natural" talent: "Listen, I got thirty-six expressions / Sweet as pie to tough as leather. / And that's six expressions more than all the Barrymores put together. / Instead of just kicking me,/ why don't they give me a lift? It must be a plot, / 'cause they're scared that I got / such a gift!" (ibid., 13).

Fanny's "gift," her talent for "being herself," becomes apparent in the film when Keeney finally relents and allows her to perform with the chorus in a roller-skating number ("I'd Rather Be Blue"). Woefully incapable of roller skating, Fanny utterly destroys the integrity of the number, but sends the audience into hysterics. She comes out on top in the end, as the stage manager pushes her on to the stage to sing "I'd Rather Be Blue," still on roller skates. Alone on the stage, she comes alive, demonstrating the star talent she had promised them. Florenz Ziegfeld decides to hire her for his famous *Follies* and gives her a song, "His Love Makes Me Beautiful," which Fanny is supposed to sing, dressed as a beautiful bride, against a backdrop of stunning women, all taller, more elegant, and less ethnic-looking than herself. Fanny protests that this will never work, that the audience will laugh at her. He insists that she do it anyway. She agrees, but at the last moment, stuffs a pillow under her dress, pretending she is pregnant and turning the number into a hugely successful comic turn. Ziegfeld is furious, but Fanny is delighted. She made use of a clever bit of stagecraft—a costume change—to escape a difficult situation. But the escape only insures that she will be perceived *as herself*, with her clearly Jewish looks, and that she will not be seen as a poseur trying to pass as someone else.

When Fanny actually tries to "act," the results are disastrous. We get a hint of this in the second half of the film, when, on a transatlantic ship with Nick, she attends one of his poker games. While Nick is the master of the poker face, Fanny is hopelessly expressive. She cannot contain herself; her face betrays anxiety, excitement, and all of the other emotions good poker players are supposed to keep to themselves. For an actress, she is remarkably incapable of playing anyone but herself. This inability to act trips her up much more seriously as the story progresses. Fanny attempts to help Nick with a business deal behind his back. The subterfuge is soon exposed, and the relationship deteriorates. The narrative marks this moment of emasculation for Nick, who detests being supported by his famous wife, as the beginning of his downfall as well. He turns to petty crime and is ultimately sent to jail for embezzling. Fanny is punished for her attempt to "act" with the destruction of her marriage. As we have seen in so many works of theatrical liberalism, men are free to self-fashion within and outside of marriage; actresses, however, once married, are limited to playing a single role.

Like the daughters in *Fiddler on the Roof*, Fanny is torn between the comfort of communal obligation and the lure of individualism. Her two best-known songs encapsulate that tension. She introduces Nick to her old neighborhood, Henry Street in Brooklyn, with the song "People," about the close-knit community she loves. When Nick tells Fanny that he avoids entanglements, that he likes "to feel free," Fanny replies, "You can get lonesome—being that free." Then she sings: "Just let one kid fall down / And seven mothers faint." Convinced that "people who need people are the luckiest people in the world," Fanny nonetheless is totally taken in by Nick's promise of glamour, wealth, and the material pursuit of happiness (ibid., 61–62). Influenced by Nick, Fanny becomes increasingly convinced of the importance of individual happiness, even at the expense of her communal, her theatrical, obligations. In love with Nick, she drops the show and runs off to be with him. Like Hodel and Maria, she too must blindly follow her heart. She sings triumphantly,

> Get ready for me, love,
> 'Cause I'm a "comer,"
> I simply gotta march,
> My heart's a drummer.
> Nobody, no nobody,
> Is gonna rain on my parade! (ibid., 86)

Fanny is seduced by the pleasures of the heart and the purse by a consummate con man of just the sort that Erving Goffman describes. The irony here is that, while Fanny is a professional actress, she is, in Goffman's terms, utterly sincere. She believes herself, and she believes those around her. Nick, on the other hand, is the perfect example of the cynical performer. As her friend Eddie says, as she runs off after Nick, "You don't know one damn thing about him except that he's good-looking, wears fancy clothes, talks big and struts around as if he owns the world! And if you don't think that can't be an act, you're crazy!"(ibid., 83). Nick's act eventually falls apart, and Fanny's blindness to his theatricality, her inability to be a part of his "team," leads to the disintegration of her marriage.

Fanny Brice (Barbra Streisand) trying to control her poker face in *Funny Girl*.

The play is deeply confused about the moral status of Nick's theatricality. Mrs. Brice accuses her daughter of emasculating him by refusing to see him as he is: "You should have loved him a little less—and helped him a little more! Helped him be *himself*! A man—like other men!" (ibid., 126). But Fanny's charm and her star quality lies in her naïve faith that the world around her is *real*. Her fundamental inability to refashion herself into a cynical performer allows her to go back out on that stage in triumph in the end. Her authenticity makes her a star.

The actress chosen to portray Fanny Brice (a young Barbra Streisand) was particularly well suited to portray just this sort of ethnic authenticity. With her oft-noted "semitic profile," Streisand was unmistakably Jewish, and indeed her looks and her chutzpah became a symbol of Jewish ethnic pride for an entire generation. So perfectly did she fit the role that producers have not yet been able to find a replacement, and *Funny Girl* has never been revived on Broadway. Fanny Brice and Barbra Streisand became closely identified with one another, with a single exception: Brice eventually decided to have a nose job, to tone down her ethnic profile. As Dorothy Parker famously quipped, she "cut off her nose to spite her race." This decision to literally refashion her face seriously hurt Brice's career. Streisand never made this mistake. She knew that it was her nose—and the ethnic distinctiveness that it implied— that made her a Jewish star.

5

Theatricality and Idolatry

In the voracious quest for authenticity that characterized not only the ethnic revival but also the radical politics of the later 1960s, many Jewish and American culture makers became increasingly interested in breaking down the boundaries that they believed impeded communication among individuals and propped up corrupt systems of power. Experimental theater, political protests, and popular commercial incarnations of these kinds of performances tested the borders between secular theater and religious ritual, and between performers and spectators, reimagining the theater in its "original" or "authentic" purpose as a site for mystical communion and societal rebirth. Few of these writers or directors self-consciously made use of Jewish symbology; most found Buddhist, Hindu, and Native American rituals more conducive to their experimentation. But the largely anti-theatrical experimental theater practices and radical politics that characterized this move in the popular culture, as encapsulated in the acting theory and performance pieces of Richard Schechner and the Performance Group (TPG) (as well as the popular representation of this theory in the Broadway musical *Hair*), were rooted in the specific rejection or reinterpretation of the Judaic principles of theatrical liberalism. Schechner's work was in tension with that of other popular Jewish artists such as Norman Mailer, Allen Ginsberg, and Abbie Hoffman, who, while also concerned with authenticity, were more ambivalent or playful about theatricality in their engagements with and responses to the 1967 march on the Pentagon. The polemical essays of the late 1960s and early 1970s by Cynthia Ozick responded to this celebration of authenticity in explicitly Judaic terms, accusing many of idolatry and heresy. And some Jewish writers, performers, and scholars of the era resisted the mystical embrace of authenticity altogether through commercial works of popular entertainment, which continued to explore the pros and cons of theatrical self-fashioning. Mel Brooks and Gene Wilder's parody *Young Franken-stein* (1974), for example, offered an explicitly Jewish comic critique of the cult of authenticity, which was echoed in the trenchant writing of the Jewish literary critic Lionel Trilling in *Sincerity and Authenticity* (1972). In short, Jewish artists and intellectuals were obsessed during these volatile decades with determining the moral status of theatricality in an era in which the definition of *reality* was increasingly elusive.

By the mid-1960s Jewish suburbia, which had provided enthusiastic audiences for *Fiddler on the Roof* and *Funny Girl*, had become an incubator for discontent and alienation, especially among the first genera-tion raised there. This sense of alienation was one of the factors fueling a renewed sense of urgency around "authentic" identity and spiritual-ity; it also quickly became a force behind the growing countercultural movement, which included large numbers of young disaffected subur-ban Jews. These young Jews accused their parents of having lost their souls to suburban conformity, a critique that extended far beyond the Jewish community and formed a core complaint of the generation. In a distinctly anti-theatrical move, this generation of Jews rejected the assimilationist impulses of their parents, claiming that the practice of Judaism in the mid-twentieth century was devoid of authentic spiritual-ity and had devolved into a meaningless set of empty symbols. Grow-ing numbers chose to intermarry with non-Jews while others turned to Eastern religions for spiritual fulfillment. This quest for authenticity also led a number of young Jews to yearn for more Jewishness, not less. Many embraced various forms of ethnic expression while others began to revitalize the practice of Judaism itself, founding the Jewish renewal movement in the 1970s.[1]

An enormous gulf opened between young Jews raised in the suburbs and their parents. Those who came of age in the pre-war era remained deeply sensitive to anti-Semitism and acutely aware of exclusion, even as overt demonstrations of prejudice began to decline. Admissions quo-tas, exclusionary rules, and other forms of subtle and unsubtle anti-Semitism still existed through the 1950s, and many Jews had responded to these barriers by denying or at least concealing their background by changing their names and otherwise attempting to pass as non-Jews—in other words, by performing a role. As institutionalized anti-Semitism declined, many in the older generation were therefore hesitant about embracing or celebrating their "real" ethnic and religious identities, and found it inexplicable when their children aggressively critiqued the "phoniness" of these assimilationist performances. Younger people born into a far more tolerant post-war climate expressed amazement (if not disgust) at the hesitations of their parents to take a risky political position, to speak openly, to stand out in a crowd. Countless young Jews rejected what they perceived as the conventional, middle-class values of their parents by becoming deeply involved in liberal movements for civil rights (for blacks, women, homosexuals) and in radical protests against the Vietnam War and all forms of social and sexual conformity.[2]

* * *

In 1970 the essayist and novelist Cynthia Ozick gave a lecture at the Weizmann Institute in Rehovoth, Israel, titled simply "America," which spoke directly to the question of the American Jewish future in light of debates over ethnic pride, authenticity, and countercultural expression. In this lecture, reprinted later that same year in the journal *Judaism* as "Toward a New Yiddish," Ozick argued for a remarkable reconception of Diaspora Jewish culture. Vigorously denouncing the popular post-war universalism of Jewish intellectuals like Arthur Miller and many others, and equally vigorously rejecting the 1960s turn toward what she called the "ugly and intolerable term 'ethnic,'" Ozick proposed instead a Jewish culture based in Judaism itself but written and discussed in the language of secular American Jews.[3] The New Yiddish, for Ozick, would be English, but a very particular kind of English, "attentive to the implications of Covenant and Commandment." Ozick imagined a kind of Jewish culture, which was simultaneously holy and secular: "We can, even in America, try to be a holy people, and let the holiness shine for others in a Jewish language which is nevertheless generally accessible" (ibid., 177). Ozick does not speak specifically of popular entertainment and popular culture; indeed, the cultural program she proposes emerges from her vehement rejection of popular culture in the 1960s. And yet, the Judaically inflected secular culture she describes in "Toward a New Yiddish" bears a striking—if unself-conscious—relationship to theatrical liberalism. The essay is a remarkable historical document because it offers us a window onto the tensions dividing Jewish writers and intellectuals in the 1960s, who attacked liberalism from both sides: radicals denouncing the liberal state as the engine of war and repression, and neo-conservatives denouncing the culture of permissiveness and irresponsibility liberalism had made possible.

Ozick begins her discussion of Diaspora Jewish culture by accusing the theatrical Jews active in the New Left of idolatry. Critiquing the street demonstrations and alternative lifestyles of Jewish counterculture figures such as Abbie Hoffman and Allen Ginsberg, Ozick determines that, although the movement is often seen as Jewish because of its commitment to social justice, it actually is deeply anti-Jewish. Like their radical Jewish forebears, the hippies are anti-government, "they dream the old nightmares of the czars," but their protests are without context. They do not realize "that they dream these nightmares *because they are Jews*" (ibid., 160). These hippies represent yet another generation in a long Jewish tradition of protest, and their "moral anesthesia," as Ozick calls it, is the result of a deep ignorance about their own history, a result of the quintessentially American embrace of the new:

> Exhilarated by insurrectionist and treasonable invective, the young imagine themselves to be profoundly new, unheard-of, romantically zany and strange, the first of their kind. Whereas they are only the de-Judaized shadows of their great-grandfathers in the Pale. (ibid., 160)

How does this ignorance of history represent a turn toward idolatry? By elevating this radical newness, this alternative lifestyle, to the level of poetry by aestheticizing it, these young hippies end up not only fashioning new selves but imagining that these selves are divorced both from history and from any kind of communal obligations. To create a self that is outside of history and community is to create an idol. Ozick observes that this self-involved ecstatic movement embraces *being* with an idolatrous passion (she is particularly critical of the phenomenon of the "be-in"), but ignores action; hippies worship the "here and now" through the use of drugs but ignore the burdens of the past and the consequences that lie in the future. This is the terrifying result of liberal individualism pushed to its extreme; a freedom without obligations.

For an example of the type of heresy she describes, Ozick turns to the most recognized Jewish poet of the peace movement, Allen Ginsberg.

She is particularly incensed by his claim that his countercultural "life-style" is a kind of poetry. "Lifestyle," Ozick complains, "implies a hope for revolution to be effected through a community of manners." Knowing all we do at this point about the close relationship between Judaism and action, this seems an odd criticism. Isn't Judaism also a community of manners? Definitely not, Ozick asserts. *Manners* are Christian; *Acts* are Jewish:

> Manners are endemically and emphatically in the realm of poetry and outside the realm of acts: the poem is the incarnation of the deed, the romance of belief stands for the act. Manners are gesture, gesture is theater and magic. . . . Revolutionary lifestyle incorporates very literally a eucharistic, not a Jewish, urge. What Ginsberg in his testimony called "psychedelic consciousness" is what the Christian used to call grace. (ibid., 161)

For Ozick, then, granting sacred status to gestures and manners, which aim to embody meaning in and of themselves, is a deeply non-Jewish choice. She is particularly horrified when, at a "be-in" in Chicago, Ginsberg aestheticizes and de-historicizes the Christian cross:

> At the be-in, a group of ministers and rabbis elevated a ten-foot cross high into a cloud of tear gas thrown by rioting police. When Ginsberg saw this he turned to his friend and said: "They have gassed the cross of Christ." Perhaps for the first time since Rome an elevated cross was on the receiving end of a pogrom, but the fact remains that for the rabbis who carried it and for Ginsberg who pitied it the cross had been divested of its historical freight. It had been transubstantiated from a sign of the real acts of a community into the vehicle of a moment rich in aesthetic contrast, Christian grace, psychedelic consciousness, theatrical and poetical magic—like that moment in our national anthem when the Star-Spangled Banner waves gloriously through a smoky night of shell-fire. (ibid., 162)

Ozick is horrified that a bunch of Jewish artists, protestors, and rabbis could so easily forget the "historical freight" of that cross for Jews and see it simply as an abstract sign of peace; that Jews could so easily idolize the cross. She connects this kind of amnesia with the impulse to universalism, Allen Ginsberg's idea that all religions of the world are the same, "allee samee" as he says, and so it makes no difference if you recite mantras, love the cross, or immerse yourself in Hasidic mysticism (all of which Ginsberg did). To Ozick, however, it makes a huge difference. Sinai—the site and content of Jewish revelation—is all about rejecting cultishness and ecstasy. It is simply *not* the same as what came before . . . or after: "[Y]ou cannot comprehend Sinai and still say 'allee samee.' Sinai . . . commands deed, conduct, act, and says No to any impulse that would impede a community of justice." What Ginsberg wants to do, according to Ozick, is to absorb the Jewish passion for peace, mercy, and justice within a larger universalism. He wants to profess these Jewish values by transcending them. But then, she argues, what he's doing isn't Jewish at all:

> Allen Ginsberg retains the Jewish passion for peacefulness, mercy, and justice, but he imagines that by transcending its Jewish character he will be better empowered to infuse it into all men: an acutely Christian formulation. In transcending the Jewish *behavioral* character of the vision, he transcends the social vision itself, floating off into various modes of release and abandonment. He recapitulates the Hellenization of Jewish Christianity. He restates the justification by faith that is at the core of Pauline Protestantism. (ibid., 162)

Ozick criticizes Ginsberg for substituting ecstasy for *mitzvot*, presence for action. She accuses him of ultimately desiring transubstantiation through mind-altering drugs: "There is no need for a covenant with God if God can enter flesh" (ibid., 163). And she places him outside of the Jewish cosmos by accusing him of that very definition of religion that Moses Mendelssohn and so many Jewish thinkers after him resisted: the ultimately Christian "justification by faith."

She then turns her attention to literature, making similar accusations about post-modern aesthetics, which she sees as "self-sustaining, enclosed, lyrical and magical—like the eucharistic moment, wherein the word makes flesh" (ibid., 165). She scoffs at Jewish writers who write in this vein, and especially those who appear to write only to achieve fleeting fame in a non-Jewish world. Ozick particularly lambastes

Norman Mailer as "a tragic American exemplar of wasted powers and large-scale denial" (ibid., 170). She notes his "lust to be Esau," to sell his Jewish birthright for a few meagre years of Diaspora flattery. Only in his turn to journalism (a vaguely Jewish art according to Ozick because it involves judging Gentile culture rather than trying to personify it) in *Armies of the Night* (Mailer's 1968 report on the march on the Pentagon) does Ozick see Mailer "swinging round" to the role of Jacob: "[W]ith old Jacob's eye he begins to judge Gentile culture. . . . Esau gains the short run, but the long run belongs to Jacob" (ibid., 170). For Ozick, the legacy of Jacob is much like that described earlier: the ability to approach the truth in circuitous ways, to understand the uses of performance without succumbing to its seduction, to inhabit multiple names and never to imagine the self as wholly new.

In response to the twin idolatrous pursuits of the hippie lifestyle and post-modern aesthetics, Ozick imagines a Diaspora Jewish culture of what she calls "Jewish liturgical literature." Her definition of liturgical is surprising. It doesn't mean prayer, although prayer might be included. It means literature with "a choral voice," which speaks to and responds to the judgments of a community, a literature open and responsive to the call of history, a literature concerned with "conduct and the consequences of conduct," with "a society of will and commandment" (ibid., 164). And above all, she insists, "the liturgical mode will itself induce new forms, will in fact *be* a new form; and beyond that, given the nature of liturgy, a *public* rather than a coterie form" (ibid., 175). What Ozick describes is theatrical liberalism. She describes a Jewish culture, which is simultaneously secular and holy, which privileges action and conduct, which is communal and based on obligation. Like theatrical liberalism, the Jewish culture she describes has boundaries that are practically invisible; after all, this culture is conducted in English and assumes the basic freedoms of liberalism. It appears, to all intents and purposes, to be American. She notes that, like theatrical liberalism, this culture has its enemies, who refer to it obliquely not as Jewish but as the work of "New York Intellectuals" (which echoes critiques of "Hollywood" and "New York liberal culture"). "Opposition," she wryly asserts, "is at least proof of reality" (ibid., 176). What Ozick fails to recognize is that the culture she yearns for has enjoyed a rich and full existence at least since the early twentieth century in the realm of popular entertainment.

The very figures whom she excommunicates in her essay—Ginsberg, Hoffman, Norman Mailer, Philip Roth—as well as the creators of *Fiddler on the Roof* whom she critiques elsewhere, write with many of the liturgical impulses she promotes.[4]

* * *

Ozick's critique of hippie-dom and post-modernism offers only one of many Jewish perspectives on 1960s popular culture. The 1967 march on the Pentagon served as a focal point for many Jewish artists, writers, directors, and performers of the late 1960s and '70s. It was a theatrical event, but it also spawned artistic reflection, in both the experimental and popular culture arenas, and in many ways created the pop culture cliché of "the sixties" we still live with today. In *Revolution for the Hell of It,* one of the major leaders of the counterculture and the founder of the yippies, Abbie Hoffman, explores the impulses and actions that led up to the march and the techniques he created to make the political protest both effective and consistent with his aesthetic principles. These techniques are rooted in Jewish-created popular entertainment; they draw on aspects of theatrical liberalism for their power. Hoffman is, for example, obsessed with changeability and self-fashioning, as he notes in this description of the ways various groups perceive the yippies:

> This reluctance to define ourselves gives us glorious freedom in which to fuck with the system. We become communist-racist-acid-headed freaks, holding flowers in one hand and bombs in the other. The Old Left says we work for the CIA. Ex-Marines stomp on us as Pinkos. Newport police jail us as smut peddlers. Newark cops arrest us as riot inciters. (These four events were all triggered by passing out free copies of the same poem). So what the hell are we doing, you ask? We are dynamiting brain cells. We are putting people through changes. The key to the puzzle lies in theater.[5]

Resisting Ozick's charge of idolatry, Hoffman here defines freedom the way theatrical liberals defined it for much of the twentieth century: freedom involves the right not to be pinned down to a single identity definition, the right to self-transformation. Like a hippie Bugs Bunny,

Hoffman hops from identity to identity, escaping traps by allowing his audience to perceive him as multiple and impossible to define. Unlike Willy Loman, however, Hoffman is utterly unconcerned with being well liked. His only goal is to incite people to action: "The aim is not to earn the respect, admiration, and love of everybody—it's to get people to do, to participate, whether positively or negatively" (ibid.). Hoffman draws on the conventions of film comedy and vaudeville for his techniques:

> Do it all fast. Like slapstick movies. Make sure everyone has a good time. People love to laugh–it's a riot. Riot—that's an interesting word-game if you want to play it. Don't be for or against. Riots–environmental and psychological–are Holy, so don't screw around with explanations. Theater also has some advantages. (ibid.)

Riots are holy—laugh riots are also holy. As in theatrical liberalism, theater and political engagement are sacred acts:

> Don't rely on words. Words are the absolute in horseshit. Rely on doing— go all the way every time. . . . Move fast. . . .Get their attention, leave a few clues and vanish. Change your costume, use the props around you. Each morning begin naked. Destroy your name, become unlisted, go underground. (ibid., 29–30)

Hoffman's theatricality was also self-consciously Jewish. In a stunt at the New York Stock Exchange a few months before the march on the Pentagon, Hoffman showed up with eighteen friends and was confronted at the door by a guard who, noticing the way they were dressed, accused them of being hippies staging a demonstration. Hoffman replied:

> "Who's a hippie? I'm Jewish and besides we don't do demonstrations, see we have no picket signs," I shot back. The guards decided it was not a good idea to keep a Jew out of the Stock Exchange, so they agreed we could go in. (ibid., 32)

Hoffman decided that the best way to protest the Vietnam War was to exorcise the evil from the Pentagon by forming a circle of people around it, chanting, and "levitating" it. In an extraordinary chronicle of the march, *Armies of the Night,* Norman Mailer describes Hoffman's theatrical brilliance:

> Now they [the band The Fugs] were dressed in orange and yellow and rose colored capes and looked at once like Hindu gurus, French musketeers, and Southern cavalry captains, and the girls watching them, indeed sharing the platform with them were wearing love beads and leather bells—sandals, blossoms, and little steel-rimmed spectacles abounded, and the music, no rather the play, had begun, almost Shakespearean in its sinister announcement of great pleasures to come. Now the Participant [Mailer] recognized that this was the beginning of the exorcism of the Pentagon, yes the papers had made much of the permit requested by a hippie leader named Abbie Hoffman to encircle the Pentagon with twelve hundred men in order to form a ring of exorcism sufficiently powerful to raise the Pentagon three hundred feet. In the air the Pentagon would then, went the presumption, turn orange and vibrate until all evil emissions had fled this levitation. At that point the war in Vietnam would end.[6]

Hoffman was a brilliant theater director, and Mailer relishes every detail of the spectacle Hoffman created. Mailer describes the mimeographed handout that was distributed to the crowd, outlining the procedure for levitation. The pseudo-religious, "allee samee" language contained in the document was exactly the kind of universalism that made Cynthia Ozick so angry:

> We Freemen, of all colors of the spectrum, in the name of God, Ra, Jehovah, Anubis, Osiris, Tlaloc, Quetzalcoatl, Thoth, Ptah, Allah, Krishna, Chango, Chimeke, Chukwu, Olisa-Bulu-Uwa, Imales, Orisasu, Odudua, Kali, Shiva-Shakra, Great Spirit, Dionysus, Yahweh, Thor, Bacchus, Isis, Jesus Christ, Maitreya, Buddha, Rama do exorcise and cast out the EVIL which has walled and captured the pentacle of power. . . . We are demanding that the pentacle of power once again be used to serve the interests of GOD manifest in the world as man. (ibid. 139–140)

Cynthia Ozick assumed this sort of religious incitement was unironic and therefore she perceived in it a direct threat to Judaism, especially on the part of its Jewish practitioners. Mailer is not so sure. He marvels at the grand theatrical gestures of these young protestors, of the absurd yet brilliant ability Hoffman, Ginsberg, and others had to capture the imagination of the crowd and to draw even those lingering on the sidelines into the demonstration in the hopes of effecting real change through theater. As the exorcism begins and the group begins chanting along with the musicians, "Out, Demons, out!" Mailer finds himself drawn into the experience:

> He detested community sing—an old violation of his childhood had been the bouncing ball on the movie screen; he had wanted to watch a movie, not sing—but the invocation delivered some message to his throat. "Out, demons, out," he whispered, "out, demons, out." And his foot—simple American foot—was, of course, tapping. (ibid., 141)

The urge to "sing along" becomes too great for Mailer, and he joins in. He turns to his companion, the poet Robert Lowell, whom he has earlier compared to a Puritan and a Harvard don, and remarks, "You know I like this" (ibid., 143). Lowell, with the Anglo-Saxon Protestant composure that Mailer both envies and despises, resists the theatrical pull of the crowd. Throughout his eyewitness report, Mailer remains acutely aware of his Jewishness, and Lowell serves as a kind of WASPy straight man who sets off Mailer's hotheaded Jewish theatricality. Unlike Ginsberg, whom Mailer agrees is hopelessly hypnotized by his own chanting,[7] Mailer is always self-conscious of being slightly out of place, aware of looking with "old Jacob's eye," as Ozick observes in "Toward a New Yiddish."[8]

The book Mailer wrote partakes of the post-modern techniques which Ozick rejects, but does so in such a way as to draw attention to Mailer's difference, his self-conscious theatricality, and his suspicion of the very same ecstatic communal reveries that Ozick critiques. Mailer's *Armies of the Night* is part journalism, part fiction. Most of the book ("History as a Novel") describes the events leading up to and including the march (and Mailer's arrest) as if it were a novel; referring to Mailer in the third person but telling the entire story from his particular point of view. The protagonist is a self-conscious theatrical performer, playing his role(s) on the stages of history with ironic amusement. We learn in the opening pages that

Mailer had the most developed sense of image; if not, he would have been a figure of deficiency, for people had been regarding him by his public image since he was twenty-five years old. He had in fact learned to live in the sarcophagus of his image—at night, in his sleep, he might dart out, and paint improvements on the sarcophagus. (Mailer, *Armies of the Night*, 16)

Much of the opening section deals with an actual performance, on a stage, in which Mailer and others give speeches, read poetry, play music, and tell jokes for protestors who have assembled for the march, which is to take place the following day. At no point does Mailer stop performing and just "be himself." This is an impossibility within the structure of the book he has created, and is also a central point of the book.

The final section ("The Novel as History") pulls back from the perspective of the individual and attempts to tell the "facts" of the event, in an objective and impartial manner. Of course, the fact that the story has already been told from one particular perspective undermines any attempt at objectivity, and instead reveals the subjective nature of the multiple and contradictory media reports about the march. Sounding much like his forefather Jacob (as well as the architects of Babel), Mailer describes the "crooked perspective" that he has created, and the ways in which that way of looking will continue to inform even the dry language of historical fact:

The Novelist in passing his baton to the Historian has a happy smile. He has been faster than you think. As a working craftsman, a journeyman artist, he is not without his guile; he has come to decide that if you would see the horizon from a forest, you must build a tower. If the horizon will reveal most of what is significant, an hour of examination can yet do the job—it is the tower which takes months to build. So the Novelist working in secret collaboration with the Historian has perhaps tried to build with his novel a tower fully equipped with telescopes to study—at the greatest advantage—our own horizon. Of course, the tower is crooked, and the telescopes warped. (ibid., 245)

Mailer is a performer. As a writer, he self-consciously adopts multiple roles, as Novelist, Historian, Norman Mailer, etc., and demonstrates the ways in which those roles allow him the freedom to play multiple parts in history and to see history from multiple perspectives. At the same time, Mailer is acutely aware of the way in which his position as a Jew locks him into certain identity definitions and restricts his ability to perform freely. When Mailer emerges from the courtroom, a free man after his brief stay in jail, he encounters a bevy of reporters on the lawn outside the courthouse. He is overcome by a feeling of joy, of love for his fellow prisoners, for his country, for his wife. He thinks this must be what Christians felt "when they spoke of Christ within them" (ibid., 238). So following on the heels of a Presbyterian chaplain, Mailer gives a short speech to the reporters, expressing the sort of universal (but actually Christian) feelings of grace that Ozick ascribes to Ginsberg:

> "You see, dear fellow Americans, it is Sunday, and we are burning the body and blood of Christ in Vietnam. Yes, we are burning him there, and as we do, we destroy the foundation of this Republic, which is its love and trust in Christ." He was silent. Wow. (ibid., 239)

Mailer notices how pleased all the reporters look, and he himself is pleased with his speech and with the day. He returns home and a few days later sees his speech on Christ printed in the *Washington Post,* with a few modifications:

> In his courtroom speech, Mailer said, "They are burning the body and blood of Christ in Vietnam." . . . Mailer said he believed that the war in Vietnam "will destroy the foundation of this republic, which is its love and trust in Christ." Mailer is a Jew. (ibid., 240)

No matter how inspired Mailer may be, at that moment, by the universalism of a Christian ethos of peace and love, this is *not* his ethos, and he will never be allowed to inhabit it. Performance is powerful as long as the audience is convinced; Mailer's freedom to fashion himself as an American is limited by the perspective of the journalists who report on his antics. This is where Ozick is both unnecessarily cautious (his audience never allows Mailer to be truly idolatrous), and also prescient (Mailer is likewise never allowed to forget he is a Jew). Jews can speak of universalism all they want; but if those with whom they converse continue to see them as Jews, this universalism is revealed as nothing but, as Ozick notes, "the ultimate Jewish parochialism. It is mainly Jews who profess it" (Ozick, 153).

* * *

In describing the idolatrous and ecstatic demonstrations of the late 1960s, Ozick would have found an ideal target in Richard Schechner. He was the founder of The Performance Group (TPG) and director of their most famous piece *Dionysus in '69*, an extremely influential creator of "environmental theater," which became standard operating practice for experimental theater in the 1960s and '70s (and beyond), and one of the founding scholars of the field of Performance Studies. Born in 1934, Schechner spent his childhood in the same Jewish Newark neighborhood (Weequahic) as Philip Roth, and was raised in a Jewishly active and observant household. He attended Oheb Shalom Synagogue and religious school in Newark through his teenage years, where his father also served for a number of years as president of the congregation. Like many of the writers and thinkers we have encountered in this book, Schechner has been a confirmed atheist for much of his adult life, but at the same time he has never fully abandoned his Jewish background.[9]

Schechner's influential first book, *Environmental Theater,* while overtly a rejection of popular entertainment, is nonetheless engaged with all of the tenets of theatrical liberalism, reacting to, and creatively revising the theories of the theater that predominated in American popular culture of the first half of the twentieth century. Despite their avant-garde context, Schechner's theories drew on popular theatrical modes of the past and deeply influenced the popular entertainment that emerged in its wake. Claimed by all manner of radical performance theorists, Schechner's work nonetheless fits squarely into the story of theatrical liberalism.[10] Schechner initially outlined his theory in a brief 1967 document titled "Six Axioms," in which he describes the broad spectrum of public events that he considers "theater," depicting a continuum, which ranges from public street demonstrations to traditional theatrical performance on a stage. Environmental theater lies somewhere in the middle.

The first axiom defines the goals of actors and the relationship between actors and audience. In street demonstrations, actors are just playing themselves. In traditional theater, they are playing someone else. In environmental theater, Schechner argues, actors *use* characters to *reveal* themselves. Similarly, in street demonstrations everyone is simultaneously participant and spectator while in traditional theater, the line between audience members and performers is clearly delineated. In environmental theater, however, the line between performers and spectators is fluid; audiences move between being spectators and participants in the action. Using the march on the Pentagon as an example, Schechner describes how the line between troops and protestors was constantly shifting; as some protestors were arrested, others, who had been onlookers, took their places as actors. The same happened with the soldiers. At times, soldiers even left the line to become protestors. Other axioms deal with theatrical space. Schechner resists the traditional bifurcation of space into stage and audience seating. Environmental theater aims for closer, more personal and intimate contact between audience and performers, and so seating is interspersed with performance areas and can shift during a performance. Environmental theater likewise can happen anywhere—traditional theater buildings are not necessary.[11] In these found spaces, nothing is disguised: there are no curtains or backdrops designed to hide the elements of the space. Production elements are incorporated into the performance. Lighting, sound, and video technicians are "performers" who rehearse along with the cast and are visible participants in the theatrical event. As Schechner notes in axioms four and five, the focus of the performance is multiple and variable—audiences don't necessarily know where to look. Different audience members will experience different shows, depending on where they are seated. Finally, in axiom six, the status of text is called into question: what we would traditionally recognize as a play is neither the starting point nor the goal of the performance, although plays often form the inspiration for a performance piece.

The environmental theater Schechner describes in his book takes up each aspect of theatrical liberalism (albeit unself-consciously) and shows how this established ideology can be reimagined for more radical purposes. First, he directly and forcefully reasserts the connection between theater and religion. He reanimates the notion of theater as a sacred space, which we saw in *The Jazz Singer*: the idea that performance is akin to communal ritual. Schechner was deeply influenced by anthropological work on theatrical and ritualistic practices in aboriginal communities, and it is no accident that he chose as the inspirational text for one of his first performance pieces *The Bacchae* by Euripides.[12] Schechner was interested in recapturing the religious passion and ritual associated with the classical Greek theater and finding a way to revive it for contemporary audiences. For Schechner's TPG and for the audiences who attended performances of *Dionysus in '69,* the theatrical event did indeed take on the quality of a sacred practice, and the line between theatrical performance and religious ritual was deliberately blurred:

> Many who saw *Dionysus* thought it was a celebration of our own religion and that the symbolic events of the play—the birth, taunting, orgies, torture, and killing—were a kind of new Mass; participating in *Dionysus in '69* was a way of performing an arcane ritual in the catacombs of Wooster Street. The audience was not altogether wrong. Members of the Group shared the needs of the audience. What the audience projected onto the play was matched by what the players projected back onto the audience. We all assumed a religion, if we had none.[13]

The question of course arises: *what* religion did they assume? Is this Judaism, Christianity, paganism, theatrical liberalism, or some new religion of the radical Left? What both audiences and performers were looking for, according to Schechner, was a kind of communalism, a desperate desire to be a part of a group, of The Group, to overcome the solipsism of American individualism. And participating in *Dionysus in '69* became a way of demonstrating faith in that possibility:

> Joining in *Dionysus*–like declaring for Christ at a revival meeting—was an act of the body publicly signalling one's faith. Participation and belief supported each other—on any given night the strength of feeling created by joining participation to belief could be such that everything else was swept away. (ibid., 43)

When "everything else is swept away," you get a kind of ecstatic experience of the very sort that Cynthia Ozick warned against. Schechner embraced ecstasy as an aspect of performance. Drawing on his research on shamans and on aboriginal performances, Schechner deduces that "performance itself is a heightened activity, an exalted state that is intermittent, sacred, mythic, and masked. . . . The performer has qualities of the healer and the ecstatic" (ibid., 172). For Schechner, the ecstatic involves a breakdown of the distinction between "real life" and "performance reality." In a wholly authentic performance experience, this distinction collapses and the action of the performance *becomes* real and vice versa:

> Unlike orthodox theater where the *willing* suspension of disbelief means that always there is a second reality—"the real world" shadowing the performance reality, there is in the aborigine performance a change in realities so that during the performance there is *only one reality*: the one being performed. (ibid., 178)

Although Schechner was nostalgic for this kind of authenticity, he also acknowledged its impossibility in a twentieth-century American context. Writing only a few years after *Dionysus in '69,* Schechner is already acutely aware of the folly of imagining that real community can emerge from the artificial context of a single theatrical performance:

> The performance was often trans-theatrical in a way that could not last, because American society in 1969 was not actually communal. *Dionysus* was overwhelming to the degree that audiences believed it was not a play and found that belief confirmed by the Group. This belief in the play's actuality was corroborated by its participatory elements. . . . But, as Euripides himself reminds us in *The Bacchae,* "we are not gods, but men." (ibid., 43)

Schechner is far more aware of the dangers of idolatry, especially the hubris of mistaking the self for a deity, than Ozick gives anyone on the radical Left credit for. He is also deeply interested in the "choral" voice of Ozick's liturgical mode. But what he discovers is that this choral, communal voice must be carefully circumscribed in order to have moral impact. He describes how, during the run of *Dionysus in '69,* the communal impulses of the audience ultimately had to be squelched in favor of a much more scripted and controlled theatrical event. The theater experience was still religious, but not democratic: the high priests, that is, the actors, performed the rituals for the congregation, which had to be content with merely watching, not actively participating.

Schechner's engagement with theater as a form of religious ritual is complicated by his relationship to texts. He asserts that the religion of the theater, as it has been practiced in much of the twentieth century, is related to both the Jewish and Christian practice of exegesis:

> In his original form an exegete is a guide, a director, an interpreter. . . .
> The tradition of exegesis is firmly enough rooted in European culture
> that it was relatively easy to make the transformation: The playwright
> became God (often absent but always all-powerful), his play the Bible,
> the director the exegete, the actors the celebrants, and the audience the
> congregation of the faithful. (ibid., 237)

When presented with a text to direct himself (Sam Shepard's *Tooth of Crime*), Schechner must figure out how the environmental theater might engage with this ritual of exegesis. He ultimately contradicts his own axiom that "play texts were mere pretexts out of which the performance is made; material to be used, distorted, dismembered, reassembled" (ibid., 242). While insisting that the play should never assume the status of a sacred text, Schechner argues for the reintroduction of plays back into the environmental theater. What becomes sacred for Schechner is not the text, but the process by which that text comes alive and is presented to an audience.

The rehearsal process, more than any other aspect of environmental theater, relies on an understanding of action, which closely mirrors that of theatrical liberalism. Schechner's TPG valued the process of making theater as much as, if not more than, the final product: "Process—a term used often in environmental theater—means '*getting* there' rather than 'getting *there*,' emphasis on the doing, not the done. . . . The task of environmental theater is to make process part of each performance" (ibid., 131). To this end, they established a system of open rehearsals in which small audiences could witness the process of theater making in action. Schechner's idea of "process" is closely related to Abraham Joshua Heschel's theories of religious action. Schechner also believed that spontaneity was an important part of the theater experience, but that it had to be combined with discipline and practice: "[P]rocess is a conversation between spontaneity and discipline. Discipline without process is mechanical; process without discipline is impossible"(ibid., 132). To teach discipline, Schechner had his actors perform simple ritualized tasks and speak nonsense words repeatedly, until they became suffused with meaning. Eventually, the simple rituals would be replaced by detailed actions that made sense in the context of the performance but also gave performers access to deeper meaning. While Schechner clearly differs in style from the fictional director Oscar Jaffe in *Twentieth Century,* or his real-life counterpart David Belasco, they all agree on the importance of repeated action as a way of achieving greater understanding of a role and ultimately of communicating more expressively with the audience. In describing various training exercises that focus on repeated actions, Schechner notes, "[W]hile the performer's conscious attention is occupied by a simple task, deeper things come through" (ibid., 149). Like Heschel, Schechner also viewed Judaism as a religion of action and behavior. In discussing a proposal for a (never completed) theater piece titled "The Jewish Piece," Schechner wrote to his collaborator: "I have experienced Judaism as a fundamentally ethical religion—that is concerned with behavior in the world, and not a theological religion."[14] For Schechner, as for Heschel, *action* takes priority over belief (in God or plays). By doing actions, one will automatically come to know the meaning of those actions:

> [T]he question for the performer is not "*Why* do I stab Lizzie?" but "*How* do I stab Lizzie?" . . . If each detail of the action is in place, if the connections between the details are strong and logical, then the whole action will be so together that *any answer to the question of "why" is correct.* (Or, to put it another way, knowing "how" makes knowing "why"' unnecessary.) (Schechner, *Environ. Theater,* 162)

We do not need to demonstrate "why"; we just need to do the actions which lead to "why." So in helping actors to prepare their roles, Schechner focuses on action, not on plumbing the psychological depths of a character in the way Lee Strasberg might have recommended: "Theatrical logic is about *doing, showing, impersonating, singing, dancing, and playing.* These are the resources a performer calls on when preparing a role." At the same time, Schechner does reach for the same kinds of realism and immediacy that Strasberg preached, and he similarly sees theater as the only art form that offers real, *live,* reality: "He is his own material; he does not have the buffer of a medium. Theater is not an art that detaches itself from its creators at the point of completion; there is no way of exhibiting a performance without at the same time exhibiting the performers" (ibid., 165). To achieve the kind of authenticity TPG desired, "exhibiting the performer" was often interpreted quite literally: nudity became a central feature of many of the shows, a way of insisting that nothing was hidden from the audience.

When audience members attended a TPG show, or repeated open rehearsals, as was often the case, they became familiar with the members of TPG. The audience always saw double—the performer, and the character, were simultaneously present in the show. This was Schechner's goal: "The orthodox actor vanishes inside his role. The environmental theater performer is in a perceivable relationship with the role. What the audience experiences is neither the performer nor the role but the relationship between the two" (ibid., 166). This idea has resonance not only for the experimental theater of 1960s Lower Manhattan, but also for the popular theater of Midtown Manhattan (and the screens of Hollywood). Throughout the twentieth century, the star system operated with many similar features. Stars may have moved from role to role, but they were always present for their audiences, who felt that they "knew" them despite the part they might be playing.[15] This star effect was heightened in the 1960s, especially with the advent of ethnic pride. One of the things that made *Fiddler on the Roof* and *Funny Girl* so successful was this relationship between performer and role. The relationship between Zero Mostel and Tevye or Barbra Streisand and Fanny Brice was as much as if not more important than the "realistic" representation of the roles themselves. The superimposition of proud Jews of the 1960s with the charismatic Jewish performers of earlier historical eras turns these musicals into powerful works of ethnic pride rather than simply historical period pieces. While Schechner would certainly protest that his performers were revealing truths about themselves, while commercial stars merely revealed another constructed version of themselves, the distinction does not hold upon close inspection. What Schechner's performers and Hollywood stars are doing is exteriorizing the process of self-fashioning, drawing attention to the (possibly specious) distinction between self and character. The difference is that Schechner and his performers firmly believed that they possessed a "real" authentic self. The stars of the commercial stage and screen don't seem to care.

For Richard Schechner, theater is, above all, an expression of community. While he debated whether TPG could ever truly be a community, and whether audiences had a role to play in the creation of theatrical community, he was, nonetheless, committed to the fundamental obligations of a communal practice. The exercises that he used to train performers emphasized trust and continually reinforced the obligations that group members have to one another: "Many exercises can be invented from the principle that the individual needs the group and that each member of the group needs every other member" (Schechner, *Environ. Theater*, 155). Schechner took the notion of obligation to the theatrical community that was so crucial to the early works of theatrical liberalism and transformed it for the experimental theater, but it also never strayed far from the initial Judaic impulses that gave it life.

* * *

Schechner's ideas about the theater emerged almost simultaneously in the Broadway musical. In 1967 the musical *Hair* was staged at the Public Theater, and a year later it enjoyed a successful four-year run on Broadway. The musical structure, performance style, and politics of the play all mirrored the values of environmental theater and yet also worked remarkably well for Broadway theater audiences. And while more traditionally structured musicals continued to appear on Broadway through the 1960s and 1970s, *Hair* fundamentally changed expectations about what a musical could be. *Hair* was conceived by two actors, James Rado and Gerome Ragni, neither of whom was Jewish but both were deeply influenced by Jewish theater practitioners. Rado yearned to be a composer of Rodgers and Hammerstein–style musicals, and tried his hand at many musical revues while in college. After college, he chose to study Method acting at Lee Strasberg's studio and achieved minor success as an actor on Broadway. Ragni, on the other hand, was smitten with the experimental theater of the 1960s and worked with The Open Theater, a group devoted to the same kinds of improvisational performance promoted by Schechner. Indeed, *Hair* demonstrates the ways in which theatrical liberalism had become a broad American phenomenon, practiced by non-Jews as well as Jews. At the same time, *Hair* took the musical theater in a revolutionary new direction, which ultimately signaled the end of the dominance of theatrical liberalism on the Broadway stage.[16]

Ragni and Rado met when they were performing in a short-lived Off-Broadway play and began conceptualizing the idea for a musical based on their own lives and those of the other hippies who populated the streets of Manhattan's East Village. The piece—composed by a third member of the team, Galt McDermott—was eventually picked up by Joseph Papp (who was Jewish); he produced it at his new Public Theater in the East Village in 1967. It then moved to a Midtown discotheque and finally to Broadway, where it opened at the Biltmore Theater in 1968 to excellent reviews and was nominated for the Tony Award for Best Musical that year. Rado and Ragni imagined the play as a demonstration of the lifestyle of the hippies, a kind of religious ritual (they call it "a group-tribal activity") and a political project designed to convert audiences to the morality and ideology of the hippies.[17] Their goals closely mirrored those of Allen Ginsberg. They firmly believed that a demonstration of the *lifestyle* of the Tribe of kids in the play was sufficient to convince audience members of a worldview. As they noted in the stage directions:

> The Kids are a tribe. At the same time, for the purpose of HAIR, they know they are on a stage in a theater, performing for an audience, demonstrating their way of life, in a sense, telling a story, in order to persuade those who watch of their intentions, to perhaps gain greater understanding, support, and tolerance, and thus perhaps expand their horizons of active participation toward a better, saner, peace-full, love-full world. They are trying to turn on the audience. (ibid., ix)

As in environmental theater, the set for *Hair* exposes the entire stage and allows for no masking, curtains, or pretense of theatrical illusion. There are only two set pieces on the stage, both designed to make Cynthia Ozick cringe: a Totem Pole, and a Crucifix-Tree complete with a glowing, electrified Jesus. The goal of the actors is, as in environmental theater, to use their characters to expose themselves, to demonstrate "their way of life," and at times literally to expose their bodies, as in the famous nude scene at the end of act 1. Many scenes in the play were developed through the kinds of improvisational exercises Schechner describes, and early in its run, actors interacted directly with the audience, jumping into the seats to hand out flyers and flowers for the "be-in."

Hair drew on the principles of environmental theater, but it also had enormous commercial appeal. By applying these experimental principles to the traditional backstage musical form, *Hair* reveals the remarkable flexibility of aspects of theatrical liberalism; while openly espousing radical change, the play indirectly expresses core liberal values, which are characteristic of backstage musicals. Characters celebrate conscious self-fashioning with their choice of hairstyles and costumes foregrounded throughout the play, and a song about "hair" serving as a theatrical centerpiece. The most terrifying loss of freedom in the play is the threat of conformity represented by the army. While the character Claude is of course frightened by the violence of war itself, this fear is expressed through a hatred of conformity, of being locked into a single identity definition, and is viscerally illustrated when he emerges at the end with short hair. He presents his shorn hair in a bag to his best friend Berger, a gift that represents the theatrical freedom he has relinquished. His deepest hope is that he will be able to regain this freedom upon his return: "Keep it for me," he says, "Maybe I can have a wig made when I get out" (ibid., 200). This is immediately followed by a parody of ethnic authenticity, as a sergeant calls the roll: "Irish . . . Italian . . . Jew . . . German . . . English . . . Puerto Rican . . . Polish . . ." (ibid., 202–203). Each time he rattles off an ethnic identity, a random soldier responds, "Present, sir." But Claude has not yet fully relinquished his individuality and freedom. He does not respond to the label "Polish." The sergeant must call him by name, "Claude Bukowski" (ibid., 203). He finally responds, like the others, "Present, sir" and marches in lockstep off the stage. His ability to self-fashion has been utterly squashed by the weight of conformity demanded by the army.

The role of action in the play is somewhat more complex. The key determining action in the play—political, spiritual, and theatrical—is the burning of draft cards. Much of the first act moves toward a political demonstration against the war in Vietnam. This scene directly involves the audience, who receive flowers, incense, and fruit, and are invited to participate in the demonstration. After a brief nude scene in which Berger strips and then is surrounded by puppet policemen, the Tribe produces two symbols of American liberty. The first is a flag from 1776 with the revolutionary slogan "Don't Tread on Me" emblazoned on it, which serves as a backdrop to the scene. The second is a makeshift Statue of Liberty, performed by the leading female character Sheila: She holds "a flaming Maxwell House coffee can in her right hand above her head. She strikes a Statue of Liberty pose." The Tribe introduces her as "Democracy's Daughter!" And then the action begins:

> In her other hand, Sheila holds a bunch of daffodils. One by one, each guy comes forward, lighting their draft cards, dropping the remains into the can. As each card is burned, The Tribe cheers. Sheila gives each guy a daffodil in exchange. Claude is last; he approaches the can, hesitates a moment, holds his card above it, it catches fire and he pulls it back quickly, extinguishing the flame. (ibid., 116–117)

Unable to complete the action, Claude bursts into one of the best known songs in the show, "Where do I go?" The song expresses his deep need to know *why* he should act so that he has the courage to act:

> Where is the something
> Where is the someone
> That tells me why
> I live and die ? (ibid., 118)

Of course, Claude has it backwards. If he acts, *then* he will discover why. But he is not capable of acting (the many *Hamlet* references in the play have led some to call him the "melancholy hippie").[18] And it's his lack of courage to take the leap of action that leads to his downfall. Claude is unable to feed Lady Liberty's flame and so loses the privilege to act at all; he becomes an automaton as he marches off to war.

Hair references the form of the backstage musical from the beginning. The opening notes indicate that "the entire opening of the show . . . from the moment the audience enters the theater, is The Tribe preparing for the ceremony, the ritual, the war dance (the peace dance), the play—HAIR" (*Hair*, ix). As the play opens, the Tribe is revealed on stage getting their costumes on, painting their faces, warming up their voices and their instruments. The first song, as in most Broadway musicals, is a rousing group number, "Aquarius," quickly followed by a series of four songs ("Manchester," "Manhattan," "Colored Spade," and "Sodomy") establishing the central characters Claude, Berger, Hud, and Woof. As the second act begins, we hear a scratchy rendition of the Cole Porter song, "Anything Goes," played on an antique windup Victrola. The song morphs into a loud rock number "Electric Blues," indicating the distance *and* the connection between *Hair* and the earlier musical form. The second act even features a dream ballet, in this case disguised as an acid trip. Terrified of what the army will demand of him, but also terrified to act outside the law as a war resistor, Claude dreams of the various horrible scenarios that await him. As in other musicals, the dream ballet seems to help him make up his mind. As he emerges from the trip, he tells Berger he's not going into the army, but within moments, he admits that he can't actually sustain the kind of freedom implicit in the hippie life: "It's too difficult. I can't open myself up like that. I can't make this moment to moment living on the streets" (*Hair*, 162). Berger, on the other hand, is perfectly happy with the instability: "I'm gonna go to India . . . float around . . . live in little huts in Beirut . . . feed the poor Indians in a little village somewhere . . . like Albert Schweitzer . . . bake bread. I'm gonna stay high forever" (*Hair*, 162). A hippie Huck Finn, comfortable floating from persona to persona, situation to situation, Berger is the reincarnation of the virtuoso transformative performer of early vaudeville. Like Huck Finn, the play *Hair* both rejects and embraces the civilization from which it emerged–in this case the backstage musical and the values of theatrical liberalism. As an example of radical environmental theater, *Hair* dismisses as artificial the boundaries between the stage and the real lifestyle of the hippies it depicts. But *Hair* also works in the context of theatrical liberalism, integrating the freedom of individual self-transformation into a radical framework and promoting the liberal values of communal obligation and *action* within the context of a cultural moment far more concerned with being than acting.

* * *

Two years after the march on the Pentagon, and ten years after Erving Goffman's work was published, the Columbia literature professor and Jewish intellectual Lionel Trilling took up the contradictions at the heart of *My Fair Lady* and *Hair,* in a series of lectures at Harvard University in the 1969–70 academic year. Published as *Sincerity and Authenticity* in 1971, Trilling's work explores liberal culture's love/hate relationship with theatricality, offering a historical account of views of theatrical self-making from the Renaissance invention of sincerity to the 1960s love affair with authenticity. With Trilling, we once again encounter a Jewish intellectual concerned with the moral status of the "authentic" self, performance, and theatricality. Like Goffman, Trilling is interested in performance in everyday life, although he focuses on the moral implications of such performance within fiction, poetry, and drama. Goffman, on the other hand, concentrates on the mechanics of performance in the real world. In *Sincerity and Authenticity,* Trilling historicizes these complex terms and in doing so writes a kind of psychic history of liberalism. He argues that with the development of modernity, and of the liberalism that emerged alongside it, comes a new idea of the self, an idea of a self that is multiple, that can be different things at different times. This leads to a need to morally regulate the presentation of self—to insist on sincerity as a moral bulwark against theatricality. "At a certain point in its history," Trilling tells us, "the moral life of Europe added to itself a new element, the state or quality of the self which we call sincerity."[19] By sincerity, Trilling means, "a congruence between avowal and actual feeling," a way of being that assumes that the truth lies inside, and that our outsides perfectly express what we think or feel on the inside. He locates the rise of sincerity as a moral value in European culture in the sixteenth century and explains that this new morality is a response to changes in social life. Urbanization and increasing social mobility, the Renaissance notion of the individual, and the Protestant Reformation's embrace of plain speaking all contributed to this shift.

Trilling notes that in the late sixteenth century, "it became more and more possible for people to leave the class into which they were born. The middle class rose, not only in its old habitual way but unprecedentedly" (ibid., 15). This new mobility, facilitated by the anonymity of urban life, led to a new concern that people might *pretend* to be of a station other than that to which they were born. The antidote to the uncertainty bred by this instability was an increasing value placed upon plain speaking, a value enforced by many aspects of the Protestant Reformation and illustrated most clearly in one of the greatest plays of the time, *King Lear*. Renaissance self-fashioning, as described by Stephen Greenblatt a couple of decades after Trilling's work appeared, is deeply indebted to the same historical factors. As Trilling puts it, "at a certain point in history men became individuals" (ibid., 24). He quickly goes on to explain that a wholly new notion of the self emerged at this time. People became increasingly aware of the internal space of the self and began to imagine themselves as inhabiting more than one role, and of having control over which role they might perform at any given social encounter; they saw that the distinction between private and public space and individuality was enhanced by the presence of mirrors, which allowed people to see themselves as others might see them and to make necessary adjustments to what Goffman called the personal front. We encountered Trilling's historical notion of the development of the self in Avivah Zornberg's discussion of Jacob and Esau. There, she notes that Trilling uses the biblical Abraham as an example of a character who predates the rise of sincerity. Abraham cannot be considered either sincere or insincere as these qualities require a sense of an internal self: a modern notion utterly foreign to such an early biblical figure. Zornberg convincingly argues, however, that Jacob does fit Trilling's model.

In the early seventeenth century, Trilling notes, people began to use the word "self" as an autonomous noun and to write a new literary form, that of autobiography. And it is in autobiography that the importance of sincerity is directly expressed:

> The subject of an autobiography is just such a self, bent on revealing himself in all his truth, bent, that is to say, on demonstrating his sincerity. His conception of his private and uniquely interesting individuality, together with his impulse to reveal his self, to demonstrate that in it which is to be admired and trusted, are, we may believe, his response to the newly available sense of an audience, of that public which society created. (ibid., 25)

Trilling is highly self-conscious about his use of words such as "role" and "audience" and at numerous points makes a direct connection between sincerity and theatricality. "It is surely no accident," he writes, "that the idea of sincerity, of the own self and the difficulty of knowing and showing it, should have arisen to vex men's minds in the epoch that saw the sudden efflorescence of the theater" (ibid., 10). Trilling is one of many Jewish intellectuals who connect Renaissance theater and theatricality more generally with the rise of individualism and liberalism.[20] For Jews, this story has a special urgency. Jews simply could not be the "plain speakers" demanded by the Protestant Reformation. To speak plainly about their lack of faith in Jesus, for example, would have likely led to either forced conversion or death. Jews figured prominently among the rising merchant class and had a strong investment in the class mobility promised by the modern notion of role-playing Trilling describes. Assimilating and modernizing Jews were also accused of insincerity; the parvenu is, after all, the insincere socialite. The early modern embrace of sincerity mirrors the concurrent rise of anti-theatricality and anti-Semitism described by Jonas Barish in *The Antitheatrical Prejudice.*

But, Trilling continues, in the later twentieth century, sincerity no longer holds the moral power it once did. Responding directly to Goffman, Trilling notes, that "in this enterprise of presenting the self, of putting ourselves on the social stage, sincerity itself plays a curiously compromised part" (Trilling, *Sincerity*, 10). Society requires us to be sincere, and the best way to be sincere is to give what Goffman calls a sincere performance, or in Trilling's words, to "sincerely act the part of the sincere person." The problem is that if we are playing a role, "a judgement may be passed upon our sincerity that it is not authentic" (ibid., 11). The idea of a theatrical role contains within it the judgement that if we are playing roles, there must be a true *self* underneath those roles: "somewhere under all the roles there is Me, that poor old ultimate actuality, who, when all the roles have been played, would like to murmur, 'Off, off, you lendings!' and settle down with his own original actual self" (ibid., 10). Modern art and morality asks why we should pretend to be something we are not. They assume an essential self and require that we do everything possible, as Biff demands in *Death of a Salesman*, to throw off posing and phoniness, and reveal who we really are. The embrace of authenticity, Trilling indicates, involves "a more strenuous moral experience than sincerity," requiring that we follow a "downward movement through all the cultural superstructures to some place where all movement ends, and begins," to Conrad's "heart of darkness," or Yeats's "foul rag-and-bone shop of the heart" (ibid., 12). Authenticity is the thing that exists before culture or after culture is stripped away. This has led to a remarkable reversal of values:

> At the behest of the criterion of authenticity, much that was once thought to make up the very fabric of culture has come to seem of little account, mere fantasy or ritual, or downright falsification. Conversely, much that culture traditionally condemned and sought to exclude is accorded a considerable moral authority by reason of the authenticity claimed for it, for example, disorder, violence, unreason. (ibid., 11)

Trilling is highly suspicious of this embrace of authenticity, which seems to celebrate freedom from the manners and strictures of society, but actually condemns us to a radical individualism that would make liberal society untenable.

Shocked by student riots at Columbia and the calls from countercultural artists, including his own student, Allen Ginsberg, for a release of a more primitive, less artificial authentic self, Trilling savagely critiques his contemporaries Norman O. Brown, Michel Foucault, and R. D. Laing for their wanton embrace of madness as the ultimate form of authenticity and freedom. While Trilling never explicitly accuses them of idolatry, as Ozick does, he takes issue with the same ecstatic and ahistoric Christianity that seems to inform so much of this late 1960s embrace of authenticity. He quotes David Cooper's introduction to Foucault's *Madness and Civilization*, which describes Foucault's celebration of madness as prophetic vision: "'Madness, for instance, is a matter of voicing the realization that I am (or you are) Christ.'" And Trilling sardonically replies, "So far from being an illness, a deprivation of any kind . . . madness is health fully realized at last" (ibid., 170). Furious at what he sees as a facile and immoral equation of liberation with madness, Trilling concludes his book with a passionate, deeply personal, and implicitly Jewish critique of the alienated post-modern intellectuals who have so irresponsibly rejected the gifts of liberalism in favor of an unconsidered radicalism:

But who that has spoken, or tried to speak, with a psychotic friend will consent to betray the masked pain of his bewilderment and solitude by making it the paradigm of liberation from the imprisoning falsehoods of an alienated social reality? Who that finds intelligible the sentences which describe madness (to use the word that cant prefers) in terms of transcendence and charisma will fail to penetrate to the great refusal of human connection that they express, the appalling belief that human existence is made authentic by the possession of a power, or the persuasion of its possession, which is not to be qualified or restricted by the co-ordinate existence of any fellow man? (ibid., 171)

What kind of individualism privileges the painful alienation of insanity? Trilling asks. Morally repulsed, he directly accuses his contemporaries of an irresponsible Christianity, one which has strayed too far from the Hebraism from which it emerged, which forsakes the Judaic principles of action and obligation that are at the heart of theatrical liberalism:

The falsities of an alienated social reality are rejected in favor of an upward psychopathic mobility to the point of divinity, each one of us a Christ—but with none of the inconveniences of undertaking to intercede, of being a sacrifice, of reasoning with rabbis, of making sermons, of having disciples, of going to weddings and to funerals, of beginning something and at a certain point remarking that it is finished. (ibid., 172)

Deeply concerned with the moral consequences of freedom, Trilling cannot embrace this ecstatic, and fundamentally un-Jewish, cult of the individual.

* * *

Trilling is deeply aware of the dangers of celebrating authenticity. If the authentic, essential self is the only honest expression of self, then it becomes easy to accuse anyone interested in social mobility of dishonesty. The writer and director Mel Brooks explores some of the same moral concerns as Trilling, but through the medium of comic parody and with an explicitly Jewish storyline. *Young Frankenstein,* one of Brooks's most celebrated films, simultaneously celebrates and critiques

Jewish and American ideas about identity formation, and especially focuses on the interrelated issues of ethnicity, authenticity, and destiny. Written by Mel Brooks and Gene Wilder and produced by Twentieth Century Fox, *Young Frankenstein* follows the story of Frederick Frankenstein (pronounced Fronkensteen and played by Gene Wilder), an American scientist and the great-grandson of the notoriously "cuckoo" Baron von Frankenstein of Transylvania, who is compelled to journey to Transylvania to discover what destiny holds for him. There, with the help of the humpbacked Igor (Marty Feldman), the voluptuous Inga (Teri Garr), and creepy Frau Blücher (Cloris Leachman), he discovers his great-grandfather's old notebooks, decides the experiment in fashioning life could work, and proceeds to create a man (Peter Boyle). As in the original *Frankenstein* movie (1931) directed by James Whale, things don't go quite according to plan: the creature gets the wrong brain and eventually escapes to terrorize the town. Frederick, unwilling to give up, captures the creature and tries to train him to be civilized (via the disciplines of musical comedy) but eventually can only rectify his errors by sharing some of his own life-essence with the creature, and vice versa. The movie retells this famous story with many winks and nods at the audience, continually referencing earlier Hollywood versions of the Frankenstein myth (the scene when the monster comes to life is played on the very same lab equipment used in the original 1931 movie), and providing levity with copious Jewish jokes. But the very act of parody involves criticism, and Brooks's target is the very same cult of authenticity that Trilling decries, albeit with far more explicitly Jewish content.

As the movie begins, we witness Dr. Frederick Frankenstein giving a lecture on voluntary and involuntary action to his medical school students. One particularly persistent student addresses him by name, only to be told that the doctor's name is pronounced "Fronkensteen." The student goes on to ask about Frederick's notorious ancestor, and Frederick dismisses his great-grandfather's work as Old Country superstition. Here we see the anxiously assimilated third-generation American, who has changed his name and disowned his past, only to have it come back and haunt him. It's worth noting here that both Mel Brooks (formerly Melvin Kaminsky) and Gene Wilder (born Jerome Silberman) also changed their names to appear more American. They were intimately familiar with the anxieties of inclusion Frederick exhibits in this scene, and the theatrical self-fashioning designed to overcome it. Immediately following his lecture about "the will," in which he hilariously demonstrates the difference between voluntary and involuntary action, Frederick is presented with his great-grandfather's will, and seems to be drawn—involuntarily—to the Old Country to investigate his inheritance. Frederick undertakes a roots journey to discover who he "really" is, one which mirrors a newly emerging interest in Old World Eastern Europe among third-generation American Jews, as evidenced by Irving Howe's best-selling love letter to immigrant Jewish life, *World of Our Fathers,* not to mention the success of *Fiddler on the Roof* on stage and screen. Frederick's real identity (which is explicitly "scientist," implicitly Jewish) is the very one he was trying to escape when he changed his name and disowned his ancestors. As he journeys to Transylvania (by train!), he passes first through New York, and then arrives almost instantly in Eastern Europe, all the while accompanied by an old couple whose language changes from English to some vaguely Slavic tongue as the journey progresses. Matthew Jacobson's book *Roots Too* describes the increasingly popular yearning for a connection with one's Old Country roots in 1970s America, a yearning that often resulted in a journey to the site of Americanization at Ellis Island or to obscure European villages.[21] Frederick too travels backwards through a metaphorical Ellis Island to an Old Country, which is oddly familiar. Not only is it the same Transylvania represented in the 1930s Frankenstein movies, but it is also peopled by Hollywood-style Old World anti-Semites (who are only thinly veiled as "anti-scientists"). In a clichéd "town meeting" scene, each member of the community speaks with a different European accent—from cockney to German—but all of them share a hatred of "scientists," epitomized by the Frankenstein family. As one villager remarks, in painfully familiar rhetoric: "He's a Frankenstein, and they're all the same. It's in their blood, they can't help it. All those scientists, they're all alike. They say they're working for us, but what they really want to do is rule the world!" Brooks takes aim here at the nostalgic notion that things were better in the Old Country and that if one only accepted one's ethnic heritage, all prejudice would dissolve.

Yet it is only in the Old Country that Frederick can fully realize his potential. During his first night in the family castle, he suffers nightmares in which he struggles with his famous ancestor. He tosses in bed, melodramatically mumbling, "No no no . . . I'm not a Frankenstein. I'm a Fronkensteen. Don't give me that. I don't believe in fate, and I won't say it. Alright, you win . . . I'll say it, I'll say it . . . Destiny, destiny, no escaping that for me. Destiny, destiny. . . . " Frederick must embrace his "destiny," which is to accept his identity as a Frankenstein and, by extension, to take on the task of fashioning a living, breathing self. The irony, of course, is that Frederick's essential identity involves the most extreme form of self-fashioning (or fashioning selves). He is helped along in this project by Igor, the great-grandson of the original Igor, who serves as the consummate unmasker, an Old World Jew who sees through Frederick's assimilationist performance. When Igor welcomes Frederick at the train station as "Dr. Frankenstein," Frederick corrects his pronunciation:

> IGOR: Frederick Frankenstein?
> FREDDY: Fron kon steen!
> IGOR: Are you putting me on?
> FREDDY: No, it's pronounced Fron konsteen.
> IGOR: And do you also say Fro dereck?
> FREDDY: No, Fred ereck.
> IGOR: Why isn't it Frodereck Fronkon steen?
> FREDDY: It's not. It's Fredereck Fronkonsteen.
> IGOR: I see.[22]

Igor takes in Frederick's name change, and then with a look that only Marty Feldman can perform, demands Frederick call him Aye-gor, thereby revealing the absurdity of this sort of pretension. Frederick's acceptance of his "real" name is the equivalent of Brooks and Wilder—and everyone else in Hollywood—reclaiming Kaminsky and Silberman. He goes on to further reclaim his heritage by acknowledging an obligation not only to his grandfather but also to his grandfather's creation, the creature. The film parodies both the naïve embrace of one's "authentic" identity that ignores the realities of racial prejudice, and the earlier assimilationist impulse that made this roots journey necessary in the first place.

Brooks also takes aim at the cult of psychic authenticity that Trilling describes in *Sincerity and Authenticity*, the essential part of ourselves that exists *before* culture. As Frederick notes in his opening lecture, our selves consist of both our voluntary will and reflexive, pre-cultural, biological reactions over which we have no control. But early in the film, Frederick seems to think that he is not subject to involuntary reactions. He believes that his "self" is completely constructed by an act of will and that he has perfect control over the performance of his own identity. He has created himself in opposition to his family heritage, in keeping with American norms and the rational dictates of science. Even when, at a particularly climactic moment in the lecture, he accidentally stabs a scalpel into his thigh, he doesn't flinch, demonstrating his perfect control over his reflexive impulses. But then his carefully fashioned "will" comes into conflict with another will, the will of his late great-grandfather. And Frederick is lured, against his own will, into another world.

In this world he creates a creature, which embodies Trilling's definition of authenticity—the "monster" is without culture, without civilization, driven only by primitive impulses of the Freudian id (hunger, sex, and violence). He is all reflex and lacks voluntary will. He is everything Frederick is not. But Brooks does not romanticize this kind of authenticity. Rather, he makes fun of it and, by extension, of those who do romanticize it. At the very moments in which the monster is being his most horribly authentic self (with an innocent little girl we assume he will push into a well or as he is about to rape Frederick's fiancée Elizabeth) Brooks has him demonstrate to us that not only is this a repetition of a scene from another movie, and therefore hardly an expression of primitive authenticity, but that the monster actually knows this and is self-consciously performing a role. When, after throwing a bunch of flowers into the well, the little girl innocently asks, "Oh, dear, nothing left. What shall we throw in now?" the creature glances at us through the camera lens and raises an eyebrow. This supposedly authentic being is, of course, theatrical, an actor playing a role, a product of civilization. Brooks, like Trilling, rejects the possibility of an authenticity that exists outside of culture, and through parody demonstrates the dangers inherent in romanticizing that kind of essentialism.

As a parodist, Brooks is also concerned with formal authenticity. Making a career of spoofing entertainment genres, Brooks both celebrates and critiques the notion of original artistic invention.[23] For

Brooks, as for so many other Jewish artists of the era, American Jewish cultural authenticity resides in the first half of the twentieth century, the era that saw the birth of theatrical liberalism and a host of other entertainment genres, which emerged to express its values. It is no accident that so many of the "Jewish" films of the period reach back to Jewish-created entertainment of an earlier era (*Funny Girl, Young Frankenstein,* and *Zelig* are only a few of many examples). In choosing to parody a film from 1931, the heyday of Jewish Hollywood, Brooks is reaching back to a time when Jews were enamored of the principles of theatrical liberalism. The film makes this debt to the period of theatrical liberalism evident in its careful reproduction of the period style, but even more so in the way that Frederick decides to demonstrate that he has "civilized" the monster. He and the creature perform a song-and-dance routine, "Puttin' on the Ritz," lifted from the eponymous movie musical of 1930 (starring Fred Astaire) and complete with top hat, white tie, and tails.

To be civilized, for Frederick, is to perform in the fashion of theatrical liberalism. But it turns out that, like Eliza Doolittle's first appearance at the horse races in *My Fair Lady,* the monster is incompletely trained in the skills of theatrical liberalism. Frightened by a bit of stage lighting, he stops dancing, screams menacingly, and goes careening down the aisle and out of the theater as the audience recoils in horror. The creature violently destroys the sanctity of the theater. Motivated by his internal fears rather than his external dance moves, he is unable to fulfill his obligation to his theatrical community and instead destroys the theatrical illusion completely. The civilizing mode of theatrical liberalism is not powerful enough to overcome the primitive forces unleashed by Frederick's act of creation. Something is missing. Later, the creature is lured back to the castle by Frederick playing the violin. The scene is yet another parody: With his floppy hat and beard, Gene Wilder resembles nothing so much as the fiddler from *Fiddler on the Roof,* luring his beast back home with a bit of Jewish music. But again, simply playing the music is not sufficient. The creature must be actively refashioned through a risky process, which involves Frederick giving up control over his own self-fashioned self.

There is something ridiculous about the repressed Frederick at the beginning of the film: his vehemence about his name change, his refusal

Frederick (Gene Wilder) presents The Creature (Peter Boyle) in a suave performance of "Puttin' on the Ritz" in *Young Frankenstein*.

to acknowledge his past, his desexualized relationship with his fiancée Elizabeth are all markers of insecurity. His need to police the boundaries of this constructed identity is a problem that Frederick ultimately solves by tapping into the authenticity of the creature. Toward the end of the film, through a complex operation involving multiple operating tables, helmets, and bubbling fluids, Frederick finds a way to "equalize" both his and the monster's imbalance between voluntary will and reflexive primitivism, thereby turning both of them into healthy, civilized individuals. Saved by a bit of the monster's primitivism (and Inga's sensual response to it), Frederick is no longer a neurotic Jew. Redeemed by a dose of Frederick's verbal gifts and ethical sophistication, as well as Elizabeth's concern with manners, the creature is no longer a psychotic savage. In this gothic laboratory in Transylvania, Brooks has fashioned the perfect formula for a healthy mid-twentieth-century Jewish man. Take an ounce of imposing physical bulk (stolen from post-1967 Israeli machismo as much as from the creature), add to it a pound of Nobel Prize–winning scientific genius, stir it for decades on Broadway and in Hollywood, add a dash of *shikse* sexuality, and you have the perfect recipe for fashioning a non-neurotic Jew! There is nothing "authentic" about this—recipes are by nature constructions.

Frederick's self-fashioning and his fashioning of another self in *Young Frankenstein* begin as theatrical and external acts, much like the kind of self-fashioning exhibited in works of theatrical liberalism from the earlier twentieth century, but his project turns out to be only partially successful. The movie's conclusion combines high theatricality with a dangerous operation conducted upon real bodies in which real fluids are exchanged (at least as real as one can get in a Mel Brooks movie). The experiment is risky and its outcome unassured. Indeed, due to an unforeseen interruption, the process is ultimately incomplete. In Cynthia Ozick's provocative essay, "Toward a New Yiddish," she accused the counterculture of idolatry, claiming that in fashioning images, selves, and literature under the naïve assumption that one might stand outside of history, or reinvent it, these artists usurped the role of God as the ultimate creator. Brooks is also concerned with the arrogance potentially inherent in self-creation, and he addresses that concern in the very way Ozick recommends. Far from romanticizing the authenticity of the creature or valorizing Frederick as a self-made man, Brooks insists that we are always indebted to the past; even the creature has a past. Through parody—the comic acknowledgment of the power of history—Brooks gives Frederick and the creature the chance to live something approximating a moral life.

6

I Am a Theater

CECILIA: Tom's perfect.
GIL: Yeah, but he's not real. What good is perfect if the man's
    not real?
TOM: I can learn to be real. There's nothing to it. Being real
    comes very naturally to me.
GIL: You can't learn to be real. It's like learning to be a
    midget.
    —*Purple Rose of Cairo,* by Woody Allen (1985)

Woody Allen's 1985 film *Purple Rose of Cairo,* explicitly dramatizes
the connection hinted at in *Young Frankenstein* between self-creation
and theatricality. The film once again thrusts us back into the temporal homeland of theatrical liberalism, into a Depression-era movie
house where an RKO Astaire-Rogers style film is playing. Cecilia, who
has seen the movie countless times, watches raptly from the audience.
Suddenly, one of the characters on the screen turns directly to her and
begins to speak. He "escapes" the film, claiming he is in love with her.
The minor Hollywood actor Gil Shepherd is shocked and angry to learn
that the character he created, Tom Baxter, has walked off the screen.
He has been working hard, in true theatrical liberal fashion, to create
a persona and yet it seems that he, like Frederick Frankenstein, cannot
control his own creations. Gil (the actor) chastises Tom (the character):

GIL: I took you from the printed page and made you live.
TOM: So I'm living.
GIL: Yes, but for the screen only. Please . . .
TOM: I want my freedom.
GIL: I don't want another me running around.
TOM: Why? Are you afraid I'll embarrass you?

GIL: Yes, frankly . . .

TOM: But you created me.

GIL: All right, look. Be reasonable here. I'm starting to build a career. Is life up on the screen so terrible?[1]

Like the creature in *Young Frankenstein,* the character Tom wants to be real. While the ethical concerns of Gil and Frederick Frankenstein around their relationship to a character they have fashioned bear some similarity to one another, the central conflict differs dramatically. In *Young Frankenstein,* there is no question that Frederick's creation is real. Indeed, this is the central problem of the Frankenstein story. He has a real body, dug up from a grave, and a real, if abnormal, brain. He is capable of causing real damage, having real sex, and ultimately becoming a real, civilized husband. *Young Frankenstein* and *My Fair Lady* raise questions about the authenticity of particular incarnations of self—especially those which are explicitly theatrical, involving costume, accent, and gesture—but somewhere within these selves is a real, living, breathing authentic person. Tom, on the other hand, is explicitly *not* real. He gets in a fight but never messes up his hair. He does not understand sex, and carries around play money. He does not understand the rules of reality. He is not, as Gil says, human. Gil's argument is complicated, of course, by the fact that Gil is also not "real" and neither is Cecilia. All of them are characters on a screen.

In the 1980s and '90s, post-modern ideas about self-fashioning and an intense concern with questions of identity spilled out from the esoteric writing of scholars onto the screens, stages, and pages of popular entertainment. These works used popular forms to investigate the boundaries of the self, teetering between righteous assertions of the morality of authenticity and equally knowing insistence on the absolute constructedness of the self. Following Goffman and Trilling, Jewish intellectuals continued to be leaders in this discussion. Debates among scholars of cultural studies, Jewish studies, race, ethnicity, and sexuality surrounding representations of the Holocaust, the racial category of Jews, the place of Jews—and Jewish victimhood—in American identity politics, and the relationship between anti-Semitism and sexuality roiled campuses and spilled over into American politics, journalism, and popular culture.[2] Sexuality became, more than ever before, a core interest of scholars of performance and identity; the study of sexuality centers, after all, on the relationship between internal psychological desire and embodied action. Self-identified lesbian Jewish theorists such as Judith Butler, Eve Kosofsky Sedgwick, and Marjorie Garber developed new narratives about the construction of identity via performance by focusing their attention on the representation of sexuality in literary, popular, and political culture, often using Jewish self-representation as an emblematic case study.[3] While directly critiquing liberalism, these critics nonetheless played an important role in articulating a new version of theatrical liberalism for the late-twentieth century, one which touted the freedom performance made possible, but it was simultaneously characterized by a deep ambivalence about the role of action (refigured as "agency" in critical theory) in fashioning selves.

Curiously, the interest in gender and sexuality in those two decades among cultural critics (many of them women) led to very few new representations of Jewish women in popular culture; instead the mostly male writers of works of theatrical liberalism expanded their focus on Jewish men's sexuality to include both gay and straight characters. "Jews" in popular culture continued to be largely male, and the freedom to self-fashion continued to be problematic for female characters. Barbra Streisand's performance as the cross-dressing Anshel in *Yentl* is the exception that proves the rule. Streisand's portrayal of Yentl in many ways resembles her Fanny Brice: her performance is simply a way of being *more herself*. While her cross-dressing does allow her to study in a yeshiva, briefly, it also gets her into serious ethical dilemmas. As soon as she finds an opportunity to be herself *without* the costume (in America), she quickly dispenses with it. Far from being celebrated, Yentl's refashioning of herself as Anshel is a problem to be solved.[4]

While many Jewish writers and performers continued to produce popular works of theatrical liberalism, which focused on everyday behavior, self-fashioning, and obligation—television shows like *Seinfeld* and *Friends* are among the most obvious examples—the more popular works geared to more intellectual audiences raised questions about the power of theatricality and external action to secure individual freedom or to create ethical community. With the work of Judith Butler in particular, the performance of self explored by Goffman, and the role-playing described by Trilling were transformed into the more amorphous acts of self-creation that she defined as performativity. Although Butler has never explicitly described her work as such, we can see her books from the 1990s as continuing a conversation among American Jewish intellectuals about the importance of performance and theatricality to an understanding of identity in the modern world (particularly, but not limited to, Jewish identity). In two influential books, *Gender Trouble* (1990) and *Bodies That Matter* (1993), Butler outlined a philosophy of gender, and later all subjectivity, which builds on earlier work on the performance of identity while insisting it bears no relationship to the theater at all. Butler was deeply influenced by post-structuralist European thinkers Michel Foucault and Jacques Derrida, as well as a number of feminist and psychoanalytic critics. But what is striking about Butler's ideas—radical as they are—is how relevant they are to this deeply American narrative about theatrical liberalism. Butler is nearly silent about her own Jewishness in her early work, as well as her Americanness, but her focus on *action* places her work squarely within our story. And as she makes explicit later in her career, her Jewish upbringing, her family history, and her current practice of Judaism are all inextricable from her philosophical work.[5]

In *Gender Trouble* Butler argued that society constructs all aspects of identity. We have no essential self and no natural gender that resides outside of the society in which we live. There is, for Butler, no such thing as authenticity. In an attempt to clarify this point, Butler wrote in the preface to the tenth-anniversary edition of the book: "[W]hat we take to be an internal essence of gender is manufactured through a sustained set of acts, posited through the gendered stylization of the body" (Butler, *Gender Trouble*, xv). This sustained set of acts is what Butler calls performativity, a highly ritualized mode of identity formation conditioned by societal expectations and power relations. "Performativity," she writes, "is not a singular act, but a repetition and a ritual, which achieves its effects through its naturalization in the context of a body, understood, in part, as a culturally sustained temporal duration" (ibid., xv). A self is a series of acts, repeated over time, which become understood as natural, as "a real self." These acts are repeated so often, with so little self-consciousness, that they become transparent, they become our description of self and reality. When a baby is born, Butler argues, the process of "gendering" begins. With the announcement "it's a girl!" or "it's a boy!" the baby is immediately placed within a cultural web of meaning, which will then be repeatedly reinforced throughout his or her life, in the way this person is treated, in the range of choices of dress, gesture, voice, and self-presentation available to him or her, in the options this person has available in terms of relationships, career, and every other aspect of life.

Perhaps most relevant for our purposes here is that Butler sees "gender" as a verb; *action* constructs identity. She is impatient with feminist and ethnic multicultural politics of the 1980s, which insist that a subject must first embrace his or her authentic racial, ethnic, sexual, or other identities before acting politically in relation to them (the very kind of authenticity that Schechner encouraged and that Trilling and Ozick recoiled from). No self exists for Butler outside of the performance of that self: "The foundationalist reasoning of identity politics tends to assume that an identity must first be in place in order for political interests to be elaborated and, subsequently, political action to be taken. My argument is that there need not be a 'doer behind the deed,' but that the 'doer' is variably constructed in and through the deed" (*Gender Trouble*, 181). For Butler, performance comes first; identity second. In other words, unlike Goffman, who argues that we are actors performing roles, Butler insists that there is no pre-existing performer who does deeds. The doing of the deeds *constructs* the performer, rather than the other way around. This is why Butler uses the term "performativity" rather than performance. She is wary of theatrical metaphors, which assume a stable actor who plays a series of roles. Butler certainly believes there is a subject, but this subject does not exist separate from or before the roles it enacts. In many ways, Butler pushes the focus on action in theatrical liberalism to its logical conclusion. Instead of focusing on the tension between external actions and internal feelings, she sidesteps this opposition, rejecting the internal altogether and insisting that without external action, no subject exists at all. When we look at the works of Woody Allen, Tony Kushner, and Philip Roth, however, performativity by no means excludes the more prosaic understanding of performance; indeed, it continues to depend upon it.

Butler's ideas have a less congenial relationship to theatrical liberalism's understanding of individual freedom. In *My Fair Lady, Blazing Saddles, Young Frankenstein,* and *The Purple Rose of Cairo,* central characters struggle with whether they are free to determine their own identities, to resist the pull of their creators, to break out of the prescribed narrative that determines their roles in the films. Performance, as we have understood it throughout this book, is fundamentally an expression of freedom: the ability to transform oneself *is* freedom for so many of the characters we have met on our journey. Remember Bugs Bunny's quick changes, Pseudolus's song "Free" in *A Funny Thing Happened on the Way to the Forum*, Anna's song "I Whistle A Happy Tune" in *The King and I*, or Willy Loman's hallucinations in *Death of A Salesman*; all of these characters cherished their transformative abilities and saw them, for better or worse, as a guarantee of their freedom as an individual liberal subject. Judith Butler is decidedly opposed to this notion of a subject that exercises free will in this way. As she writes in the preface to *Bodies That Matter*:

> [I]f I were to argue that genders are performative, that could mean that I thought that one woke in the morning, perused the closet or some more open space for the gender of choice, donned that gender for the day, and then restored the garment to its place at night. Such a willful and instrumental subject, one who decides *on* its gender, is clearly not its gender from the start and fails to realize that its existence is already decided *by* gender. (*Bodies That Matter*, x)

For Butler, "relations of power" and "normativity constraints" determine gender. We don't have the individual agency to do this for ourselves. In fact, we could say that Butler sees all of us as characters in a play, our actions determined by a limited set of possible scripts and a clearly defined set of approved costumes. Subversion happens for Butler when we draw attention to these limited choices and hence become aware of the fact of limitation. She is particularly interested in drag, for example, which, through a highly stylized and theatrical performance, makes us aware of the constructed quality not only of the character of the drag performer but of all gender identities. Butler also turns to the malleability and instability of language as a tool of political subversion. We saw earlier how Lorenz Hart turned words into actors playing multiple roles. In his acrobatic and playful lyrics, he both celebrated and warned against the instability at the "heart" of the theatrical venture.

Butler likewise sees the transformative quality of language as the key to political action, if not freedom, within a system of power that is otherwise hopelessly constricting. Turning to the work of the deconstructionist Jacques Derrida on the multiple and complex ways in which words (which he calls signs) can be "resignified" or made to mean differently in different contexts, Butler, in her book *Excitable Speech,* treats words in much the same way as she treats identity. Exploiting the instability of words and meaning, Butler sees an opening for political action, which she calls "the political promise of the performative."[6] She encourages, for example, the reappropriation of formerly destructive terms such as "queer" by the very groups who have been hurt by these derogatory terms. While acknowledging that these terms will always carry traces of their painful histories, she feels that the risk is counterbalanced by the opportunity this "resignification" offers to undermine the dominant power structure that otherwise claims ownership of the term. Lorenz Hart celebrated the freedom inherent in the theatricality of both performance and language but also worried about the instability this theatricality implied. Butler, on the other hand, sees the instability as the very source of freedom and resists any attempt to shut down the free play of meaning via censorship, politically correct or otherwise.[7]

* * *

While Judith Butler was developing her ideas on the construction of identity and the freedom of the subject, Jewish-created popular entertainment was similarly exploring the relationship between stable identity and unstable theatrical characters, and wondering about the power of these characters to define reality on their own terms. Appearing seven years before *Gender Trouble,* Woody Allen's "mockumentary" *Zelig* explores the multiple theatrical ways in which a real life might be constructed. Returning to the 1920s—the film begins in 1928, that pre-Depression moment to which so many of the works we have looked at obsessively return—*Zelig* uses all of the familiar tropes of a biographical documentary to construct a story of a man who was known as a "chameleon." Leonard Zelig (Woody Allen), a nondescript Jewish man from Brooklyn, became an early twentieth-century sensation because he would transform himself, apparently against his will, into a member

of whatever group he was with at the moment. Zelig's transforma-
tions are remarkably convincing; they transcend racial, ethnic, physical, and psychological boundaries with apparent ease. With fat men, he
becomes fat. With a black jazz band, he becomes black, and a passable
trumpet player as well. With rabbis, he grows a beard and discusses Talmud. *Zelig* constructs Leonard's story as a curious tale of sickness and
cure with a happy ending. The film self-consciously and often hilariously adopts documentary film conventions of the late 1970s such as
an authoritative narrator (with a vaguely upper-class accent), the use
of stock footage to evoke an era, and the careful perusal of still photo-
graphs for clues to the secret of Zelig's malady. In order to understand
Zelig's significance to the popular culture, Woody Allen assembles a
cast of real Jewish intellectuals: Susan Sontag, Irving Howe, Saul Bellow, and others all play themselves with utter seriousness, commenting
sagely on Zelig's peculiar psychological condition and its relationship to
his Jewishness, anti-Semitism, jazz-age culture, and the rise of fascism.
The combined effect of all of these familiar tropes of the documentary
film is to develop a believable story and to raise our consciousness
about how such life stories are constructed. By parodying the documentary form, Woody Allen forces the viewer to consider the ways in
which *all* life stories, indeed *all lives*, are constructed by narrative and
shaped by the storytelling conventions of the era. In *Zelig*, Woody Allen
argues, like Judith Butler, that all identity is constructed, although as a
filmmaker, Allen is more interested in the power of particular narrative
forms and particular ways of viewing than in the role of language in
this process.

Like Willy Loman, Leonard Zelig is introduced early in the film as
a patient with a mental illness resulting from an unnatural belief in the
values we have been discussing as the hallmarks of theatrical liberalism.
His compulsion to transform himself is presented as a problem with
potentially disastrous moral consequences. He is constantly misrepre-
senting himself. One minute he is an upper-class Republican, the next
a working-class Democrat. One minute he is a white gangster, the next
a black musician. Raised during the heyday of theatrical liberalism, the
son of a Yiddish actor, Zelig appears to have taken the ethos of theatrical liberalism one or two steps too far. He has become a walking
illustration of the power of theatrical liberalism pushed to its logical

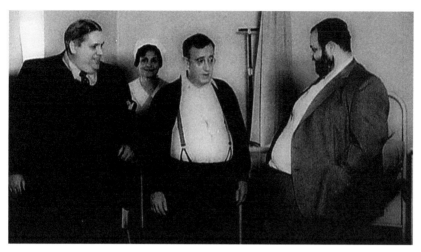

With fat men, Zelig (Woody Allen) becomes fat.

conclusion. He has no apparent identity aside from the multiple identities he adopts. He is all external action—he has no interior self. From the perspective of the film, and especially of its stentorian narrator, this is a sickness in need of a cure. Caught infiltrating the Yankees' training camp, and later an opium den in Chinatown, Zelig is apprehended and brought to a mental hospital for observation. The doctors debate the reasons for his condition, suggesting that it is "glandular," the result of a tumor, a response to Mexican food, or, according to the lovely doctor who ends up treating him, due to his "unstable makeup."

Dr. Eudora Fletcher (Mia Farrow) takes his case, and works hard to unearth the cause of Zelig's strange malady. Under hypnosis, he reveals that as a child he was beaten by his parents (and the neighbors and everyone else) and that he was bullied by anti-Semites (his parents sided with the anti-Semites). The reason he transforms himself is because, as he intones, "It is safe to be like the others. I want to be liked." Like Willy Loman, Leonard Zelig has determined that the guarantee of success in American society is to be well liked. Just as Dr. Fletcher is on the verge of figuring out how to heal Zelig, however, his half-sister and her shady lover appear and, asserting their legal rights, whisk him out of the hospital and market his talents as a sideshow attraction, "the human chameleon." Zelig is thrust into the very Jewish world of show business to which he is best adapted and becomes an overnight sensation. Songs and dances are named after him, and merchandisers have a field day making "chameleon" aprons, clocks, and board games. Zelig performs with Eddie Cantor on the vaudeville stage, meets Fanny Brice, and is offered a film contract by Hollywood producers. His transformative talent seems to have found its proper outlet. However, all of this show business "success" is represented in the film as inhuman and abusive. According to the narrator, Zelig has no will of his own; his sister and her lover orchestrate everything and make all the money. Over a shot of Zelig, calmly sitting alone in a room and eating, the narrator intones:

> Zelig's own existence is a non-existence. Devoid of personality, his human qualities long since lost in the shuffle of life, he sits alone, quietly staring into space. A cipher. A non-person. A performing freak. He who wanted only to fit in, to belong, to go unseen by his enemies and be loved neither fits in nor belongs.[8]

The scene offers a multilayered commentary on documentary film and biography, celebrity, and the ways in which narratives and selves are constructed. The footage of Zelig is remarkably benign. He sits quietly, and apparently happily, munching something that looks like a cookie. He shows no sign of mistreatment, restraint, or discomfort. It is the narration that ascribes meaning to the scene. This narrator, who has no evidence for the claims he makes, shapes our understanding of this phase of Zelig's life. Zelig's half-sister was of dubious moral character and died under suspicious circumstances; Zelig, on the other hand, is the hero of the story. The narration works hard to make Zelig a pure victim, caught in a web of evil and forced to perform against his will. The narration assumes that a life on the stage must be a non-life. But the carefully doctored film clips of Leonard with Fanny Brice, Clara Bow, Jack Dempsey, and Josephine Baker belie this simple moral fable, showing Leonard apparently perfectly happy in his celebrity. The film also forces us to ask why Leonard's theatrical career is inhuman, but all the celebrities he encounters, those about whom countless similar bio-pics were made, represent the pinnacle of success, the American dream. The narrative arc of the film, which has an overt anti-theatrical slant, needs Leonard to be a victim, so that he can be "cured" and the story neatly resolved. Leonard's own relationship to his theatricality remains murky throughout this section.

After the sudden and dramatic deaths of his half-sister and her lover, Zelig disappears, only to be rediscovered on a dais with the pope, having transformed himself into a very convincing bishop. Unmasked as an imposter, Zelig is returned to New York Hospital where he is once again under the care of Dr. Fletcher. She decides to bring Leonard to her home in the country for intensive therapy. Knowing full well that the work she is doing is important, she arranges to film the treatment, a record that comes to be known as the "White Room Sessions." With this device, Allen both creates the explanation for the existence of the footage necessary to tell a compelling story and calls attention to another sort of performance. Zelig never ceases to be a performer, even within the apparent privacy of the therapy room. We have to assume that Dr. Fletcher, who was "interviewed" for the film and therefore is presumably still alive, has agreed to make the record of Zelig's treatment available to the "director" of this documentary. Zelig, as we later come to learn, is her late husband, and the release of this intimate material indicates Dr. Fletcher is not immune to the fascination with celebrity and performance, and the voyeuristic pleasures of watching other people play themselves.

Eudora Fletcher's careful attention to Leonard Zelig appears to work. By giving him unconditional love, while encouraging him to reveal aspects of his past under hypnosis, she slowly cures him of the need to transform himself. They fall in love, and he becomes "himself." As the narrator intones, he is "at last his own man. His point of view is his own. He's an individual. A human being." Leonard and Eudora enjoy instant celebrity once again—and are feted by scientists, literati, and Hollywood celebrities. But what exactly does it mean that Leonard has a "point of view" and has become "his own man"? It means, apparently, that he has learned to speak in the bland platitudes expected of American politicians. When asked if he has anything to say to the children of America, Leonard replies:

> Be yourself. You can't act like anybody else just because you think they have all the answers and you don't. You have to be your own man and learn to speak up and say what's on your mind. Now maybe they're not free to do that in foreign countries but that's the American way. (ibid.)

Who is Leonard now? He no longer transforms himself into others, apparently because he no longer needs to. He has achieved the most successful transformation of all, one that requires no further performances. Under the influence of the upper-class Protestant Eudora, Leonard has changed into a "typical" American man, and both he and Eudora are celebrated by all for his remarkable "cure." Leonard has adopted the guise of a member of Eudora's class and background, but this performance is so "natural" as to be invisible. As long as Leonard remains a stable and assimilated character who looks and acts like a "typical American," no matter how bland and uninteresting, he is considered "cured."

But when he and Eudora announce marriage plans, his activities as a chameleon come back to haunt him. It turns out Leonard is already married . . . multiple times. Lawsuits, negative publicity, accusations of immorality follow these revelations, and Leonard slips back into his transforming, performing ways. Leonard once again disappears, only to turn up finally in Nazi Germany—as a Nazi. So far backwards has he slid, or so talented at impersonation is he, that he has managed to convince those who would most desire to destroy him. Through an improbable meeting at a Nazi rally, Eudora and Leonard reconnect, and Leonard manages a remarkable escape. They steal a plane and although Eudora, a skilled flyer, passes out, Leonard transforms himself into a pilot like Eudora and flies the two of them home nonstop across the Atlantic Ocean (upside down) in a none-too-subtle tribute to the similar escape of the Polish theater troupe in Lubitsch's 1942 *To Be or Not to Be*.[9] Much celebration ensues once again, they are finally married, and apparently live happily ever after. What remains unclear at the end of the film, however, is who exactly Leonard *is* in this happy ending. As Saul Bellow comments in his final clip: "What enabled him to perform this astounding feat [flying the airplane] was his ability to transform himself. His sickness was also at the root of his salvation. It was his disorder that made a hero of him." So what remains of Leonard Zelig when he is "cured" of the disorder (which is also his salvation) and apparently the only reason he is interesting at all? Does he exist outside of his compulsion to transform himself, to do imitations? In many ways, he is an ideal example of Butler's argument. There is no *essential* Zelig, no doer behind the deed. Zelig becomes Zelig through the act of performing. And he also becomes the cured, assimilated, and happy Leonard through an act of performance, albeit one which is less obvious and less abnormal. By repeatedly learning to go through the motions of stability, Leonard eventually achieves it, or at least the appearance of it, for himself.

The opinion of the narrator and of the fake documentary *Zelig* is clear. Leonard is cured, and the world is saved from the dangerous and destabilizing impact of an obsessive performer. The question that lingers at the end of the film, however, is how exactly Woody Allen wants *us* to judge Zelig. It is no secret that Allen is thoroughly enamored of the era and attitudes of theatrical liberalism. Countless films—not only *Zelig* but also *Broadway Danny Rose, Radio Days, The Purple Rose of Cairo,* and many others—extol the theatrical values of the earlier years of the twentieth century, the marvellous freedom of transformation, the centrality of action and acting to a moral life, the obligations members of a theatrical community agree to adopt. At the same time, Allen is one of the most famous patients of psychoanalysis in America. Are these two value systems irreconcilable? Can one embrace both the transformative power of external performance *and* believe in the shaping force of the internal psyche?[10] At the end of the film, Leonard and Eudora receive the keys to New York City and are told by the mayor: "You are a great inspiration to the young of this nation who will one day grow up to be great doctors and great patients." What does it mean to be a "great patient"? For Zelig, it meant to raise assimilative performance to such an exquisite art that his performance became naturalized and invisible, that the evidence of being cured of the neurosis of performance is, in fact, pulling off the best performance ever.

* * *

Philip Roth's post-modern novel *The Counterlife* (1986) offers another approach to late-twentieth-century liberal Jewish identity in America. Like Judith Butler and Woody Allen, Roth engages directly with the complications of a theatrical performance of self in a post-modern context. Narrated by Roth's longtime alter ego, the author Nathan Zuckerman, the novel investigates a pressing intellectual issue of the 1980s, multiculturalism and identity politics—particularly the unexamined embrace of authenticity that Trilling critiqued—by having Nathan and his brother Henry encounter, inhabit, and reject multiple versions of

Jewish identity. Each of the five chapters bears the name of a spatial location or metaphor, which evokes a corresponding dream of Jewish authenticity. Chapter 1, "Basel," represents the Jewish dream of assimilation to a European ideal; chapter 2, "Judea," represents the opposite dream of Jewish ethnic and national purity. "Aloft," which takes place on an airplane, quite literally dramatizes the problems of the *luftmensch* ("air man"), living in a world of ideas rather than action; while "Gloucestershire" and "Christendom" offer two more symbolic locations in which the novel's Jewish characters confront Christianity and Jewish difference. But each chapter is also undercut by the others; facts, names, and characters change from chapter to chapter, never allowing the reader to relax into a single narrative or identity for any of the characters. While the story twists and turns, characters die and then reappear, medical troubles and lovers (all named Maria) migrate from Henry to Nathan and back again, and characters threaten to destroy the novel or leave it altogether, one central theme remains intact. The novel tracks, relentlessly and brilliantly, Roth's deep interest in self-creation and particularly the challenges of *Jewish* self-creation in liberal America. This problem is most directly addressed by a series of recurring tensions in the novel between *thought* and *action,* flesh and spirit, the heart and the penis, Jew and Christian.

Engaging with the literary theory of deconstruction so popular in the mid-1980s, Roth proposes these binary oppositions and then proceeds to break them down, showing how these apparently disparate ideas or objects supplement and define one another. The novel opens, for example, by setting up a clear opposition between the heart and the penis. Like Lorenz Hart, Philip Roth is also concerned with "the heart of the matter," and in this case, that heart is a literal one, pumping blood deep within the body but is also associated metaphorically with marital fidelity and familial obligation (but not romantic love). The penis, on the other hand, is externally visible and associated with sexuality, power, creativity, and freedom. In *The Counterlife,* the relationship between the two is both dependent and antagonistic. The book begins with Nathan's eulogy for his brother Henry, who has died of heart bypass surgery, undertaken because he became so frustrated with the impotence caused by his heart disease drugs. The impotence prevents him from carrying on an affair with Wendy, his dental assistant, and therefore makes it impossible for him to imagine himself anew. Without the sexual escape from his everyday life that Wendy provides, and that his earlier affair with a Swiss woman named Maria also provided, Henry is stuck in a single definition of himself as a faithful husband and father and responsible dentist. He is also stuck in another binary opposition between Jew and Gentile. His affair with Maria (who is from Basel, hence the title of this section), opened up to him the possibility of being different, of escaping the ethnic identity prescribed for him by his family and community. But his heart has betrayed him. Without his potency, it seems, he cannot fulfill these dreams of escape. The affair with Maria ended long ago, not due to Henry's physical impotence but rather due to an internal lack of will to burst free of his ethnic obligations, to create himself anew. Henry recalls that he spoke with Maria after she returned to Basel, and she asked him if Christmas was helping to ease the pain of separation. Henry replies, to his later mortification, that he doesn't observe Christmas. Upon learning of this, Nathan is awestruck at his brother's inability to break free of binary ways of thinking:

> How absurd, how awful, if the woman who'd awakened in him the desire to live differently, who meant to him a break with the past, a revolution against an old way of life that had reached an emotional standstill—against the belief that life is a series of duties to be perfectly performed—if that woman was to be nothing more or less than the humiliating memory of his first (and last) great fling *because she observed Christmas and we do not.*[11]

Henry firmly believes that the stress of letting Maria go, of failing to re-create himself, is what led to his heart trouble in the first place. In other words, his failure to break down one opposition led to his imprisonment by another. As Nathan observes, "If Henry had been right about the origins of his disease, if it did indeed result from the stress of that onerous defeat and those arduous feelings of self-contempt that dogged him long after her return to Basel, then, curiously enough, it was being a Jew that had killed him" (ibid., 41).

In the second half of the novel, the position of the brothers is reversed. Nathan has the heart problem, which likewise renders him impotent. Nathan is also having an affair, albeit platonic, with a married English woman, also named Maria, and desperately wants to marry her and become a father. He, too, wants to create himself anew with a Gentile woman and to father a child. His weak heart serves to insure Maria's fidelity to her husband, so he takes the same risk Henry took and opts for bypass surgery. When he, like Henry, dies on the operating table, he loses not only his ability to father a child but also his control over his novel. Both Henry and Maria wander through the novel after Nathan's death, plundering his manuscripts and (briefly) taking control of the narrative. In both cases, the heart and the penis are connected yet cannot seem to work together: the brothers can have one or the other, but not both. The freedom of self-invention promised by the penis is prevented by the malfunctioning of the heart. Sex is directly linked in the novel to creativity. As Nathan recalls, "his sessions with Wendy had been Henry's art; his dental office, after hours, his atelier; and his impotence . . . like an artist's artistic life drying up for good" (ibid., 35). And creativity in this novel is the guarantor of freedom, the most important freedom being the theatrical ability to play roles, to imagine oneself, and others, as *different* (hence the counterlives of the title). The heart insures fidelity while the penis insures freedom. Both need to function, however, to insure life.

In its quest to understand the nature of modern subjectivity, *The Counterlife* sets up yet another opposition, between the body (flesh, blood, guts) and the mind (the inventive imagination, the space of thought and writing). At the heart of this book is a question about the nature of the self that has inspired philosophers for centuries: Is it located in the mind or the body? Roth acknowledges the power of the Cartesian assumption that the mind brings the self into being and the much more modern assumption that all selves are constructed through language (as per Butler), but he also raises incisive questions about these assumptions. The ability to write counterlives for oneself, to break out of one story of the self and create another, is central to Nathan's sense of what it means to have agency in the world, and he seems determined, at the beginning of the novel, to protect that belief. But the failure of Henry to rewrite himself, figured as a bodily failure caused by heart disease and impotence, leads Nathan to question his own assumptions about the power of the head over the body. Toward the end of the first chapter, Nathan is accosted at his brother's funeral by Barry Shuskin, who has decided to have his body frozen, waiting for the moment when science will be able to thaw him out and offer him immortality. Humorously introducing the issue that will obsess Nathan for much of the book, Shuskin describes the different approaches of cryonics facilities on the East and West Coasts:

> What they're doing on the West Coast, because of their feeling that the body is not what's important, that your identity is all up here, so they separate the head from the body. . . . It's cheaper than freezing and storing the whole body . . . I don't go for it myself. I want my whole body frozen. Why? Because I personally believe your experience is very much connected to your memories that every cell in your body has. You don't separate the mind from the body. The body and the mind are one. (ibid., 46)

Throughout the novel, characters like Shuskin appear who shake Nathan's faith in the agency afforded by the mind, by thinking and writing. These characters represent the blood, guts, bodies, viscera of humanity. When Henry encounters Nathan's manuscript about Henry's (fictional) death, he is appalled at the way Nathan imagines him and his sexual fantasies:

> [W]hen I am doing an implant, and the whole mouth is torn open, and the tissue detached from the bone, and the teeth, the roots, all exposed, and the assistant's hands are in there with mine, when I've got four, even six, hands working on the patient, the *last* thing I'm thinking about is sex. You stop concentrating, you let that enter, and you fuck up—and I'm not a dentist who fucks up. I am a success, Nathan. I don't live all day vicariously in my head—I live with saliva, blood, bone, teeth, my hands in mouths as raw and real as the meat in the butcher's window! (ibid., 235–236)

The novel is saturated with Nathan's anxiety that the blood and guts Henry works with are more "real" than the writing Nathan does. Nathan comes face to face with characters who, unlike himself, are engaged in the process of living lives defined explicitly by their literal or metaphorical engagement with real flesh. At Henry's funeral, Nathan runs into an old cousin, Shimmy Kirsch, a man who never fails to remind Nathan of the lightness of his own being:

> [T]hese drearily banal and conventional Shimmys displayed all the ruthlessness of the renegade, their teeth ripping a chunk out of life's raw rump, then dragging that around with them everywhere, all else paling in significance beside the bleeding flesh between their jaws. . . . Their lack of all nuance or doubt, of an ordinary mortal's sense of futility or despair, made it tempting sometimes to consider them inhuman, and yet they were men about whom it was impossible to say that they were anything *other* than human: they were what human really is. (ibid., 38)

If these men of the flesh are human, what does that make men like Nathan, who live a life of the mind? While Nathan clearly enjoys the power he wields as a writer, he worries that his focus on creating selves through language might be mere solipsism. He is anxious that as a writer, he has become alienated from a real world in which he could take real action and have real impact.

Here the mind/body opposition gives way to an opposition between two types of Jewish men: the scholar/intellectual, who lives a life of the mind spent indoors, reading, studying, and writing, and the man of action, who spends his time in the world, engaged in business or politics. This opposition can be traced once again all the way back to the pair of brothers Jacob and Esau. Nathan, the writer and intellectual, "lives in tents" like Jacob and, also like Jacob, is crafty and theatrical. He plays numerous parts and creates parts for others to play. Henry, while not exactly a hunter in the fields like Esau, is a dentist who deals in blood and guts. Shimmy, likewise, has

> No questions, no excuses, none of this who-am-I, what-am-I, where-am-I crap, not a grain of self-mistrust or the slightest impulse toward spiritual distinction; rather, like so many of his generation out of Newark's old Jewish slums, a man . . . completely in accord with the ways and means of the earth. (ibid., 37)

Early in the novel, then, Nathan seems to divide the world of Jewish men between those who think and those who act. He continually tests himself against those who appear to personify one or the other extreme, searching for a way to reconcile them. When he comes face to face with pale yeshiva boys in Israel, or with his own cousin who is a Holocaust survivor, for example, he clearly worries that he is just another version of the weak victimized bookish Jew, so focused on Torah study or the secular equivalent as to be incapable of engaging with the physical world around him. When an Israeli secret service agent saves Nathan and other passengers from a hijacking aboard an El Al plane, Nathan is appropriately admiring, but also mistrustful. The agent introduces himself as "a very simple guy," one who, as he says, "[doesn't] even bother . . . to point the accusing finger to justify what I do. *I just do it*. I say, 'That's what I want, I'm entitled,' and I *act*" (ibid., 177, emphasis in original). Repulsed as he is by this demonstration of unexamined conviction, Nathan is at the same time grateful that in the case of the attempted hijacking, the agent did not stop to think but just acted on impulse.

As the novel develops, however, this easy opposition begins to break down. Jacob, after all, is *both* a thinker and a theatrical actor, and so are many of the characters in this novel: the yeshiva student Jimmy ben-Joseph transforms himself into a dangerous terrorist before Nathan's eyes. The yeshiva outfit turns out to be the ideal costume for smuggling weapons aboard a plane: "a yeshiva *bucher* they don't check out the same way," Jimmy explains (ibid., 164). Nathan has a particularly difficult time with Mordecai Lippman, a self-proclaimed man of action who ironically speaks at length about the uselessness of words. An Orthodox reactionary, Lippman, in the chapter titled "Judea," seduces Henry (who, in this chapter, survived the bypass operation but fell into depression afterward) into leaving his family, living in a settlement on the West Bank, carrying a gun, speaking Hebrew, and fighting Arabs for a living. Lippman posits his philosophy of certainty against what he calls Nathan's culture of doubt and his life of action against Nathan's life of the mind. "History and reality will make the future and not pieces of paper!" he exclaims, criticizing the proposed Arab/Israeli peace agreement but also none too subtly dismissing Nathan's occupation as a writer (ibid., 117). Totally enthralled by Lippman's potency and assurance, Henry explains to Nathan that Israel is, for him, an escape from the self-involved world of psychology and *thought* that characterized his life in the Diaspora (this is a different version of Henry than the one who insisted his dentistry brought him into contact with the blood and guts of life). "There's a world outside the Oedipal swamp," he insists, "where what matters isn't what made you do it *but what it is you do!*" (ibid., 140, emphasis in original). By the end of this scene, however, Nathan is beaten by Lippman at his own game: "[F]ollowing Lippman's seminar, language didn't really seem my domain any longer . . . I was outclassed" (ibid., 130).

Despite being drawn to these men who assert their freedom to act without thinking, Nathan passionately exposes what he sees as the fatal flaws in the arguments of these powerful, all-too-human figures. In countless passages, he reasserts the importance of complexity, multiplicity, and self-examination to the moral and creative life. Impressed as he is by these characters' ability to assert themselves in uncomplicated ways, and to act on these assertions without deliberation, he finds he simply cannot endorse the unexamined, albeit effective, life. After three chapters spent confronting flesh and blood *actors,* in the penultimate chapter, "Gloucestershire," Nathan and his reader retreat into an orgy of talking, writing, editing, inventing, and reinventing. The platonic affair with Maria takes place entirely within his apartment building. He never leaves the house. So complete is his estrangement from the world of flesh and action that when Nathan dies toward the end of this chapter, an admirer laments that his death was so neat and bloodless:

> A sanitized death, a travesty of a eulogy, and no ceremony at all—completely secular, having nothing to do with the way Jews bury people. At least a good cry around the hole, a little remorse as they lower the coffin, but no, no one even allowed to go off with the body. Burn it. There is no body. (ibid., 218–219)

Nathan has achieved here the complete annihilation of his body, but his manuscripts live on, the triumph of the mind over the body, thought over action. Pieces of paper can make a difference in the world, as Nathan learns when a young admirer uses his ideas as the basis for a planned terrorist attack, or as Henry acknowledges when he rips out chapters from Nathan's manuscript to make sure that his wife will never encounter the evidence of his infidelity. Illusion matters.

So now we begin to understand why we are spending so much attention on this novel in a book on popular entertainment. In the final chapter of *The Counterlife*, Nathan comes to realize that the only way to reconcile these oppositions is through the metaphor and reality of performance. Nathan comes to realize that only in theater can one marry action and thought, reality and illusion, body and mind, and ultimately Christian and Jew. This last chapter, "Christendom," is both philosophical and theological, redefining basic tenets of theatrical liberalism about action, freedom, and obligation for post-modern American culture. It may perhaps seem strange that one of the most dramatic and passionate expressions of theatrical liberalism of the late-twentieth century comes not from Hollywood or Broadway but from the pen of a literary intellectual. *The Counterlife* is neither a popular play nor a movie, but it nonetheless provides an example of theatrical liberalism remarkable for its strong defense of theatricality in the face of powerful forces arguing for multicultural authenticity, not to mention its razor-sharp comic wit. Before it even begins to argue for the theatricality of identity, the novel itself reveals an acute awareness of its intervention into theatrical modes, and it often draws deliberate attention to itself as a kind of play. When Nathan takes a drive with Henry in the West Bank, he is startled by the fact that his newly Zionist brother brings a pistol along:

> [M]y mind remained on his pistol, and on Chekhov's famous dictum that a pistol hanging on the wall in Act One must eventually go off in Act Three. I wondered what act we were in, not to mention which play—domestic tragedy, historical epic, or just straight farce? (ibid., 108)

Nathan can only imagine the pistol in the context of dramatic structure. Indeed, pistols, penises, and words all share creative theatrical force in this novel. The book opens with a description of a "narrative . . . burn[ing] a hole in Zuckerman's pocket" (ibid., 13). Moments later Nathan worries that Henry might shoot him, thereby determining the genre to be Greek tragedy (complete with a five-act Aristotelian structure): "What if who he shoots is me? What if that was to be Act Three's awful surprise, the Zuckerman differences ending in blood, as though our family were Agamemnon's?" (ibid., 108). In the next chapter, or act, Nathan encounters Jimmy, the hijacker, on a flight from Israel to

England, and remarks once again on the pistol he brandishes and the dramatic genre it indicates:

> It was the pistol, Henry's first-act pistol. This then must be the third act in which it is fired. "Forget Remembering" is the title of the play and the assassin is the self-appointed son who learned all he knows at my great feet. Farce is the genre, climaxing in blood. (ibid., 171)

But then again, maybe this is not a farce but a high-stakes adventure movie or a surreal Italian art film. Nathan notes of the secret service agent who saves him and the rest of the passengers on the plane:

> [I]n the highly freckled skin and thinning orangey hair I half sensed something illusionary, as though perhaps he was wigged and completely made-up and underneath was a colorless albino. I was under the impression that it was all a performance and nonetheless was terrified out of my wits. (ibid., 173)

Nathan has come to realize that a performance—even if it is illusion—nonetheless can have real consequences. He was really "terrified out of [his] wits." As the theatrical imagery continues to intensify after this chapter, Nathan comes to realize that the illusion of performance may in fact *be* reality, or at least the closest to reality anyone ever gets.

Roth rejects the essentialism that characterized the identity politics dominating popular discourse in 1980s America with as much passion and urgency as Trilling rejected authenticity a decade or so earlier. Yet he also questions the notion that all identity is constructed by language; he resists this too-easy opposition between thought and action, between mind and body. "Christendom," as befits the final chapter of *The Counterlife*, is a densely packed critique of the dangers of embracing authenticity and of what Nathan calls the pastoral, and a full-throated celebration of the powers of theatrical liberalism. In an impassioned response to Maria, who has just argued that Nathan's Jewish "preoccupation with irresolvable conflict" is driving her away, back to a tranquility she craves, a simple English pastoral life, Nathan disputes the possibility that Maria, or anyone, can ever just be themselves (ibid., 313). Echoing Erving Goffman, Nathan insists that he holds himself to the same standard of theatrical self-consciousness:

Being Zuckerman is one long performance and the very opposite of what
is thought of as *being oneself.* In fact, those who most seem to be themselves appear to me people impersonating what they think they might
like to be, believe they ought to be, or wish to be taken to be by whoever
is setting standards. So in earnest are they that they don't even recognize
that being in earnest *is the act.* For certain self-aware people, however,
this is not possible: to imagine themselves being themselves, living their
own real, authentic, or genuine life, has for them all the aspects of a hallucination. (ibid., 319)

Nathan acknowledges that this sort of hallucination is exactly the
opposite of what Western medicine considers mental health. "What
is desirable" according to psychiatrists is not the kind of self-divi-
sion Nathan describes, an imaginative theatricality that led to Willy
Loman's hallucinations and Zelig's chameleonism, as well as Nathan's
writing and Henry's love affairs; rather, it is "congruity between your
self-consciousness and your natural being," the very definition Lionel Trilling uses to explain sincerity and Jonas Barish sees as the
root of Puritan anti-theatricality (ibid., 320). But Nathan argues for
another—and to him more moral—definition of mental health, a theatrical worldview "whose sanity flows from the conscious *separation*
of those two things." In attempting to define these two things more
carefully, Nathan isn't sure the "natural being" or essential core even
exists, but like Goffman (and unlike Butler), he is unwilling to dis-
pense with it entirely. Instead he proposes a new definition for the
"irreducible self," one that supports Woody Allen's version in *Zelig,*
complicates Judith Butler's idea of performativity, and makes theatrical liberalism the core of human subjectivity:

If there even *is* a natural being, an irreducible self, it is rather small, I
think, and may even be the root of all impersonation—the natural being
may be the skill itself, the innate capacity to impersonate. I'm talking
about recognizing that one is acutely a performer, rather than swallow-
ing whole the guise of naturalness and pretending that isn't a performance but you. . . . It's *all* impersonation—in the absence of a self, one
impersonates selves, and after a while impersonates best the self that best
gets one through. (ibid., 320)

In the act of performance Nathan finds the indissoluble bit of the self that constitutes a soul. Theatricality is as close as Nathan ever gets to essentialism, and the self-conscious performance is the only act he holds sacred. As he reaffirms a page later, "I certainly have no self independent of my imposturing, artistic efforts to have one. Nor would I want one. I am a theater and nothing more than a theater" (ibid., 321).

In *The Counterlife,* the theater *is* the self. To imagine otherwise is to fall prey to what Nathan calls the "womb-dream," the pastoral myth of a "sanitized, confusionless life." To desire a world without difference, contradiction, or conflict, without the theatrical division of self, or the more violent division of peoples, a "perfectly safe, charmingly simple and satisfying environment that is desire's homeland" is, according to Nathan, not limited to the English, although they have perfected it. For Henry, Basel represented that form of redemption and for Zionists ("Fleeing now, and back to day zero and the first untainted settlement—breaking history's mold and casting off the dirty, disfiguring reality of the piled-up years"), the land of Israel also serves as a pastoral dream (ibid., 322). For Christians, of course, the "virginal vision of Momma" practically invented the genre, and even Nathan, who thought he was immune to such seductions, fell prey to a redemptive pastoral vision of fatherhood with a young English wife. "In dead seriousness," he observes with a gesture at the American dream articulated in *The Great Gatsby,* "we all create imagined worlds, often green and breastlike, where we may finally be 'ourselves'" (ibid., 322). But what Nathan has come to realize in a few short weeks in England, and after a few unpleasant encounters with British anti-Semitism, is the pressing danger of falling prey to pastoral dreams:

> In America, I thought, where people claim and disown "identities" as easily as they slap on bumper stickers—where even though there are people sitting in clubs who think it's still the land of Aryans, it just don't happen to be so—I could act like a reasonable fellow when she'd distinguished Jews from Caucasians. But here, where you were swathed permanently in what you were born with, encased for life with where you began, here in a *real* land of Aryans, with a wife whose sister, if not her mother as well, appeared to be the pointwoman for some pure-blooded phalanx out to let me know that I was not welcome and had better not come in, I couldn't let the insult pass. . . . We couldn't just be "us" and say

the hell with "them" any more than we could say to hell with the twentieth century when it intruded upon our idyll. (ibid., 308)

The pastoral fuels lovely images of New Edens, but it cannot abide
any imperfections in that pretty picture. Jewish difference is a smudge
on the British landscape. As Maria finally admits:

> I object to people clinging to an identity just for the sake of it. I don't
> think there's anything admirable about it at all. . . . I think all these ethnic
> groups—whether they are Jewish, whether they're West Indian and think
> they must keep this Caribbean thing going—simply make life more dif-
> ficult in a society where we're trying to just live amicably, like London,
> and where we are now very very diverse. (ibid., 301)

Maria's universal dream of what Nathan calls "the perfect undiluted,
unpolluted, unsmelly 'we'" is, of course, the polite rationale for fascism and
ethnic cleansing. The pastoral invites, indeed demands, violence to remove
the differences that threaten it. Nathan is shaken by his experience in England. He suddenly realizes that the freedom to write himself, to play the
narrative games of the previous chapter, depends upon a society invested
in that freedom, a version of liberalism that allows him to exercise control
over his identity, that encourages performance. This realization throws
into relief the very Americanness not only of his assumptions but those of
Judith Butler as well. Butler's critique of liberalism, and especially her limited view of individual agency, is influenced by European philosophy but
only ultimately makes sense in an American context. As Nathan discovers,
it's a lot easier to argue for the free play of language and the power of performance in a culture that privileges individual freedom, even if that freedom
necessarily remains incomplete. In England, where the values of theatrical liberalism have little power, Nathan is suddenly burdened by the limitations of a history and a people that he thought he had escaped. Nathan
has preserved himself from seduction by the simplistic, dogmatic truths of
Shimmy, Lippman, or the El Al agent, only to find himself trapped by one
of the oldest and most simplistic dogmas of them all.

What originates in the heart in this novel is realized via the penis.
And vice versa. When Nathan finally confronts a decision that *requires*
irreversible action—whether to circumcise his son in the face of his

in-laws' disapproval—he decides to take action. His justification rests *not* on an unthinking desire to reinscribe the simplistic, essentializing opposition between mind and body; in fact, he is motivated by the opposite impulse. In choosing to circumcise his son, he forcefully rejects the pastoral and makes a surprising connection between theatricality and this Jewish ritual. If the Jewish self is, as Nathan claims, a performance, ever evolving and changing, how can we account for circumcision, an irreversible mark on the body, made on a barely conscious newborn infant, which forever inscribes this boy with a particular identity? This mark in the flesh seems to reduce the child's freedom to perform counterlives and multiple roles from the very beginning. Nathan acknowledges that circumcision is deliberately limiting:

> Circumcision is startling, all right, particularly when performed by a garlicked old man upon the glory of a newborn body, but then maybe that's what the Jews had in mind and what makes the act seem quintessentially Jewish and the mark of their reality. Circumcision makes it clear as can be that you are here and not there, that you are out and not in—also that you're mine and not theirs. (ibid., 323)

But this is a limitation Nathan seems prepared to accept. Not the limitation of a particular ethnic, religious, or national identity, but rather the limitation of simply knowing there are limits. Circumcision makes clear the boundaries within which self-invention can happen and makes it impossible for Jewish boys to ever imagine themselves to be outside of history. Writing in the liturgical mode Cynthia Ozick called for, Roth articulates the communal obligations which define much of Jewish practice:

> There is no way around it: you enter history through my history and me. Circumcision is everything that the pastoral is not and, to my mind, reinforces what the world is about, which isn't strifeless unity. Quite convincingly, circumcision gives the lie to the womb-dream of life in the beautiful state of innocent prehistory, the appealing idyll of living "naturally," unencumbered by man-made ritual. To be born is to lose all that. The heavy hand of human values falls upon you right at the start, marking your genitals as its own. (ibid., 323)

Nathan embraces circumcision because it will protect his son from ever dreaming the pastoral dream, from ever being able to imagine a world without difference.

By embracing circumcision as *the opposite* of the pastoral ("the pastoral stops here and it stops with circumcision"), Nathan sets up and then breaks down one final binary opposition, the binary that in many ways shapes the entire narrative between Christian and Jew. Circumcision was one of the key rites that divided Jews from early Christians, and continued for much of Western history to serve as a mark of difference. Paul's Letter to the Romans strongly argues against the practice: "For he is not a Jew, which is one outwardly; neither is that circumcision, which is outward in the flesh: But he is a Jew, which is one inwardly; and circumcision is that of the heart, in the spirit, and not in the letter; whose praise is not of men, but of God" (Rom. 2:28–29, KJV). Paul's rejection of the commandment to circumcise the flesh in favor of circumcising the heart brings us back to the heart/penis binary, but now with additional theological significance. The Jew, according to later Protestant interpretations of Paul, continues to be tied to external actions and to a problematic idea of difference and chosenness. A good Christian, on the other hand, should circumcise the heart, make a personal covenant with God through an internal expression of faith. This kind of circumcision, according to Paul's interpreters, is universal, no longer limited to a single chosen nation. This tension between faith and action, internal and external definitions of the self, shaped not only Jewish-Christian relations but also the Jewish response to Protestant Enlightenment liberalism. The priority of action over intention articulated initially in Exodus 24 (*na'aseh v'nishma*) is repeated here in the making of a young Jewish boy: a specific ritual action, the *bris* (ritual circumcision) comes first, before the baby is even aware of his options. From this action, according to Roth, follows a series of internal developments: the awareness of difference, Jewish identity, familial obligation, and historical consciousness.

For Nathan, then, circumcision becomes a way of resisting what he sees as a Protestant impulse toward universalism and homogeneity, one which explicitly excludes him as a Jew. But at the same time, it seems to confuse his logic about performance. On the one hand, circumcision is a ritual designed to make the Jewish boy aware of difference, a mark inscribing an ethos of multiplicity right on the body and making possible the idea of counterlives around which the novel revolves. On the other hand, the baby himself has no control over his own circumcision. "The heavy hand of human values" is not the baby's hand, of course, but the father's (or his surrogate). This seems to call into question the whole ethos of self-creation that Nathan has been celebrating throughout the book. Freedom, for Nathan, is the ability to create counterlives, to invent selves, to do impersonations. Self-making is at the root of Nathan's idea of performance, and is also, of course, central to theatrical liberalism. The agency to make and remake the self guarantees the individual freedom so important to American Jews. How to reconcile this with the utter vulnerability of the baby who is, without conscious assent, marked as a member of a particular group? The father makes the baby into a Jew; the baby has nothing to do with it.

The Counterlife forces us to reconsider the liberal rhetoric of self-making and the limits of individual freedom in theatrical liberalism. Do we indeed have the power to completely make and remake ourselves from scratch? Jonathan and Daniel Boyarin argue that this idea of self-making applies differently to Protestants and Jews:

> The story of the self-made man, stripped down to its common features, starts from a zero point. It has no prehistory. It continues in linear fashion, step by step, progressively. In this version, the word "success" has lost its connotations of coming after, inheriting, taking the place of; this success, this doing well, is all about finding a high place in a capitalist hierarachy that is constantly evolving and expanding. We suggest that this American ideal is closely linked to the Christian (and especially Protestant) notion of individual salvation, and through this to the assumption of the discrete self as existing in a uniquely defined time, such that chronology is co-terminous and contingent with a sequential and progressive individual biography.[12]

To be "born again" is a similarly individual act, an expression of personal salvation which requires no physical mother or father to effect the change. Like Roth, the Boyarins turn to circumcision to help define a specifically Jewish notion of self-making. They acknowledge that for modern secular American Jews, few differences of selfhood seem to separate them from their Protestant peers. Indeed, most American boys are circumcised at birth, not just Jews. But the ritual act of circumcision differs in important ways from the "medical" version. Echoing Roth, the Boyarins note the ways in which this mark on the body situates the male Jew within history:

> Even though most Jewish men . . . do not recall their own circumcisions and are not expected to, the communally sanctioned and communally observed ceremony and the mark it leaves nevertheless serve as reminders that the world existed before one was conscious of it, and will continue to exist after one's own consciousness is extinguished. (ibid., 49)

Circumcision is a form, then, of Jewish self-making. It differs in crucial ways from the Protestant notion of the self-made man. It is fundamentally communal. It requires multiple generations and a "communally observed ceremony" to create a Jewish boy. When that Jewish boy grows up, he will have the opportunity for his own act of self-creation: he can circumcise his son. The question of wills, and will, creation and self-creation that was so pressing in *Young Frankenstein* emerges here in a more explicitly Judaic way. Roth's conflation of the freedom of performance with the obligation of circumcision leads to a new kind of self-making and a new understanding of theatrical liberalism, one which insures the freedom of multiplicity, performance and difference while always being bounded by history.

Roth's otherwise convincing argument about circumcision contains one major flaw. It only addresses the question of Jewish identity for men. As Shaye Cohen asks in his provocative study *Why Aren't Jewish Women Circumcised?*: "[I]f circumcision is an essential marker of Jewishness, what are women? Can women be Jews?"[13] Philip Roth, Woody Allen, Tony Kushner, Mel Brooks, and many other writers of this era seem to have little interest in addressing this glaring omission in their works: Jewish women play little if any role in the stories they tell. Even in the heyday of theatrical liberalism, women's theatricality was considered dangerous and destabilizing. But it is possible that Roth, in offering a new understanding of theatrical liberalism at the end of *The Counterlife,* may have, however unintentionally, also created an opening for Jewish women to enter this story as subjects in their own right. The ritual of circumcision leads Nathan to conclude that Jewish identity depends on recognizing difference while accepting the limitations of history and the obligations of community. But this correspondence of Judaism with the central features of theatrical liberalism by no means *requires* circumcision.

On the final page of *Counterlife*, Nathan makes a curious statement about identity. He says that England has made a Jew of him in only eight weeks and then qualifies this statement: "A Jew without Jews, without Judaism, without Zionism, without Jewishness, without a temple or an army or even a pistol, a Jew clearly without a home, just the object itself, like a glass or an apple" (Roth, *Counterlife*, 324). What does it mean to be "just the object itself"? What is the essence of being Jewish? After hundreds of pages of discussion, deliberation, and literary showmanship, Nathan appears to have finally settled on a definition of his own secular Jewishness. Removed from the American context, where his identity is so commonplace as to be utterly unremarkable, Nathan's Jewishness comes into focus in England, where his particular identity and worldview of theatrical liberalism turns out to be far more remarkable. The transparency of American liberalism makes it difficult to see the outlines of particular strands of that liberalism. But in England, where theatrical liberalism is a far less accepted mode, Nathan can finally begin to make out a self-definition, which then rings true for him. The object itself is a secular American Jew who may no longer even recognize himself or herself as Jewish. An individual who self-consciously performs her life, who understands the value of action, who revels in the limited freedom for self-invention, and is aware of being bounded by communal obligation and historical contingency. An individual who refuses the simplicity of binary oppositions, as Nathan realizes in the final chapter of *The Counterlife*:

> The burden isn't either/or, consciously choosing from possibilities equally difficult and regrettable—it's and/and/and/and/and as well. Life *is* and: the accidental and the immutable, the elusive and the graspable, the bizarre and the predictable, the actual and the potential, all the multiplying realities, entangled, overlapping, colliding, conjoined—plus the multiplying illusions! (ibid., 306)

This "object itself," like theatrical liberalism, does not require one to choose between opposing systems; it is neither Protestant liberalism nor Judaism but instead a unique amalgam of both.

* * *

The multiplying profusion of possibility, and the ironic focus on differ-ence itself as the source of identity in so many works of popular culture and cultural criticism, left theatrical liberalism in a confusing position on the Broadway stage as the century drew to a close. On the one hand, the embrace of multiplicity represented the culmination of the very freedom promised by theatrical liberalism. Indeed, the lasting legacy of post-modernism and performance studies is the resistance to limits on identity; to limit identity is to limit freedom, to embrace the false prom-ise of stable truths, to refuse theatricality altogether and to turn once again to essentialism. On the other hand, this refusal of limits makes it extremely difficult to make decisions about taking action and hon-oring obligations. In the last decade of the twentieth century, writers and artists who continued to embrace the tenets of theatrical liberalism, especially those who aimed to speak to an intellectual elite as well as a popular audience, found themselves twisting in knots to make the case for a still-seductive and powerful brand of liberalism without being labeled embarrassingly naïve or impossibly utopian by their more cyni-cal colleagues and critics. This project was further complicated by the re-emergence of Judaism itself in the popular culture—as an aesthetic, moral, political, and spiritual subject of inquiry. While *ethnic* Jewish-ness made a reappearance in American popular culture in the 1960s, with *Fiddler on the Roof,* it wasn't until the late 1980s and early 1990s, with the increasing focus on religion in the American public sphere, that self-identified secular Jewish artists began to look to aspects of their *religious* and *spiritual* heritage for moral and aesthetic inspiration, and to tentatively begin to incorporate the imagery, texts, and practices of Judaism into work intended for both Jewish and broadly American audiences.

Tony Kushner's Tony Award–winning play *Angels in America*—and its equally celebrated Emmy Award–winning HBO adaptation—was one of the first plays of the late twentieth century to bring aspects of Judaism into popular consciousness in this way. The play struggles to renegotiate the relationship between late-twentieth-century theatri-cal liberalism and Reagan-era identity politics using a variety of Jew-ish symbols, historical figures, characters, and rituals. Written and performed in two parts, *Millennium Approaches,* and *Perestroika,* the play tells the intersecting stories of Prior Walter, a Protestant gay man with AIDS; his Jewish lover Louis, who lacks the fortitude to confront illness and leaves Prior in part 1; Belize, a black former drag queen, best friend, and nurse to Prior; Roy Cohn, right-wing Jewish lawyer and closeted homosexual who sent the Rosenbergs to the electric chair; and a Mormon couple, Joe, a closeted Republican lawyer and Roy's protégé, who eventually has an affair with Louis; and Harper, Joe's frustrated Valium-addicted wife. The core theatrical event of the play is the arrival of an Angel from heaven, who seeks Prior as a new prophet. In part 2, Prior ends up visiting heaven, refusing the prophecy, and returning to earth with a message of love and forgiveness for his friends, the nation, and the audience.

Angels in America is a play about gay life, AIDS, American politics, and spiritual yearning, but more than anything it is a play that both embodies and illustrates late-twentieth-century ambivalence about the key principles and forms of theatrical liberalism.[14] A self-appointed heir to Arthur Miller, Kushner struggles in *Angels in America* with much of the same ambivalence that Miller expressed about theatricality, albeit through a late-twentieth-century lens, which takes into account the theatrical experiments of the 1960s and '70s, the embrace of Brechtian self-consciousness by scholars in performance studies as well as theater practitioners on the American stage, and the focus on performativity in post-structuralist critical theory.[15] Kushner aimed to make *Angels in America* both a self-consciously theatrical event *and* an immersive spiritual experience. As he indicates in a "note about the staging" at the beginning of the published play, "The moments of magic . . . are to be fully realized, as bits of wonderful *theatrical* illusion—which means it's OK if the wires show, and maybe it's good that they do, but the magic should at the same time be thoroughly amazing."[16] Deeply suspicious of sentimentality ("eschew sentiment!" he advises in the opening notes to part 2), he insures in good Brechtian fashion that the audience never has the opportunity to be lost in illusion by constantly drawing attention to the play as a work of and about popular culture.[17] Just before the Angel appears at the end of part 1, there is a fantastic light show. "Very Stephen Spielberg," Prior observes. When Prior returns from his visit to heaven in part 2, he quotes from *The Wizard of Oz,* "I've had a remarkable dream. And you were there and you . . . " (2:140). Moments of high seriousness are consistently undercut in this way; these asides provide humor, of course, but also reveal a nervous ambivalence about the power of theatricality. The laughter evoked here is a knowing laughter, the laughter of those who not only get the joke but who laugh to show that *they* are not taken in by illusion.[18]

Angels in America differs from *Death of a Salesman* in this arch self-consciousness about theatricality, but like *Salesman* it is deeply critical of the power of theatrical self-fashioning at the heart of theatrical liberalism. The celebration of the theatricality of the Angel, wires and all, belies a rigid attitude toward the performance of identity. The two figures who serve as moral centers for the play (Prior and Belize) are the two who are most clearly "true to themselves." And the truth of themselves is located in their sexuality. Neither is ever in the closet; neither is ever shown trying to pass for something he is not. While both have been in the theater in the past, they appear to have rejected performance on political grounds; they are both, significantly, *ex*-drag queens. As Belize says to Prior, "All this girl-talk shit is politically incorrect, you know. We should have dropped it back when we gave up drag" (1:61).[19] Belize is a nurse; he makes his living dealing in the harsh reality of bodies: blood, guts, and death. Prior likewise becomes particularly vehement about the false illusion of theatricality after the spectacular funeral of a drag-queen friend, complete with sequins, incense, and twenty professional Sicilian mourners: "That ludicrous spectacle in there, just a parody of the funeral of someone who *really* counted. We don't; faggots; we're just a bad dream the real world is having, and the real world's waking up. And he's *dead*" (2:42). Prior and Belize serve as moral centers and spiritual touchstones in the play *because* they have embraced the truth of themselves. Cross-dressing, for men at least, is surprisingly problematic in this play, especially in part 1. While all of the actors play a number of minor and major characters, only women appear as men (the rabbi and the doctor, for example, are played by the actor who also plays Hannah; the actor playing Harper also plays Roy's associate Martin). In part 2, there is one male to female crossover—the actor playing Louis also plays his grandmother—but this is in a scene that Kushner notes can be cut (and is cut from the HBO version). Part of the practical reason for this is likely that the women have less stage time than the men, and therefore can double or triple their roles. This just highlights another surprising feature of a work so obsessed with identity politics: male sexuality and male identity remain at the center of this narrative, which is meant to articulate a national mythology. Female sexuality is treated in a stereotypical or dismissive manner (the frustrated housewife, the uptight Mormon mother-in-law). The cross-casting is also often deliberately transparent in order to deepen our response to particular characters by emphasizing essential traits, which are inherent in the actor: Belize is nurse to Prior, but also to Harper, as Mr. Lies. The Angel is also Prior's nurse, Emily. There is a subtle but insistent embrace here of stability of identity as a necessary precursor to moral action.[20]

Other key characters do self-consciously perform multiple identities, but they end up as moral failures. Joe, a Mormon Republican lawyer, is a closeted homosexual, working hard to perform his "straight" life. Far from embracing performance as a survival and escape strategy, as so many theatrical liberal characters did in the past, Joe is tortured by the lie of his existence. As he tells his desperate wife, Harper: "Does it make any difference? That I might be one thing deep within, no matter how wrong or ugly that thing is, so long as I have fought, with everything I have, to kill it. . . . For God's sake, there's nothing left, I'm a shell. . . . As long as my behavior is what I know it has to be. Decent. Correct. That alone in the eyes of God" (1:40). For Joe, performance is akin to murder. He has killed his true self in his effort to conform to his religious beliefs. The play clearly takes a stand here *against* action as the source of the moral self. Joe's idea of "correct" behavior is decent only through what Kushner considers the skewed eyes of organized religion. In the world of the play, the lack of correspondence (or "identity") between his internal self (his sexuality) and his external behavior damns him. Joe's self-delusion is the cause not only of his but also of his wife's unhappiness. Harper's addiction to Valium, and the comforting hallucinations the drug induces, are the result of Joe's less sympathetic delusions. Harper is not really held responsible for her playacting, and as soon as Joe reveals his true identity to her, she is freed to be herself as well. She leaves her stash of pills with Joe and flies off to San Francisco to find herself. A Mormon and a Republican, Joe is unable to fully "come out of the closet" and is therefore excised from the redemption promised at the end of the play.

Roy Cohn is denied redemption for similar reasons. Certainly his anti-communist, right-wing politics make him an unsympathetic figure. But what really damns him is hypocrisy, and specifically the personal hypocrisy of living life in the closet. Early in the first part of the play, Roy has an appointment with his doctor. The doctor tells him that he has AIDS. Roy refuses the diagnosis in a remarkably powerful speech about the construction of identity:

> Your problem, Henry, is that you are hung up on words, on labels, that you believe they mean what they seem to mean. AIDS. Homosexual. Gay. Lesbian. You think these are names that tell you who someone sleeps with but they don't tell you that. . . . Like all labels they tell you one thing and one thing only: where does an individual so identified fit in the food chain, in the pecking order? . . . Now to someone who does not understand this, homosexual is what I am because I have sex with men. But really this is wrong. Homosexuals are not men who sleep with other men. Homosexuals are men who in fifteen years of trying cannot get a pissant antidiscrimination bill through City Council. . . . This is not sophistry. And this is not hypocrisy. This is reality. I have sex with men. But unlike nearly every other man of whom this is true, I bring the guy I'm screwing to the White House and President Reagan smiles at us and shakes his hand. Because what I am is defined entirely by who I am. Roy Cohn is not a homosexual. Roy Cohn is a heterosexual man, Henry, who fucks around with guys. (1:45–46)

Roy freely admits to having sex with men. But he has no intention of being identified by his private sexual behavior; indeed, he insists that his public actions define him. The doctor replies, simply and directly, that it doesn't matter what Roy calls his disease or his actions, and it doesn't matter what strings Roy pulls—he is going to die anyway. His body will become his truth. And Roy apparently gets his comeuppance in the end: he is disbarred, tortured by the ghost of Ethel Rosenberg (for whose execution he is held responsible), and dies a painful, horrible death. In the worldview of *Angels in America,* Roy's theatricality renders him as evil as his politics. Unlike Joe, he is not tortured by performance. He has made an art of self-fashioning and has no moral problem with it; he is, in many ways, the representative of theatrical liberalism in the play. And because of this, he is, as Louis insists "the polestar of human evil" (2:95). But Roy is also, like Willy Loman, the star of the play. Roy directs scenes (feeding lines to his doctor about his illness, telling Joe how to behave when he is blessing him, "faking" death to get Ethel to sing), and his death scenes are among the most dramatic moments in the play. In the Tony Awards for part 1, and the Golden Globes and Emmys for the HBO adaptation, the actors playing Roy Cohn (Ron Liebman and Al Pacino) won awards for best actor. Others were nominated in supporting roles. Like *Death of a Salesman*, *Angels in America* achieves dramatic success on the back of the very performance virtuosity it otherwise seems to abhor.

This ambivalence about theatricality becomes especially pronounced in the moments when the play turns to Judaism and the Hebrew Bible for its powerful millennial imagery. Once again, in *Angels in America* we encounter the story of Jacob as a kind of mythological backdrop to late-twentieth-century politics and culture. But the play presents us with two distinctly different versions of Jacob—the theatrical son who deceived his father to get a blessing, and the prophet who wrestled with an angel and became Israel—and asks us to choose between them. Early in part 1, Joe uses the story of Jacob to tell Harper about his personal struggles with sexuality:

> I had a book of Bible stories when I was a kid. There was a picture I'd look at twenty times every day: Jacob wrestles with the angel. I don't really remember the story, or why the wrestling—just the picture. . . . I still dream about it. Many nights. I'm . . . It's me. In that struggle. (1:49)

For Joe, the angel is a symbol of his homosexuality, and the wrestling becomes his desperate attempt to overcome it. But Joe is an unwilling and unsuitable prophet. As a closeted homosexual pretending to be straight, he is aligned with the younger, more theatrical Jacob. In part 2, Joe visits Roy, who is dying of AIDS, in the hospital. On his deathbed Roy decides to bless Joe: The stage directions state, *Roy motions for Joe to come over, then for him to kneel. He puts his hand on Joe's forehead.* Joe has come to visit Roy in order to tell him that he is gay. "Roy, I . . . I need to talk to you about. . . ."

Roy Cohn (Al Pacino) giving Joe (Patrick Wilson) a "brokhe" in *Angels in America.*

he interrupts, not recognizing the scene Roy is re-enacting. Roy
directs him: "Ssshah. Schmendrick. Don't fuck up the magic"(2:82).
Roy notes that Joe gets his blessing openly; he doesn't have to jump
through the hoops that Jacob did: "A *Brokhe.* You don't even have to
trick it out of me, like what's-his-name in the Bible." Roy is the one
character in the play who fully supports—and enacts—Jacob's dramatic cunning: "A ruthless motherfucker, some bald runt, but he laid
hold of his birthright with his claws and his teeth" (2:83). Roy wants
to pass the legacy of Jacob on to Joe, but he himself doesn't want to
be Isaac ("The sacrifice. That jerk," he says). But Joe can't stand to fool
Roy; he feels that he, like Jacob, *has* tricked the blessing out of Roy.
And so he tells Roy that he is living with a man. Roy goes crazy, yanks
out his IV tube, and starts yelling at Joe, insisting that he return to his
wife. "You already got my blessing—WHAT MORE DO YOU WANT
FROM ME?" he screams. At the end of his life, Roy discovers that he,
like Isaac, has been deceived. But the deception is not a straightforward one. He is not upset that Joe is sleeping with a man; he is upset
that Joe rejects the ruthless and dramatic potential that Jacob represents. Instead, Joe has bought into identity politics; he feels the need
to come out of the closet and turn his private sexual behavior into
his public identity. Roy wants a spiritual son, a legacy who shares his
embrace of performance and external action as a means of shaping

identity. Roy thought he blessed Jacob only to discover that Joe more closely resembles Esau, the simple man of the fields ("Marlboro Man," Prior calls him).

Prior, on the other hand, is Jacob the prophet. Prior wrestles with the angel, hurts the angel's leg, demands a blessing, and gets it. Prior jumps directly to the second blessing; he has no need for the initial, falsely acquired one. Whereas Joe is the Jacob of the deception, Prior is the mystical prefiguration of Jesus, the Jacob who wrestles with the angel and not only wins but refuses the initial book, gains access to heaven, and bargains for a new covenant, a new prophecy. The angels want him to preach a prophecy of stasis and purity to the late-twentieth-century world in which he lives. The Angel sees into a future, in which a world abandoned by God continues to descend into suffering and destruction. "Stop moving!" she commands. "Forsake the Open Road; Neither Mix nor Intermarry; Let Deep Roots Grow; If you do not MINGLE you will Cease to Progress" (2:52). For the Angel, progress must be stopped in order to avoid destruction. Prior rejects this prophecy: "We can't just stop," he tells the angels. "We're not rocks—progress, migration, motion is . . . modernity. It's *animate,* it's what living things do" (2:132). Prior insists that he will return to earth, in spite of the pain and suffering that he and the rest of the world will inevitably experience. He wants a new blessing and a different prophecy: "Bless me anyway," he demands, "I want more life" (2:135).[21]

Judaism is explicitly invoked in this play in a way we have rarely seen in a century of Jewish-created popular entertainment. But while Kushner makes use of Jewish mysticism to signal Prior's authentic transformation and rebirth (via the flaming Aleph), he simultaneously recoils from the more human theatricality of Jews and Jewish practice represented by Roy Cohn and Louis. The opening scene in *Angels* with the rabbi, various references to Hebrew and the Hebrew Bible, Roy's blessing, Ethel Rosenberg's Yiddish lullabies, and the recitation of the Kaddish toward the end of part 2 are either awkward reminders of a world that has disappeared or isolated elements floating free of their theological context. Kushner is, to be fair, critical of all organized religion; Mormonism also comes in for its share of critique. But the play turns an explicitly Anglo-Saxon Protestant man into a version of a Jewish prophet and offers only deeply morally flawed Jewish characters, Roy and Louis, who at times verge on anti-Semitic stereotypes. Louis only ends up reciting Kaddish for Roy because Belize, the other (Christian) moral center of the play, insists on it. Louis doesn't even know the words; he is helped by the ghostly presence of Ethel Rosenberg, a representative not only of left-wing Jewish politics but also of an Old World Yiddish tradition, which has long disappeared.

Toward the end of the play, Prior, in the guise of Jacob the prophet, after having been betrayed and denied by his Jewish lover, travels to heaven and back, and emerges changed by his experience, imbued with love, forgiveness, and grace. *Angels in America* offers one possible ending for this history of theatrical liberalism: in turning an "original" Protestant American—Prior, the one who came before—into a version of Jacob, indeed of Israel, triumphing over the Angel, and preaching a theology of progress and rebirth, the play expresses the logical conclusion of the merging of Judaism and Protestantism at the heart of American national mythology. But the play's subtle and paradoxical anti-theatricality, its rejection of sentiment, its critique of the self-fashioning embodied by Roy, and by "the closet," indeed its moral abhorrence of the theatrical Jacob in any form, make it—like *Death of a Salesman*—an uneasy expression of theatrical liberalism. Like many writers and artists at the end of the century (Jewish or not), Kushner is inspired by the spiritual passion that animates secular discussions of identity and politics. But by insisting on a kind of authentic spirituality as the answer to America's political and cultural crises, and simultaneously rejecting theatrical self-fashioning as immoral, *Angels in America* ends up losing sight of what makes American popular culture so powerfully and spiritually engaging. The binary opposition between religion and theatricality, as we have seen, is a false one. Spiritual concerns clearly motivate American national identity and American popular entertainment. But *Angels in America* looks too far afield for these spiritual expressions, which were actually being applauded nightly on the so-called secular stages of the Broadway theaters that surrounded the Walter Kerr Theater (where *Angels* opened in 1993), in productions of musicals such as *Guys and Dolls, My Fair Lady, Carousel,* and *Damn Yankees,* all of which were playing on Broadway at the same time. The ceaseless revival of American musicals on Broadway is one of American culture's most dependably practiced religious rituals, and the place to look for expressions of American Jewish spirituality are in those plays, not in Hasidic mysticism. After a hundred years, theatrical liberalism had become a secular religion in its own right, one whose origins were deeply rooted in Judaism and American liberalism but which, at the dawn of the twenty-first century, wielded a theatrical and spiritual power all its own.

Curtain Call

On March 24, 2011, Ben Brantley wrote in the *New York Times* about a new musical that had just opened on Broadway:

> This is to all the doubters and deniers out there, the ones who say that heaven on Broadway does not exist, that it's only some myth our ancestors dreamed up. I am here to report that a newborn, old-fashioned, pleasure-giving musical has arrived at the Eugene O'Neill Theater, the kind our grandparents told us left them walking on air if not on water. So hie thee hence, nonbelievers (and believers too), to "The Book of Mormon," and feast upon its sweetness. . . . "The Book of Mormon" achieves something like a miracle. . . . the religion of the musical, which lends ecstatic shape and symmetry to a world that often feels overwhelmingly formless. . . . All the folks involved in "Mormon" prove themselves worthy, dues-paying members of the church of Broadway.[1]

As this review makes abundantly clear, theatrical liberalism remains alive and well in America. Ben Brantley's hyperbolically religious language is inspired by the content of the show itself, which centers on the relationship between religion, theater, and reality. In "I Believe," in the second act of *Book of Mormon,* the main character performs his faith through the mechanism of a showstopping musical number, eliding the difference between religion and theater. The early twenty-first century saw a rejuvenation of the rhetoric of theatrical liberalism. A new musical from Mel Brooks arrived on Broadway (*The Producers*)[2], and a few years later, *Glee,* a show about musical theater, became a popular television series. With the advent of reality television, American popular culture continued to embrace the idea of the "backstage" story, albeit often with troubling implications. Over the past couple of decades, Jewish artists, writers, directors, and performers have given popular culture forms new life by filling them with explicitly Judaic religious content. Many of these recent works mirror the approach of *Angels in America,* using mysticism or other aspects of Jewish thought and practice as symbols of authenticity. For example, Madonna's turn to Kabbalah or, in the case of "Heeb" culture, turning what had been marginalizing about Jewish culture in America into a standard of hipness, without fully engaging in the living possibilities of this spiritual tradition. Others, however, have begun to gesture at the potential inherent in a fully self-conscious acknowledgement of the place of religion in secular culture.

In 2005, I co-organized a conference and cultural festival at the University of Toronto entitled "ReJewvenation," which reflected on the renaissance of Diaspora Jewish culture in the early years of the twenty-first century. Encompassing overtly Jewish expression in popular music, performance art, theater, digital media, movies, television, and literature, the conference explored the complex fabric of contemporary Jewish avant-garde and popular culture. Rather than signaling the demise of Jewish identity and the triumph of assimilation, or the triumph of Jewish identity but the demise of Judaism—both of which had long been predicted to occur in Diaspora Jewish life by the end of the twentieth century—conference participants found that the artists whose work we encountered and discussed that weekend were unexpectedly immersed in the texts, values, rhetorical modes, rituals, and artistic heritage of Judaism and Jewish life. Equally surprising, they were often doing so through popular forms with deep roots in American culture: comic books, popular music, Hollywood film, stand-up comedy, and television sitcoms. It struck me at the time how effectively the forms of American popular culture, in particular, served to express these Judaic ideas, and I began to wonder if perhaps these "secular" forms might not have some deeper relationship to Judaism and Jewish culture. The vibrant Jewish culture of the early twenty-first century spurred me to look back in American Jewish history, to search for the roots of this connection between Jews and popular entertainment in America in the rich religious and political soil of American liberalism and secular Judaism.

Amichai Lau-Lavie, the founder of the performance group Storahtelling, opened the conference on Friday night with his show "The Sabbath Queen." Inhabiting the persona of an ultra-orthodox

Holocaust survivor, the Rebbetzin Haddasah Gross (a widow of six rabbis, all named Gross), Lau-Lavie proceeded to usher in the Sabbath with prayer, song, and comedy. The Rebbetzin led the audience in the blessings over the candles, wine, and challah, songs for welcoming the Sabbath Queen, and a study of the Torah portion of the week, all while keeping up a patter about love, sexuality, and faith (in a tribute to a kind of ultra-orthodox Dr. Ruth), which kept the audience laughing from start to finish. This drag performance evoked a whole history of American Jewish popular comedy from vaudeville to the Catskills to *Saturday Night Live*, but with a significant difference. The humor in this performance did not reside in a demonstration of the difference between Jew and Gentile. This Jewish character had no ambivalence about being Jewish. She fully embraced both her Jewish ethnic identity and her religious lifestyle. What made the performance hilariously funny was a much subtler kind of difference. Just as David Belasco suggested in his acting theory almost a century earlier, Lau-Lavie paid close attention to detail in building the character—her dress, gestures, accent, and religious attitudes were precisely reproduced. The character was presented respectfully and earnestly. The audience *really* prayed with her and *really* learned Torah with her. Never was the Rebbetzin held up as an object of ridicule for her religious beliefs or used as an easy punching bag for her conservative views on sexuality. The only significant difference between the Rebbetzin character and a "real" rebbetzin was that this one was actually a man. That overt act of self-fashioning, which was never directly acknowledged in the performance, offered a subtle and persistent critique of ultra-orthodox rigidity. Yet the show never advocated defiant secularism or ironic distance as the alternative to the strictures of orthodoxy. Embodying both man and woman, orthodox Rebbetzin and gay stand-up comic, Lau-Lavie created a character who demonstrated the creative potential of an American Jewish liberalism, which self-consciously rejected the distinction between the secular and the religious. The show made a powerful argument for the Jewishness of every aspect of the performance, not only the blessings and the Torah study but also the attention to gesture and accent, the careful makeup job, the humor, and the defiant act of self-transformation at the center of the piece.

The Rebbetzin Hadassah Gross. (Photograph by Keith Germark.)

Lau-Lavie's performance alerted us to the power of action, both in Judaism and on the stage, and sent me searching for the roots of this kind of action in Jewish tradition. This book has traced a history of effective *action* and *acting* from the biblical Jacob to the late-twentieth-century Roy Cohn of *Angels in America*. Dressed as Esau, Jacob defiantly transformed himself, not to distance himself from his family but to secure his position within it. When Isaac blessed Jacob, Jacob remained blessed. The blessing stuck and could not be revoked, even though the recipient of the blessing was "merely" performing. In his foundational study of performative speech, *How to Do Things With Words,* J. L. Austin described the ways in which speech can be an act, one that can affect real change in the world. When a minister says the words, "I now pronounce you man and wife," the couple are really married. Saying it makes it so. Austin qualifies this assertion, however, noting that speech acts only work when the conditions are right. Words spoken on the stage are "infelicitous": "a performative utterance will, *in a peculiar way,* be hollow or void if said by an actor on the stage." According to Austin, performances cannot be performative, they cannot make real things happen in the real world.[3] The theatricality of Lau-Lavie and of his ancient precursor Jacob, Jakie Rabinowitz's jazz singing, Magnolia's "make-believe," Willy Loman's hallucinations, Erving Goffman's dramatic sociology, Eliza Doolittle's speech lessons, and the circumcision imagined by Nathan Zuckerman all suggest the opposite. When the Rebbetzin Haddassah Gross blessed the candles and welcomed in the Sabbath, those candles were *really blessed* and the Sabbath was *really welcomed*, even though the Rebbetzin was not really a rebbetzin and the blessing happened on stage. Whether on the stage or in the street, whether performed in knowledge or naïve ignorance, whether intentional or not, acting makes a difference in the world. Action is an animating force of secular Judaism; it is also at the heart of American liberalism. One enduring legacy of theatrical liberalism is this faith in the power of acting to create selves, define communities, and fulfill obligations, a faith that continues to be shared by countless Americans, Jewish and non-Jewish alike.

After years following the circuitous paths of theatrical liberalism, however, I realize now that the power of Lau-Lavie's performance resided not only in the actions he performed on the stage but also in the embrace of contradiction that his drag performance implied. For more than a century, American Jews have created distinctively Jewish responses to the fundamental questions of liberalism and modernity. Combining Judaic views on action, individual identity, and communal obligation with Protestant Enlightenment ideas about individual freedom, they redefined the boundaries and potential of American liberalism for multiple generations. At the same time, theatrical liberalism has at its heart a healthy suspicion of the very values it promotes, a suspicion that fuels ongoing debates about freedom and obligation, sincerity and authenticity, theatricality and idolatry. From the multiplicity of Jacob, who is both devious and straightforward, both *yakov* and *ish tam*, to the dual selves of Jakie Rabinowitz and Jack Robin, from the technical brilliance of Belasco to the naturalist authenticity of Strasberg, from the anarchic theatricality of Abie Hoffman to the prescriptive restraint of Cynthia Ozick, theatrical liberalism offers not a single definition of a Jewish liberal self but rather the debate itself as the fundamental fact of Jewish liberalism. Walt Whitman celebrated American liberalism in *Leaves of Grass* by embracing contradiction: "I am large," he wrote, "I contain multitudes." Similarly, in a famous Talmudic legend, a debate between the followers of Shammai and the followers of Hillel is resolved by a voice from heaven, which insists that Jewish tradition also contains multitudes: "*both* these *and* these are the words of the living God."[4] The acceptance of multiple viewpoints does not, however, obviate the need for action, as Nathan Zuckerman feared. The heavenly voice goes on to declare that the law, in this case, sides with Hillel. But debate itself, which is ordained by God, continues. To live in a pluralist society is to live with contradictions. Theatrical liberalism offers a way to do just this, insisting on actions which change the world but never shut down the debate. It is too soon to predict the fate of this kind of secular Judaism in the twenty-first century. But one element of it seems likely to persist. The debate—and the show—must go on.

NOTES

EPIGRAPH

  1. Abraham Joshua Heschel, "The Science of Deeds," in *God in Search of Man* (New York: Farrar, Straus and Giroux, reprint, 1976), 283.

  2. David Belasco, "Acting as a Science," in *Actors on Acting*, ed. Toby Cole and Helen Krich Chinoy (New York: Crown Publishers, 1970), 579.

  3. Edna Ferber, *A Peculiar Treasure* (New York: Lancer Books, 1938, 1961), 12.

NOTES TO SETTING THE STAGE

  1. See the Library of Congress website on "God Bless America," http://lcweb2.loc.gov/diglib/ihas/loc.natlib.ihas.200000007/default.html.

  2. As Richard Corliss wrote in *Time* magazine on December 24, 2001, in "That Old Christmas Feeling: Irving America" [http://www.time.com/time/sampler/article/0,8599,189846,00.html]:

> On the afternoon of September 11, 2001, a group of Senators and Congressmen stood on the Capitol steps and sang that something-more-than-a-song. Two nights later, when Broadway turned its lights back on, the casts of "The Producers" and other shows led theatergoers in renditions of the same song. The next day, at an official requiem at the National Cathedral in Washington, it was played by the U.S. Army Orchestra. The following Monday, to mark the reopening of the New York Stock Exchange, New York Governor George Pataki and Mayor Rudolph Giuliani joined traders in singing it. That evening, as major league baseball games resumed around the country, it replaced "Take Me Out to the Ballgame" as the theme song of the seventh-inning stretch. Over the next weeks, everyone—Celine Dion, Marc Anthony, N.Y.P.D. officer Daniel Rodriguez, the whole country—sang "God Bless America."

  3. Berlin decided not to use the song in the 1918 show, but "God Bless America" did finally make it into a musical when *Yip, Yip, Yaphank* was reconceived in 1943 as the patriotic Hollywood musical *This Is the Army*.

  4. See, for example, Michael Freedland, *A Salute to Irving Berlin* (London: W. H. Allen, 1986), Laurence Bergreen, *As Thousands Cheer* (New York: Viking, 1990), especially pp. 12 and 410; and Philip Furia's *Irving Berlin* (New York: Schirmer Books, 1998), 11. For an in-depth treatise on Berlin's background and talent, see Jeffrey Magee, *Irving Berlin's American Musical Theater* (New York: Oxford

University Press, 2012*)*. Max I. Dimont's *The Jews in America: The Roots, History and Destiny of American Jews* (New York: Simon and Schuster, 1978); Howard M. Sachar's *A History of the Jews in America* (New York: Random House, 1992), 353–373; and Irving Howe's *World of Our Fathers* (New York: Schocken Books, 1976) offer examples of the rags-to-riches legends of Jewish popular entertainers.

5. The first books to appear on Jews and entertainment in America tended to offer a celebration of the contributions of Jews to American culture or an anxious commentary on the so-called power of Jews to dictate the direction of American mass culture. See Lester D. Friedman, *The Jewish Image in American Film* (Secaucus, NJ: Citadel Press, 1987); Patricia D. Erens, *The Jew in American Cinema* (Bloomington: Indiana University Press, 1984); and the articles in Sarah Blacher Cohen, ed., *From Hester Street to Hollywood* (Bloomington: Indiana University Press, 1983). The next generation of scholars and journalists built on these early studies, focusing on why Jews were drawn to particular art and media forms, how these forms aided in acculturation, and why Jews were able to create culture that spoke so successfully to the American public. My book *Making Americans: Jews and the Broadway Musical* (Cambridge, MA: Harvard University Press, 2004), falls into this category. See also Jeffrey Melnick, *A Right to Sing the Blues: African Americans, Jews, and American Popular Song* (Cambridge, MA: Harvard University Press, 1999); Michael Rogin, *Blackface, White Noise: Jewish Immigrants in the Hollywood Melting Pot* (Berkeley: University of California Press, 1996); Neal Gabler, *An Empire of Their Own: How the Jews Invented Hollywood* (New York: Doubleday, 1989); Paul Buhle, ed., *Jews and American Popular Culture* (Westport, CT: Praeger, 2007); Stephen Whitfield, *In Search of American Jewish Culture* (Hanover, NH: Brandeis University Press, 1999); Henry Bial, *Acting Jewish: Negotiating Ethnicity on the American Stage and Screen* (Ann Arbor: University of Michigan Press, 2005); Donald Weber, *Haunted in the New World: Jewish American Culture from Cahan to the Goldbergs* (Bloomington: Indiana University Press, 2005); J. Hoberman and Jeffery Shandler, *Entertaining America: Jews, Movies, and Broadcasting* (Princeton: Princeton University Press, 2003); and Vincent Brooks, *You Should See Yourself: Jewish Identity in Post-Modern American Culture* (New Brunswick, NJ: Rutgers University Press, 2006).

6. See Courtney Bender and Pamela Klassen's introduction to *After Pluralism,* (New York: Columbia University Press, 2011).

7. This view of secularization held sway for nearly a century. Max Weber first formulated a version of the secularization thesis, which he described as the "disenchantment of the world." He did not deny the shaping power of religious thought on secular life—his famous argument about the Protestant work ethic asserted it—but he noted the decline in religious practice and belief in modern Western society. Max Weber, *The Protestant Ethic and the Spirit of Capitalism* (New York: Norton, 2009). More recently, Peter Berger defined secularization as the key feature of modern life in his 1967 work *The Sacred Canopy: Elements of a Sociological Theory of Religion* (New York: Anchor Books, 1991). See Jose

Casanova, *Public Religions in the Modern World* (Chicago: University of Chicago Press, 1994), chap. 1, for a nuanced history of the rise and fall of this thesis.

8. Janet Jakobsen, "Ethics After Pluralism," in Bender and Klassen, *After Pluralism,* 31–58.

9. Jonathan Z. Smith, "Religion, Religions, Religious," in *Critical Terms for Religious Studies,* ed. Mark C. Taylor (Chicago: University of Chicago Press, 1998), 269. See also Talal Asad, *Genealogies of Religion* (Baltimore: Johns Hopkins University Press, 1993).

10. Tomoko Masuzawa, *The Invention of World Religions, or, How European Universalism Was Preserved in the Language of Pluralism and Diversity* (Chicago: University of Chicago Press, 2005). From this line of argument, a number of post-colonial critiques of the progressive nature of secularization have emerged. See Talal Asad, *Formations of the Secular: Christianity, Islam, Modernity* (Stanford, CA: Stanford University Press, 2003); and Wendy Brown, *Regulating Aversion: Tolerance in the Age of Identity and Empire* (Princeton: Princeton University Press, 2006).

11. Robert J. Baird, "Late Secularism," *Social Text* 18 no. 3 (2000): 128.

12. Janet R. Jakobsen with Ann Pellegrini, "World Secularisms at the Millenium: Introduction," *Social Text* 18 no. 3 (2000): 8.

13. Laura Levitt, "Impossible Assimilations, American Liberalism, and Jewish Difference: Revisiting Jewish Secularism," *American Quarterly* 59 no.3 (2007): 811–812.

14. Israel Friedlaender, *Past and Present* (Cincinnati: Ark Pub. Co, 1919), 267. Quoted in Mordecai Kaplan, *Judaism as a Civilization* (New York: Macmillan, 1934), vii.

15. Levitt, "Impossible Assimilations," 828. Other scholars of Jewish secularization such as Naomi Seidman and David Biale argue that Eastern European Jews resisted (or at least were ambivalent about) a secularization that so circumscribed religious identity, and they point to aspects of Eastern European Jewish literary and political culture—Hebraic, Zionist, Yiddish, Socialist—as sites of this resistance. Seidman notes that Jewish secularization occurred largely in response to external forces—the political and cultural position of Jews in European society—rather than as a response to an internal crisis of faith, as was the case for Protestants. This resulted in a change in practice rather than belief: the disintegration of religious practice among modernizing Jews and the assimilation of those same Jews, via new practices, habits, and modes of self-presentation, into the surrounding Christian community. Seidman, "Secularization and Sexuality: Theorizing the Erotic Transformation of Ashkenaz," a pre-circulated paper for a session on "Secularization and Sexuality" at the annual meeting of the Association for Jewish Studies, December 17, 2007; and David Biale, *Not in the Heavens* (Princeton: Princeton University Press, 2011).

16. This impulse was not limited to popular culture. Other arenas for this type of secular Jewish creativity include constitutional law and progressive politics

(especially the areas of civil rights, labor, environmental concerns, and social welfare). While these are not the subject of this study, it would be fascinating to see how Jewish involvement in these areas is similarly shaped by the nature of Jewish secularism.

17. Tracy Fessenden laid the foundation for such narratives by articulating the Protestant foundations of secular American literary culture against which these other secularisms have defined themselves. *Culture and Redemption: Religion, the Secular, and American Literature* (Princeton: Princeton University Press, 2007).

18. Sacvan Bercovitch, *The Puritan Origins of the American Self* (New Haven: Yale University Press, 1975).

19. Jeffrey Stout, *Democracy and Tradition* (Princeton: Princeton University Press, 2004), 19.

20. Ibid. In chap. 2, "Race and Nation," Stout describes blues spirituality. While he is more interested in its relationship to 1960s Black Nationalism, his ideas are also helpful for understanding an earlier moment in the development of American liberal culture.

21. While some of these same elements can be found in avant-garde and high culture American and Jewish works, we focus our attention almost exclusively on *popular* culture, works that were designed to appeal to a large mass of consumers, to meet the demands of "show business."

22. For a definition of "habitus," see Pierre Bourdieu, *Distinction: A Social Critique of the Judgement of Taste* (Cambridge, MA: Harvard University Press, 1984), chap. 3.

NOTES TO CHAPTER 1

1. See, for example, Marline Otte, *Jewish Identities in German Popular Entertainment, 1890-1933* (Cambridge: Cambridge University Press, 2006); Anna Shternshis, *Soviet and Kosher: Jewish Popular Culture in the Soviet Union* (Bloomington: Indiana University Press, 2006); Yuri Slezkine, *The Jewish Century* (Princeton: Princeton University Press, 2004); and Jon Stratton, *Coming Out Jewish* (London: Routledge, 2000).

2. See Joel Berkowitz, "Introduction," in *Yiddish Theater: New Approaches* (Oxford: Littman Library of Jewish Civilization, 2003), 3.

3. *Encyclopaedia Judaica*, 2nd ed., ed. Michael Berenbaum and Fred Skolnik, vol. 19 (Detroit: Macmillan Reference USA, 2007), 669–685, s.v. "Theater." See also Nahma Sandrow, *Vagabond Stars: World History of Yiddish Theater* (Syracuse: Syracuse University Press, 1995). On the purim-shpiel, see Elliot Horowitz, *Reckless Rites: Purim and the Legacy of Jewish Violence* (Princeton: Princeton University Press, 2006), chap. 9.

4. See Joshua Levinson, "Atlet Ha-Emunah: Alilot Damim ve-Alilot Medumot" ("The Athlete of Piety: Fatal Fictions in Rabbinic Literature," *Tarbiz* 68 [1999]: 61–86), especially 69, nn. 41–43.

5. The Talmud on Psalm 1:1 makes the connection between *moshav leytzim* and the theater. See *Masechet Avodah Zera*, 18b.

6. See Tosefta *Masechet Avodah Zera*, chap. 2, halachot 5–7, and Talmud Bavli *Masechet Avodah Zera* 16a, 18a.

7. See Katharine B. Free's article "Thespis and Moses," in Shimon Levy, ed., *Theater and Holy Script* (Brighton: Sussex Academic Press, 1999), 149–157.

8. *Sifre Aharei Mot*, an early first-century commentary, sec. 9, vv. 8 and 9.

9. Rambam, *Mishneh Torah*, "Avodat Cochavim," chap. 11, halacha 1.

10. There were some exceptions to this law (doctors, servants to the king [Rambam], etc.) but no mention is made of actors in this context in *Shulchan Aruch* or in other texts of the period.

11. *Shulchan Aruch*, Even Ha'Ezer, chap. 21:1.

12. Talmud Bavli *Masechet Nazir* 58b; see also Rashi's and Ibn Ezra's commentary on this verse in the Torah (Devarim 22:5).

13. See the thirteenth-century Italian biblical commentator Rekanaty on Devarim 22:5. This kabbalistic idea concerns the notion that man is the giver of light (*mashpia*) and women are receivers (*mekabelet*). If man puts on a woman's clothes, he turns the mashpia into a mekabelet, with the result that his soul may become confused in the process of reincarnation (*gilgul*). While some commentators—including Rashi, the most important of all medieval rabbinic commentators—assert that as long as the cross-dressing is not intended for the purposes of breaking sexual laws, it is not prohibited, the general attitude seems to be one of extreme caution.

14. *Shulchan Aruch*, Orach Hayyim 696, v. 8.

15. See Ahuva Belkin, "Masks and Disguises as an Expression of Anarchy," in *Theater and Holy Script,* ed. Shimon Levy (Brighton: Sussex Academic Press, 1999), 210.

16. One source connects Esau's anger at Jacob for stealing his blessing, and the later punishment of the evil Haman (by the prophet Elijah, who, according to midrash, dressed as a Persian in order to bring about Haman's death) in the Purim story. The commentator notes that as both Esau and the prophet Elijah "wore masks" or disguised their feelings in order to prevent greater evil, therefore we too wear masks on Purim. See Siach Yitzchak, *She'elot v't'shuvot,* Responsa 380.

17. See Shmuel Feiner, *The Jewish Enlightenment* (Philadelphia: University of Pennsylvania Press, 2002). Specific examples include Isaac Euchel's "A Family Portrait" and Aaron Wolfsohn's "Frivolity and Bigotry," both described in Israel Zinberg, *History of Jewish Literature,* vol. 8 (Cleveland: Case Western University Press, 1972–78), chap. 5.

18. Hutchins Hapgood, *The Spirit of the Ghetto*, rev. ed. (New York: Schocken Books, 1966), 126.

19. Nahma Sandrow, *Vagabond Stars*, 87.

20. Gershom Scholem, "Redemption through Sin," in *The Messianic Idea in Judaism* (New York: Schocken, 1971), 78–141.

21. Judah Leib Gordon, "For Whom Do I Toil?" reprinted in Paul Mendes-Flohr and Jehuda Reinharz, eds., *The Jew in the Modern World: A Documentary History* (New York: Oxford University Press, 1980), 315.

22. See Rashi's commentary on Gen 32:29: "It shall no longer be said that the blessings came to you through trickery and deceit" (*akavah*—referring again to Jacob's name), "but with nobility and openness."

23. Rashi is the acronym for Rabbi Shlomo Yitzhak, a medieval French rabbi, and author of the first and most authoritative comprehensive commentaries on the Talmud and the Hebrew Bible. So important is Rashi's commentary that it is generally included alongside the original text in published versions of these works, and children are expected to learn Rashi as they learn Torah and Talmud. Rashi refers here to *Genesis Rabbah* 78:4.

24. He cites *Genesis Rabbah* (a Talmud-era midrashic commentary) and then Taanit 29b. The Zohar, which explicitly connects Jacob with the snake in a number of places indicates, "The Garden of Eden came in with Jacob, for it is a field of holy apples."

25. Since death had not been introduced, this is Pirkei d'Rabbi Eliezer's explanation for how Adam and Even came to wear animal skins (Gen. 3:21).

26. So miraculous was this clothing that, according to another midrash, despite the fact that Esau was large and Jacob was small, when Jacob put on the clothing, it actually fit him perfectly. By this miracle, Rebekah knew that she was doing the right thing.

27. See also the passage from Jeremiah (9:3–4) mentioned earlier in which Jacob's behavior is linked not only to the deception of his father but to the later behavior of the Israelites, which Jeremiah sees as causing the destruction of the Temple.

28. An interesting comparison is made in another early midrashic source (*Esther Rabbah* 8:1) between the cries of Esau, upon learning he has lost the blessing, and the cries of Esther's uncle Mordecai, upon learning that the king has agreed to Haman's request to kill the Jews. Esau's scream was so full of anguish that it echoed through the ages, indicating God's unwillingness to forgive Jacob's sin, until the days of Mordecai, when God almost allows the Jews to be destroyed in Shushan. Only Esther's bravery assuages God's anger and saves the Jews. Jacob's sin of performance is redeemed by Esther, yet another consummate performer and the source of later Jewish theatrical traditions.

29. The rabbis of the Talmud are notoriously ahistorical. Needless to say, Torah academies did not actually exist in the time of Jacob; the Torah itself would not be given to the Jews until hundreds of years later, in the time of Moses.

30. See *Tanchuma Toledot Rabbah* 63:8 for the first and *Midrash Rabbah* for the second.

31. A medieval Spanish scholar, Rabbeinu Behaye also parses Jacob's sentence carefully in order to excuse him, but uses slightly different logic. If Jacob had simply said, "I am Esau," Behaye argues, he would have lied. But when he adds *bechorecha*, meaning "the first born," or "the one who deserves the birthright," he makes his statement true. Jacob is not representing Esau, he is representing the birthright, and because the birthright *is* his by virtue of the prophecy revealed to Rebekah, Jacob is telling the truth.

32. The shrewdness to "pretend to be what one was not" in order to survive a hostile world was, because of the particular historical circumstances Jews faced, understood by many memoirists and historians to be essential. See Mary Antin's comments in her memoir *The Promised Land*: "In your father's parlor hung a large colored portrait of Alexander III. The Czar was a cruel tyrant,—oh, it was whispered when doors were locked and shutters tightly barred, at night,—he was a Titus, a Haman, a sworn foe of all Jews,—and yet his portrait was seen in a place of honor in your father's house. You knew why. It looked well when police or government officers came on business. . . . 'It is a false world,' you heard, and you knew it was so, looking at the Czar's portrait . . . 'Never tell a police officer the truth,' was another saying, and you knew it was good advice." *The Promised Land* (Princeton: Princeton University Press, 1985), 18, 20.

33. Harold Bloom and David Rosenberg, *The Book of J* (New York: Grove Weidenfeld, 1990), 211.

34. Emanuel Levinas, *Nine Talmudic Readings*, trans. Annette Aronowicz (Bloomington: Indiana University Press, 1990), 30–50.

35. Avivah Gottlieb Zornberg, *Genesis: The Beginning of Desire* (Philadelphia: Jewish Publication Society, 1995), 144–179.

36. Lionel Trilling, *Sincerity and Authenticity* (Cambridge, MA: Harvard University Press, 1972).

37. Zornberg cites both Or Ha-haim and Sefat Emet in *Genesis*, 172.

38. The internal quote is from Nietzsche, *The Birth of Tragedy*, whom Zornberg cites as expressing a view of performance anathema to Christian dogma (Nietzsche continues: "which is *only* and will be only moral, and which, with its absolute standards for instance, its truthfulness of God, relegates—that is, disowns, convicts, condemns—art, all art, to the realm of *falsehood*"). See Zornberg, 173 and n. 79. Zornberg makes Nietzsche the unlikely voice of Jewish consciousness here.

NOTES TO CHAPTER 2

1. Moshe Leib-Halpern, *Freiheit*, April 7, 1922, quoted in Irving Howe and Kenneth Libo, *World of Our Fathers* (New York: Harcourt Brace Jovanovich, 1976), 483.

2. Warren Susman, "'Personality' and the Making of Twentieth-Century Culture," in *Culture as History* (Washington, DC: Smithsonian Institution Press, 2003), 271–285. Susman is one of a number of historians who have noted a shift in definitions of the American self in this period from "character" to "personality." See also Richard Rabinowitz, *The Spiritual Self in Everyday Life* (Boston: Northeastern University Press, 1989); Karen Halttunen, *Confidence Men and Painted Women: A Study of Middle-Class Culture in America 1830–1870* (New Haven: Yale University Press, 1982); and Alan Trachtenberg, *The Incorporation of America: Culture and Society in the Gilded Age* (New York: Hill & Wang, 1982). Most argue that economic changes led to this development; Rabinowitz and Haltunnen also look to changes in the American religious landscape. Few note the impact of

immigrant cultures, and since most of them focus on the nineteenth century, they don't generally engage with the particular qualities of Judaism (which were more pronounced in American culture with the large immigration at the turn of the twentieth century) that make this encounter particularly productive of change.

3. *The Jazz Singer* was produced on Broadway by Sam H. Harris and had a successful run of 303 performances with George Jessel in the lead role. It appeared as a film a year later, produced by Warner Brothers, directed by Alan Crosland, and featuring the vaudeville star Al Jolson. Warner Brothers chose this story to introduce their new synchronized sound technology, and its success is partially attributable to its status as the first talking picture. The film has been the subject of intense scholarly interest because of its use of blackface and the connections it draws between blacks and immigrant Jews. See Most, *Making Americans* (Cambridge: Harvard University Press, 2004), 32–39. See also Michael Rogin *Blackface, White Noise* (Berkeley: University of California Press, 1996); Matthew Frye Jacobson, *Whiteness of a Different Color* (Cambridge, MA: Harvard University Press, 1998); and W. T. Lhamon, *Raising Cain* (Cambridge, MA: Harvard University Press, 1998).

4. Samson Raphaelson, *The Jazz Singer* (New York: Brentano's, 1925), 51. Hereafter cited in text.

5. These battles were most often taken up by the orthodox Christians that Jeffrey Stout describes, rather than the Emersonian liberal Protestants. On theater censorship battles and religious involvement in the establishment of the Production Code, see James M. Skinner, *The Cross and the Cinema* (Westport, CT: Praeger, 1993); Robert K. Johnston, *Reel Spirituality* (Grand Rapids, MI: Baker Academic, 2006); Gregory D. Black, *Hollywood Censored* (Cambridge: Cambridge University Press, 1994); Frank Walsh, *Sin and Censorship* (New Haven: Yale University Press, 1996); and Francis G. Couvares, ed., *Movie Censorship and American Culture* (Amherst: University of Massachusetts Press, 2006). On anti-Semitism and censorship, see Steven Alan Carr, *Hollywood and Anti-Semitism* (New York: Cambridge University Press, 2001).

6. Jonas Barish, *The Antitheatrical Prejudice* (Berkeley: University of California Press, 1981), 1. Emphasis in original. For an illuminating discussion of Barish's notion of anti-theatricality, see introduction to *Against Theater: Creative Destructions on the Modernist Stage,* ed. Alan Ackerman and Martin Puchner (New York: Palgrave, 2006).

7. See Barish, *The Antitheatrical Prejudice,* chap. 4, 80–131.

8. Cited in ibid., 92. Emphasis in original.

9. Michael T. Gilmore, "The Literature of the Revolutionary and Early National Periods," in *Cambridge History of American Literature,* vol. 1, *1590–1820,* ed. Sacvan Bercovitch, 577.

10. Ibid., 578.

11. Anthologized in *The Jews of the United States, 1790–1840: A Documentary History,* vol. 2. ed. Joseph L. Blau and Salo W. Baron (New York: Columbia University Press, 1963), 405–409.

12. See Alan Ackerman, *The Portable Theater* (Baltimore: Johns Hopkins University Press, 1999).

13. *The Life of P. T. Barnum: Written by Himself*. Originally published 1855. (Champaign: University of Illinois Press, 2000).

14. See Ackerman, *Portable Theater* for an extended discussion of anti-theatricality in the stories by Whitman and Alcott.

15. Louisa May Alcott, *Work: A Story of Experience* (Boston: Roberts Brothers, 1873); and Anna Cora Mowatt *Autobiography of an Actress; or, Eight Years on the Stage* (Boston: Ticknor, Reed, and Fields, 1853). By the later nineteenth century, attitudes toward actors began to soften, but it was not until the early twentieth century that actors actually became a kind of model for ambitious young Americans to emulate. See Karen Halttunen, *Confidence Men and Painted Women* (New Haven: Yale University Press, 1986).

16. *The Chorus Lady,* by James Forbes (1907) [Accessed through Chadwick website, University of Toronto library]: http://gateway.proquest.com.myaccess.library. utoronto.ca/openurl/openurl?ctx_ver=Z39.88-2003&xri:pqil:res_ver=0.2&r es_id=xri:lion-us&rft_id=xri:lion:ft:dr:Z000781807:0
Cambridge, ProQuest Information and Learning, 2003>

17. *Rollo's Wild Oats,* by Clare Beecher Kummer (1920) [Accessed through U of T library website]: http://solomon.wodr.alexanderstreet.com.myaccess.library. utoronto.ca/cgi-bin/asp/philo/navigate.pl?wodr.196. Rollo's Wild Oat Electronic Edition by Alexander Street Press, L.L.C., 2012 Website: North American Women's Drama. Produced in collaboration with the University of Chicago. See also *The Torch Bearers* (1922), by George Kelly, and *The Little Clown* (1918) by Avery Hopwood.

18. As Tracy Fessenden shows, anti-Catholic bias in nineteenth-century American literature lies beneath much of this anti-theatricality. It is interesting, therefore, that by the early twentieth century, a convent could serve as a refuge from the theater. *Culture and Redemption*, chap. 3.

19. Barish, *The Antitheatrical Prejudice*, 467.

20. Friedrich Nietzsche, *The Gay Science*, ed. Bernard Williams, trans. Josefine Nauckhoff (Cambridge: Cambridge University Press, 2001), 226. For a discussion of theatricality and anti-theatricality in the late nineteenth and early twentieth centuries, especially as articulated by Nietszche, see Martin Puchner, *Stage Fright: Modernism, Anti-theatricality, and Drama* (Baltimore: Johns Hopkins University Press, 2002).

21. The rights of women and blacks were under consideration at the same time. See Lynn Hunt, *Politics, Culture, and Class in the French Revolution* (Berkeley: University of California Press, 1984).

22. The play premiered in New York in 1895 and was revived on Broadway in 1905, 1915, and 1921.

23. See Sue Lloyd, *The Man Who Was Cyrano* (Bloomington, IN: Unlimited Publishing, 2002) for background on Rostand. For a discussion of the rise of the

director in the nineteenth century, especially in relation to *Trilby* and *Cyrano de Bergerac*, see Larry Switzky, "Hearing Double: Acousmatic Authority and the Rise of the Theatre Director." *Modern Drama* 54, no. 2 (2011): 216–243.

24. The sheer number of "backstage" titles from the period is staggering. Think of *The Jazz Singer, Show Boat, The Royal Family, Stage Door, 42nd Street, Twentieth Century, On Your Toes, Babes in Arms, Annie Get Your Gun, A Night at the Opera, Jumbo, Pal Joey, Shall We Dance,* and *Holiday Inn,* to name only a few of the most memorable ones.

25. *Dames* was produced by Warner Brothers, directed by Ray Enright, with musical numbers by Busby Berkeley; it starred Warners regulars Ruby Keeler, Dick Powell, and Joan Blondell.

26. Edna Ferber and George S. Kaufman, *Stage Door*, in *Kaufman & Co: Broadway Comedies* (New York: Library of America [Penguin], 2004), 626. *Stage Door* opened at the Music Box Theater in New York in October 1936, produced by Sam H. Harris and directed by George S. Kaufman. It had a successful run of 189 performances. George S. Kaufman, a Jew from Pittsburgh, was one of the pre-eminent writers of Broadway and Hollywood comedies during the late 1920s and 1930s. He wrote satirical musicals with the Gershwins and madcap screenplays for the Marx Brothers as well as collaborations with Edna Ferber and Moss Hart. His many successful plays were nearly always about actors, the theater, and/or theatricality. Edna Ferber, a Jew from Michigan, was one of the most popular writers of her day, with numerous short stories, popular novels, and plays to her name (including her most successful, *Show Boat)*. Ferber was likewise fascinated by the theater from an early age, as she notes in her memoir *A Peculiar Treasure*: "certainly I have been stage-struck all my life" (New York: Lancer Books, 1938, 1961, 27).

27. *Twentieth Century* was co-written by Ben Hecht, Jewish screenwriter and the author of a number of overtly Jewish and Zionist novels and essays (including *A Jew in Love,* 1931*)* and Charles MacArthur, son of a Baptist minister. Hecht and MacArthur first wrote a play version, loosely based on an earlier play by Charles Bruce Millholland titled *Napoleon of Broadway,* and then the screenplay. The film was directed by Howard Hawks, produced by Columbia Pictures in 1934 starring John Barrymore and Carole Lombard. Another extremely successful collaboration between Edna Ferber and George S. Kaufman, *The Royal Family* opened in 1927, produced by Jed Harris, and ran for a remarkable 345 performances.

28. *Babes in Arms,* act 1, sc. 1, p 16. *Babes in Arms* was written by Richard Rodgers and Lorenz Hart, who had already been an extremely successful musical comedy team for more than ten years when this play was produced in 1937; the show ran for 289 performances. Both Rodgers and Hart were second generation Jews of German background.

29. Jerome Kern and Oscar Hammerstein, like Rodgers, Hart, and Ferber, were of second-generation German Jewish descent (although Hammerstein was only

half-Jewish). Kern and Hammerstein had a successful partnership in the 1920s and both also worked with other well-known writers and composers (Kern with Harbach and Hammerstein with Rodgers). *Show Boat* has long been considered groundbreaking in the history of the American musical, both for its form, which integrated songs and story more completely than many other musicals of its time, and for its progressive (albeit controversial) racial politics. The play was a commercial success (running for an unprecedented 572 performances in its first incarnation) and has had countless revivals on screen and stage since then.

30. Edna Ferber, *Show Boat* (New York: Penguin, 1926, 1994), 25. Hereafter cited in text.

31. *Show Boat,* act 1, sc. 1, p. 12, original 1927 typescript located in the Billy Rose Theater Collection, New York Public Library for the Performing Arts. Notation on the script that it was printed by the Rialto Mimeographing and Typing Service Bureau Inc. 1501 Broadway, New York, NY, and was a gift to the NYPL from Miss Anna Hill Johnstone.

32. On jazz as a style as much as a type of music, see David Savran, *Highbrow/Lowdown: Theater, Jazz and the Making of the New Middle Class* (Ann Arbor: University of Michigan Press, 2009).

33. See this URL: http://www.youtube.com/watch?v=akAEIW3rmvQ.

34. David Belasco (1853–1931), was a prolific and influential Jewish American playwright, director and producer. Two of his plays, *Madame Butterfly* and *The Girl of the Golden West*, were adapted by Puccini into operas, and more than forty of Belasco's other stage works were made into films.

35. *My Fair Lady* includes a similar scene, in which Henry Higgins teaches Eliza how to perform the part of a lady. Moss Hart, the director of *My Fair Lady* on Broadway, was said to have taught Julie Andrews to *be* Julie Andrews, in much the same way that Jaffe teaches Mildred Plotka to become Lily Garland (*Twentieth Century*), in a weekend-long marathon of technical training. Steven Bach, *Dazzler: The Life and Times of Moss Hart* (New York: Knopf, 2001), 357.

36. Babylonian Talmud, Ketubot 48a.

37. Interestingly, Jaffe is explicitly linked with Jewish theatricality (albeit in a negative way) when Lily accuses him of trying to be her "Svengali." John Barrymore, who played Jaffe, had appeared in the leading role in the Warner Brothers film *Svengali* only three years earlier (1931).

38. Abraham Joshua Heschel, *God in Search of Man* (New York: Farrar, Straus and Giroux, 1955), 345. Hereafter cited in text. Heschel was born in Warsaw, received higher education in Berlin, and immigrated to the United States in 1940 to escape the Nazis. In 1945 he became a professor of Ethics and Mysticism at the Jewish Theological Seminary in New York, where he remained until his death in 1972. Heschel is considered one of the most important Jewish theologians of the twentieth century. In addition to writing countless works of Jewish thought, Heschel also became a passionate participant in the American civil rights movement.

39. See Saba Mahmood, *Politics of Piety: The Islamic Revival and the Feminist Subject* (Princeton: Princeton University Press, 2005) for a discussion of the relationship between practice, ethics, and faith in the worldview of Muslim women.

40. Moses Mendelssohn, *Jerusalem, or, On Religious Power and Judaism*, trans. Allan Arkush (1783; repr., Hanover, NH: University Press of New England, 1983), 100. Emphasis in original.

41. Heschel takes exception to Mendelssohn's single-minded focus on action. For Heschel, intention does matter, and he cautions against interpreting Judaism as exclusively devoted to law. But the relationship of faith (or intention) to action is the issue here. For Mendelssohn and Heschel both, action is a key to understanding (and for Heschel, achieving) Jewish faith. See Heschel, *God in Search of Man,* 320–322.

42. Ex. 24:7 (author's translation).

43. See Heschel, *God in Search of Man*, 281. Other relevant commentaries on this text include a compilation of well-known midrashim on Exodus 24:7, detailed in Louis Ginzberg, *Legends of the Jews*, 2nd ed., trans. from the German by Henrietta Szold, 1909–1938 (Philadelphia: Jewish Publication Society, 2003), 593. Also see Talmud Bavli, Tractate Shabbat, 88a; Talmud Bavli, Tractate Kiddushin, 40b; and on the meaning of "sh'ma" (hearing), see also *Sefer Abudarham* (1340), "Dinay Kriat Sh'ma."

44. Sheldon Harnick, "Tradition," *Fiddler on the Roof* (New York: Limelight Editions, 2000), 2.

45. John Dewey, *A Common Faith* (New Haven: Yale University Press, 1934), 60.

46. The American religious landscape that Jewish immigrants encountered upon their arrival in America was complex and varied. For most Jewish immigrants, the relevant distinction was between "Christian" and "Jewish," with "Christian" sometimes further broken down into Protestant and Catholic. While Jewish immigrants may not have been fully aware of the differences among the many Protestant sects and churches that dotted the American landscape, it was clear that a certain mainline Protestant majority enjoyed political, financial, and cultural power in American society and were therefore the obvious model for those assimilating to American culture. American Roman Catholics like the Poles, Irish, and Italians, who also shared outsider status for much of the early twentieth century, would not have provided such a model and neither did the emerging Pentecostal churches, which, while highly theatrical, appealed to a rural population also assumed to be nativist. Most of the first -and second-generation Jewish writers and composers studied here were shaped by the values of the Protestant Social Gospel that were present in the discourse of American public schools, settlement houses, and social welfare movements located in the major cities of New York and Chicago. See Benny Kraut, "Jewish Survival in Protestant America," in *Minority Faiths and the American Protestant Mainstream,* ed. Jonathan D. Sarna, (Urbana: University of Illinois Press, 1998), 15–60.

47. This is not to say that Jews were not also extremely protective of the privacy rights guaranteed by the First Amendment. To recent immigrants, the freedoms

promised by the Constitution appeared to far outweigh the sacrifices inherent in them. Indeed, it was Louis D. Brandeis, the first Jewish Supreme Court justice, who coined the term "right to privacy."

48. The Hasidic movement emerged in the early modern period partially to protest this more scholarly approach to action, arguing instead for ecstatic, spontaneous expressions of faith, often expressed through song and dance. See Moshe Idel, *Hasidism: Between Ecstasy and Magic* (Albany: SUNY Press, 1995).

49. Richard Rodgers and Oscar Hammerstein, *The King and I,* in *Six Plays By Rodgers and Hammerstein* (New York: Random House, 1955), 373. See my analysis of this musical in *Making Americans: Jews and the Broadway Musical* (Cambridge, MA: Harvard University Press, 2004), 183–196.

50. *Show Boat,* act 1, sc. 4.

51. For further interpretations of this scene, and of the function of race in the film more generally, see Lauren Berlant, "Pax Americana: The Case of *Show Boat,*" in *Cultural Institutions of the Novel,* ed. Deidre Lynch and William B. Warner (Durham, NC: Duke University Press, 1997), 399–422; Linda Williams, *Playing the Race Card: Melodramas of Black and White from Uncle Tom to O. J. Simpson* (Princeton: Princeton University Press, 2002), chap. 4; and Todd Decker, *Show Boat: Performing Race in an American Musical* (Oxford University Press, 2013, forthcoming), which deals extensively with this subject.

52. See Steven Alan Carr, *Hollywood and Anti-Semitism* (New York: Cambridge University Press, 2001).

53. This represented a certain amount of wish-fulfillment on the part of the studio, which was in a constant battle with orthodox Protestant and Catholic critics over the moral values expressed in Hollywood movies, a battle that ended with the producers adopting a self-imposed Production Code. See Gregory D. Black, *Hollywood Censored: Morality Codes, Catholics, and the Movies* (New York: Cambridge University Press, 1994).

54. Lubitsch and the other Jewish artists were not the first to celebrate artifice in this way. Oscar Wilde is his obvious forebear, and Lubitsch was a huge fan of Wilde's (he made a particularly celebrated film of *Lady Windermere's Fan*). Lubitsch is distinctive in his ability to bring this sensibility to a place—America—which Wilde considered incapable of the kind of ironic stance necessary to appreciate it.

55. *A Funny Thing Happened on the Way to the Forum* premiered in 1962 and ran for 964 performances. The music and lyrics are by Stephen Sondheim, the book by Bert Shevelove and Larry Gelbart; all three were Jewish.

56. *A Funny Thing Happened on the Way to the Forum.* Music and lyrics by Stephen Sondheim; book by Burt Shevelove and Larry Gelbart (New York: Dodd, Mead, 1985), 31–32.

57. The exception, of course, was the Zionists, who argued not only for a national definition of Jews but for a geographical, political nation-state as well.

58. See Matthew Jacobson, *Whiteness of a Different Color: European Immigrants and the Alchemy of Race* (Cambridge, MA: Harvard University Press, 1998);

Karen Brodkin, *How Jews Became White Folks and What That Says About Race in America* (New Brunswick, NJ: Rutgers University Press, 1999); and Eric L. Goldstein, *The Price of Whiteness: Jews, Race and American Identity* (Princeton: Princeton University Press, 2007).

59. *The Jazz Singer* is one of many examples of popular culture from the early twentieth century that refers to Jews as a race. Jakie characterizes the pull he feels to return to his childhood synagogue as "the cry of my race." See Goldstein, *Price of Whiteness,* chap. 1, for a discussion of how Jews adopted a racialized identity in the late nineteenth century.

60. David Sorkin, *The Transformation of German Jewry* (New York: Oxford University Press, 1987).

61. Stephen Greenblatt locates a similar idea of "self-fashioning" in early modern England, in the theater of Shakespeare. See his *Renaissance Self-Fashioning: From More to Shakespeare* (Chicago: University of Chicago Press, 1981).

62. See for example, the ambivalence about this form of theatrical self-fashioning in the writing of Benjamin Franklin, who, on the one hand worked hard to build character but on the other considered "going to plays and other places of amusement" one of the "great errata of my life, which I should wish to correct if I were to live it over again." Benjamin Franklin, *The Autobiography and Other Writings,* ed. Kenneth Silverman (New York: Penguin, 1986), 42.

63. See extended discussions on *Whoopee* and *Girl Crazy* in Most, *Making Americans,* chap. 2.

64. On the relationship between gay men and the musical theater, see D. A. Miller, *Place for Us: Essay on the Broadway Musical* (Cambridge, MA: Harvard University Press, 1998). On lesbians and musical theater, see Stacy Wolf, *A Problem like Maria: Gender and Sexuality in the American Musical* (Ann Arbor: University of Michigan Press, 2002). On race and Irish Americans, see Noel Ignatiev, *How the Irish Became White* (New York: Routledge, 1996).

65. Edna Ferber and George S. Kaufman, *Stage Door,* in *Kaufman & Co.,* 603.

66. Ibid., 633–634.

67. Edna Ferber and George S. Kaufman, *Royal Family,* in *Kaufman & Co.,* 71.

68. As Robert Cover points out, *mitzvah* "literally means commandment, but has a general meaning closer to "incumbent obligation." Robert M. Cover, "Obligation: A Jewish Jurisprudence of the Social Order," in *Law, Politics, and Morality in Judaism,* ed. Michael Walzer (Princeton: Princeton University Press, 2004), 3.

69. *Gold Diggers of 1933.* Directed by Mervyn LeRoy; written by David Boehm and Erwin S. Gelsey; released May 27, 1933. Produced by Robert Lord and Jack L. Warner; distributed by Warner Brothers. The original play on which *Gold Diggers of 1933* was based, *The Gold Diggers,* was written by Avery Hopwood and produced and directed by David Belasco. The play, however, did not contain the same kind of conversion scene as the film, which set a pattern for the standard Warner Brothers formula. As Arthur Hove details in his introduction to the screenplay, many writers participated in the development of the screenplay,

not to mention the producers who weighed in as well. The film was ultimately directed by Mervyn LeRoy, who was Jewish (although the famous director of the musical sequences, Busby Berkeley, was not).

70. *Gold Diggers of 1933*, edited and with an introduction by Arthur Hove (Madison: University of Wisconsin Press, 1980), 94. With some small additions to the dialogue taken from the film itself.

71. Cover, "Obligation," 4.

72. Some scholars have taken issue with what they argue is Cover's too-simple binary opposition. See, for example, David Novak's *Covenantal Rights* (Princeton: Princeton University Press, 2000). But while these discussions offer a more nuanced portrait of Jewish jurisprudence, the basic difference Cover discusses is never really up for debate.

73. Cover, "Obligation," 5.

74. Ferber and Kaufman, *Royal Family*, in *Kaufman & Co.*, 14.

75. Raphaelson, *The Jazz Singer*, 109.

76. In addition to *The Jazz Singer*, see, for example, *Abie's Irish Rose*, the final scenes of *Fiddler on the Roof*, pretty much everything by Philip Roth after *Portnoy's Complaint*, most Woody Allen movies, as well as *Bridget Loves Bernie*, and countless other films and television shows of the 1960s, '70s, '80s, and '90s. For a useful discussion of the role of sociology in shaping discussions of intermarriage, see Lila Corwin Berman, "Sociology, Jews, and Intermarriage in Twentieth-Century America," *Jewish Social Studies* 14 no.2 (July 2008): 32–60.

77. Kaufman in particular was quite obsessed with this plot device. It reappears in *You Can't Take it With You* (1936) and *The Man Who Came to Dinner* (1939), both written with Moss Hart.

78. Ferber and Kaufman, *Royal Family*, in *Kaufman & Co.*, 30.

79. On the feminization of Jewish men in European culture, see Sander Gilman, *Jewish Self-Hatred* (Baltimore: Johns Hopkins University Press, 1990); and in American popular culture, see Most, *Making Americans*, chap. 2. See also Daniel Boyarin, *Unheroic Conduct: The Rise of Heterosexuality and the Invention of the Jewish Man* (Berkeley: University of California Press, 1997), who discusses the same issue in ancient times.

80. Irving Berlin, *Annie Get Your Gun* (New York: Irving Berlin Music Corporation, 1949), 22–25.

81. See Max Weber, *The Protestant Ethic and the Spirit of Capitalism*, trans. Talcott Parsons (London: Routledge, 1930, 1992), chap. 3.

NOTES TO CHAPTER 3

1. Belasco, "Acting as a Science," in *Actors on Acting*, 580.

2. Lee Strasberg, "The Actor and Himself," in Cole and Chinoy, *Actors on Acting*, 623.

3. See Murray Friedman, *The Neoconservative Revolution: Jewish Intellectuals and the Shaping of Public Policy* (New York: Cambridge University Press, 2005);

and Marc Dollinger, *Quest for Inclusion* (Princeton: Princeton University Press, 2000).

4. On immigration restriction, see David S. Wyman, *The Abandonment of the Jews* (New York: Pantheon Books, 1985); and Bill Ong Hing, *Defining America Through Immigration Policy* (Philadelphia: Temple University Press, 2004). On rising anti-Semitism in the United States during the 1930s, see Henry Feingold, *A Time for Searching* (Baltimore: Johns Hopkins University Press, 1992).

5. Richard Rodgers, *Musical Stages* (New York: Random House, 1975), 184.

6. See Richard Slotkin, "Unit Pride: Ethnic Platoons and the Myth of American Nationality," *American Literary History* 13, no.3 (Autumn 2001): 469–497, for a detailed discussion of this phenomenon and a list of films.

7. See Judith Smith, *Visions of Belonging* (New York: Columbia University Press, 2006) for an analysis of this phenomenon in post-war popular culture. See Matthew Jacobson, *Whiteness of a Different Color* (Cambridge, MA: Harvard University Press, 1999) for a discussion of how ethnic difference became whiteness in the post-war period.

8. See Mark Silk, *Spiritual Politics* (New York: Touchstone Books, 1989) for a history of the term "Judeo-Christian" and a discussion of how it functioned in post-war American culture.

9. For Rodgers and Hart's mastery of the musical stage, see the quote by Brooks Atkinson in David Ewen's *Complete Book of the American Musical Theater* (New York: Holt, Rinehart and Winston, 1959), 243. In a review of their play *I Married an Angel*, Atkinson claims that "musical comedy has met its masters." See also Ethan Mordden's comments in the *Richard Rodgers Reader*, Geoffrey Block, ed. (Oxford: Oxford University Press, 2002), 12, 19: "If the Marxes (and Eddie Cantor) mark a culmination of the twenties idea of a comic musical, Rodgers and Hart are the exponents of musical comedy."

10. Dorothy Hart and Robert Kimball, eds., *The Complete Lyrics of Lorenz Hart*, (New York: Alfred A. Knopf, 1986), 252.

11. This tension between Rodgers's sentimental music and Hart's cynical lyrics has been noted by a number of critics. Rodgers himself commented in *Musical Stages* (New York: Random House, 1975) that what made "Bewitched" so successful was "the contrast of a flowing, sentimental melody with words that are unsentimental and self-mocking" (201). See also Philip Furia, *The Poets of Tin Pan Alley* (New York: Oxford University Press, 1990), 97; Gerald Bordman, *American Musical Theater*, 2nd ed. (New York: Oxford University Press, 1992), 523; John Clum, *Something for the Boys* (New York: St. Martin's Press, 1999), 62; and Frederick Nolan, *Lorenz Hart* (New York: Oxford University Press, 1994), 274.

12. *Pal Joey* was a turning point for both Rodgers and Hart, although they turned in different directions. By 1943 Rodgers had chosen a new partner and a more sentimental musical style in his work with Oscar Hammerstein. Hart, on the other hand, drank more heavily in the years following *Pal Joey* and produced little new work. He died of pneumonia and alcohol poisoning in 1943 at the age

of forty-seven. Critics and historians, writing of *Pal Joey* in hindsight, see it as the turning point for Rodgers toward the "mature" integrated musical he was to become famous for in his work with Hammerstein. This play does lay the groundwork for the genre of the musical play (*Oklahoma!, South Pacific*, etc.) but mostly by making the musical comedy impossible. The turn toward realism had little to do with artistic maturity and much more to do with the particular political and social conditions of the 1940s. See Most, *Making Americans*, on *Oklahoma* and *South Pacific*, chaps. 4 and 6.

13. John O'Hara, Lorenz Hart, and Richard Rodgers, *Pal Joey* (New York: Random House, 1952), 16.

14. The swooping melodic archrepeats, create an effect that Alec Wilder calls "hypnotic." The contrast between the monotonous and repetitive notes of the verse and the dramatic swoops of the refrain alone creates a "heartwarming" effect in the refrain, as does the satisfying way in which the refrain finally resolves. Thanks to Rose Rosengard Subotnik for this observation. Mark N. Grant, *The Rise and Fall of the Broadway Musical* (Boston: Northeastern University Press, 2004), 115, 135–138.

15. The strings can be heard in the City Center Encores! Production cast recording, which uses the original orchestrations.

16. The lyrics may also represent a none-too-subtle critique of O'Hara's creative role in the play. He was far less involved in the writing than Rodgers and Hart had hoped, because he disappeared from the project for weeks at a time. Meryle Secrest suggests that O'Hara's tardiness in initially delivering the script inspired Hart's lyrics in this song. *Somewhere For Me: A Biography of Richard Rodgers* (New York: Knopf, 2001), 215.

17. As they were, for example, in the Prince Music Theater's 2002 production in Philadelphia.

18. The self-consciousness of this song is further reinforced by the fact that Gypsy Rose Lee's real-life sister, June Havoc, played the leading nightclub dancer in the play, Gladys Bumps.

19. The play had a modestly successful run of 374 performances in 1940–41.

20. Brooks Atkinson, review of *Pal Joey*, *New York Times*, December 26, 1940, 22.

21. Although Atkinson referred to Linda as the "only uncontaminated baggage in the cast," Rodgers and Hart had little sympathy for her. Rodgers called her "stupid" in more than one interview. See Block, *Richard Rodgers Reader*, 306.

22. This song was reinstated in the New York City Center Encores! production of 1995 (and on the resulting cast album), in the Prince Music Theater's 2002 production and in the Shaw Festival production in 2004.

23. This disillusion with theatrical liberalism was not limited to Jewish writers. We see the theme articulated across a broad spectrum of popular works of the period, such as Eugene O'Neill's *Long Day's Journey into Night* (1941) and *The Iceman Cometh* (1946), Tennessee Williams' *Streetcar Named Desire* (1947), and Ralph Ellison's *Invisible Man* (1952).

24. Brenda Murphy, *Miller: Death of a Salesman*. Plays in Production Series (New York: Cambridge University Press, 1995), 70. See also *The Cambridge Companion to Arthur Miller*, ed. Christopher Bigsby (Cambridge: Cambridge University Press, 1997) on the international popularity of the play.

25. This celebration began with Brooks Atkinson's often quoted review: "By common consent, this is one of the finest dramas in the whole range of American theater," in *The Critical Response to Arthur Miller*, ed. Steven R. Centola and Michelle Cirulli (Westport, CT: Praeger, 2006), 28. By no means was all the early criticism of the play positive, but the naysayers largely dropped by the wayside as the play's canonical status was solidified.

26. See Murphy, *Miller: Death of a Salesman*, 58–59, 70, 106–107. Matthew Roudané, in the introduction to his *Approaches to Teaching Miller's Death of a Salesman* (New York: The Modern Language Association of America, 1995), refers to *Death of a Salesman* as "one of the few plays that have helped define American literary canonicity" (4). He also reports on the wide range of classes in which survey respondents report teaching the play (18). In Harold Bloom's introduction to Bloom's Modern Critical Views: *Arthur Miller* (New York: Chelsea House, 2007), Bloom refers to the remarkable and enduring impact of the play and the "universal mode of pain" it dramatizes (5). Steven R. Centola, in the introduction to Centola and Cirulli's *The Critical Response to Arthur Miller* argues for the universality of Miller's work: "his plays transcend geographical, cultural, and ideological issues and consistently bring to the stage a potent and hauntingly memorable vision of the human experience" (6).

27. Terry Otten, in *The Temptation of Innocence in the Dramas of Arthur Miller* (Columbia: University of Missouri Press, 2002), describes how the critical obsession with *Death of a Salesman* as a tragedy is a crucial part of a larger conversation among scholars of modern drama about "the viability of tragedy in the modern age and particularly in American culture" (27). He acknowledges that to a large extent, the impetus for this single-minded focus on the question of tragedy was provided by Miller himself, in his essays "Tragedy and the Common Man" (1949) and "The Nature of Tragedy" (1949). Numerous scholars make clear the high stakes involved in the discussion, none more than Harold Bloom: "Whether it has the aesthetic dignity of tragedy is not clear, but no other American play is worthier of the term" (Bloom, 5).

28. Stella Adler, *The Art of Acting* (New York: Applause Books, 2000), 33.

29. On the Jewishness of *Death of a Salesman*, see Julius Novick, "Death of a Salesman: Deracination and Its Discontents." *American Jewish History* 91, no.1 (March 2003): 97–107. Novick also offers an overview of other critics who have discussed the Jewishness of Miller's plays. Mary McCarthy, in the introduction to *Sights and Spectacles* (New York, 1957, xiv–xv) comments on the play's Jewish cadences, and George Ross, reviewing a Yiddish version of the play for *Commentary*, February 1951, notes how the play seems to make much more sense in what he calls the Yiddish "original." He claims that the director, Joseph Buloff,

"has caught Miller in the act . . . of changing his name." Reprinted in Arthur Miller, *Death of a Salesman, Text and Criticism,* ed. Gerald Weales (New York: Penguin, 1967), 259.

30. For a useful description of the universalism of the time in relation to religion and specifically Judaism, see Will Herberg, *Protestant, Catholic, Jew: An Essay in American Religious Sociology* (Garden City, NY: Doubleday, 1960).

31. Arthur Miller, *Timebends* (New York: Penguin, 1995), 82.

32. Arthur Miller, *Death of a Salesman,* Fiftieth Anniversary ed. (New York: Penguin, 1999), xii.

33. Miller makes this point explicitly in his early novel *Focus* (1945), in which a non-Jew is mistakenly made the object of anti-Semitic prejudice. See the contemporary film *Gentleman's Agreement* (1947) based on a novel by Laura Z. Hobson as well.

34. See David Savran, "The Curse of Legitimacy," in Ackerman and Puchner, *Against Theater.*

35. Kirk Williams, "Anti-Theatricality and the Limits of Naturalism," *Modern Drama* 44, 3 (Fall 2001): 285. The two internal quotes are from Arno Holz: the first from "Evolution des Dramas," *Die neue Wortkunst: Eine Zusammenfassung ihrer ersten grundlegenden Dokumente* (Berlin: Dietz, 1925), 227; the second from "Vorwart." *Sozialaristokraten Komodie,* ed. Theo Meyer (Stuttgart: Reclam, 1981), 138.

36. "The Question of Relatedness," introduction to *All My Sons, Arthur Miller's Collected Plays* (New York: Viking, 1957), excerpted in Arthur Miller's *All My Sons,* in Bloom, *Modern Critical Interpretations,* ed. Harold Bloom (New York: Chelsea House, 1988), 9.

37. Introduction to *Arthur Miller's Collected Plays* (New York: Viking, 1957), excerpted in the Viking Critical Library edition of *Death of a Salesman* (New York: Penguin, 1996), 156–157.

38. "The Question of Relatedness," in Bloom, *All My Sons,* 10.

39. This is not as obvious as it may sound. A number of theater practitioners of the 1960s were eager to make theater *into* life: through the use of theater as ritual, as political rally, as "happening," as drug-induced trip (see chap. 5, this book).

40. Steve Vineberg, *Method Actors: Three Generations of an American Acting Style* (New York: Schirmer, 1991), 6.

41. Ibid., chap. 5. See also Henry Bial's discussion of the relationship between Method Acting and *Death of a Salesman* in which he argues that the play can be considered Jewish because the actors in the play, using the techniques of the Method, drew on their own ethnic and religious backgrounds to create their characters. Bial, *Acting Jewish,* 49–58.

42. Cole and Chinoy, *Actors on Acting,* 616.

43. Lee Strasberg, "The Actor and Himself," in *Actors on Acting,* 623.

44. "The American Theater," by Arthur Miller, reprinted in *Death of a Salesman,* Viking Critical Edition (New York: Penguin, 1996), 154.

45. And maybe even the theatrics themselves were not as obscured as Miller thought. See Tracy C. Davis, Thomas Postlewait, "Theatricality: An Introduction," in *Theatricality* (Cambridge: Cambridge University Press, 2004), 39, n. 2.

46. Miller, *Timebends*, 109. Hereafter cited in text.

47. Toby Zinnman discusses how Miller turns to vaudeville much later in his career, but makes no mention of the impact of vaudeville on his most popular work. "Vaudeville at the Edge of the Cliff," in *Arthur Miller's America: Theater and Culture in a Time of Change*, ed. Enoch Brater (Ann Arbor: University of Michigan Press, 2005). D. A. Miller laments the turn to naturalism in the post-war musical, wishing that the musical had colonized Arthur Miller's work rather than the other way around. I am arguing that in some ways, it did. *Place for Us*, 2.

48. In the 1940s, musical theater was praised for conforming to realist standards so comparison between the two forms is particularly fruitful in this decade. As Freudian psychoanalysis took hold in America, it became popular to use musical numbers to depict the subconscious. The most explicit representation of this was in the Kurt Weill/Ira Gershwin musical *Lady in the Dark* (1941). Each number emerges out of a dream that the main character relates to her psychiatrist. A few years later in *Oklahoma!* (1943), the dream ballet represents the character's desires and fears. The success of that dream ballet led the form to become almost ubiquitous, and finally a cliché, in musicals of the 1940s and '50s.

49. The fact that Willy's "songs" reveal his inadequacies does not make them less theatrically successful. The musical theater is full of such songs and performances. In *Pal Joey*, Joey Evans is a second-rate actor who thinks he can be a star. "I Could Write a Book" is nonetheless a show-stopping number. Consider also *Gypsy*: "Rose's Turn" reveals Rose's deluded sense of her own potential but is designed to bring down the house. Likewise, "Mr. Cellophane," in *Chicago*, is a song about invisibility, yet it makes the character intensely visible and earned John C. Reilly an Academy Award nomination for his performance in the 2002 film version.

50. Arthur Miller, *Death of a Salesman* (New York: Penguin, 1998), 16. Hereafter cited in text.

51. Ethel Merman's performance of "I Got Rhythm" in *Girl Crazy* (1930), for example, stopped the show seven times. In the same play, the comedian Willie Howard stepped out of character to do impressions and even ended up taking requests from the audience. Tales of audience participation in the Yiddish theater are legendary. Lulla Adler Rosenfeld, in *The Yiddish Theater and Jacob P. Adler* (New York: Shapolsky Publishers, 1977) writes: "in Thomashefsky's theater in Baltimore, when a second act curtain rose on Jewish prisoners freezing in Siberia, groans and wails went up in the audience, and some old women took off their shawls and threw them to the actors on stage" (230).

52. The set was designed by Jo Mielziner, who also designed most of the Rodgers and Hart musicals, including *Pal Joey*, as well as the somewhat similar set

for *Streetcar Named Desire*. Mielziner was the half-Jewish grandson of famous Talmudist Moses Mielziner of Hebrew Union College.

53. Joseph Buloff, the actor who originated the part of Ali Hakim in *Oklahoma* on Broadway, directed and starred in the Yiddish version of *Death of a Salesman* in 1951 (*Toyt fun a Salesman*). As George Ross reported in *Commentary* (February, 1951, 184–86), Buloff played Willy with more self-conscious theatricality ("larger, more lavish realism" and a "physically generous style") and in doing so brought out the underlying Jewishness of the play, which relies, according to Ross, on pathos and irony, not tragedy.

54. Arthur Miller, "Tragedy and the Common Man," (1949), in *The Theater Essays of Arthur Miller* (New York: Viking Press, 1978), 3–7.

55. The play confounds a number of generic expectations. Bernstein's score veers toward the operatic and deviates from standard musical-theater conventions of its day, which tended to make clear distinctions between story and song. Jerome Robbins's choreography obscures the lines between musical theater and ballet. All professional productions of *West Side Story* are required to maintain not only the Bernstein score and the Laurents libretto but also the Robbins choreography, a practice common in classical ballet but unheard of in the musical theater.

56. The literature on Shakespeare adaptations, and even just on adaptations of *Romeo and Juliet*, is enormous. For an excellent overview, see Jill Levenson, "The Adaptations of Juliet and her Romeo," in *Adaptation and American Studies: Perspectives on Research and Teaching*, ed. Nassim W. Balestrini, American Studies: A Monograph Series. (Heidelberg: Universitätsverlag Winter, 2011), 216.

57. Norris Houghton, ed., *Romeo and Juliet/West Side Story* (New York: Dell, 1965), 179. Hereafter cited in text.

58. *The Complete Lyrics of Lorenz Hart*, ed. Dorothy Hart and Robert Kimball (New York: Knopf, 1986), 253. See also George and Ira Gershwin's "Blah Blah Blah," from *Delicious*, which mocks the same language of romantic love.

59. This type of scene was not uncommon in early modern drama, since (in real life) the necessity and authority of church weddings to make marriages legally binding was still in question; see, for example, Rosalind and Orlando's betrothal in *As You Like It*. In 1950s America, this assumption of authority by the lovers is seen as rebellious (marriage can take place only under the proper institutional structures) but also morally acceptable (in a democracy like the United States, rebellion is sometimes necessary to insure rights). For Tony and Maria, free choice in romantic love authorizes them to make their own decisions.

60. *South Pacific* (1949), also by Rodgers and Hammerstein, explored the violence emerging from racial prejudice, but the ending of that play offered a utopian image of the triumph of tolerance over racial prejudice through the redeeming power of romantic love.

61. J. L. Austin, *How to Do Things with Words*, 2nd ed. William James Lectures (Cambridge, MA: Harvard University Press, 1962). Austin notes that "a

performative utterance will . . . be *in a peculiar* way hollow or void if said by an actor or spoken in a soliloquy" (22). But in this case the concern is with the performative speech of the characters, not the actors playing those characters.

62. Action bears some resemblance here to Stanley Kowalski, from A *Streetcar Named Desire*, a character both sympathetic in his authenticity and reprehensible in his inability to control his animal instincts.

63. Riff's embrace of performance as the most sensible way to deal with provocation must have resonated with the writers, three of whom later openly acknowledged their homosexuality. All were in the closet when they were writing the show, however.

64. We see here as well a none-too-subtle critique of the extremely popular behaviorist psychology of the 1950s, developed and popularized by B. F. Skinner, as well as the ongoing debates between psychoanalysts and behaviorists about where to locate the "truth" of the self.

65. Raymond Williams, *Modern Tragedy* (Stanford: Stanford University Press, 1966), 87–89.

66. "There's a place for us / somewhere a place for us. Peace and quiet and open air / wait for us / somewhere" (Houghton, *West Side Story*, 201).

NOTES TO CHAPTER 4

1. Erving Goffman, *The Presentation of Self in Everyday Life* (New York: Doubleday, 1959). Hereafter cited in text.

2. For the influence of Brecht, Artaud, Grotowski, Schechner, and other experimental theater artists on the field, see Henry Bial, ed. *The Performance Studies Reader* (New York: Routledge, 2004); and Richard Schechner, *Performance Studies: An Introduction* (New York: Routledge, 2006).

3. On twentieth-century parody, see Linda Hutcheon, *A Theory of Parody: The Teachings of Twentieth-Century Art Forms* (New York: Methuen, 1985).

4. The writers who worked on *Your Show of Shows* were among the biggest names in comedy in the ensuing decades. Among them were Woody Allen, Mel Brooks, Larry Gelbart, Carl Reiner, and Neil Simon, Jewish writers all.

5. This comic device remained popular in television through the final decades of the twentieth century, although at a certain point Hebrew came to serve as the insider language rather than Yiddish. In the film *Borat* (2006), for example, Sacha Baron Cohen used Hebrew as his fake "Kazakh" language, occasioning knowing winks and laughter from Jewish viewers. For an analysis of this sort of ethnic "double coding," see Bial, *Acting Jewish*.

6. The stage version was directed by Moss Hart with Julie Andrews as Eliza Doolittle and Rex Harrison as Henry Higgins. Both Lerner and Loewe were Jewish, as was Hart. Lerner was the grandson of Russian Jewish immigrants; Frederick Loewe was born in Germany, the son of a famous Viennese operetta star. The play won the Tony Award for Best Musical (and both lead actors were also nominated for the award; Harrison won) and set a record for the longest run of a

Broadway musical to date. The film version, directed by George Cukor and starring Audrey Hepburn, was equally successful, garnering eight Academy Awards
including Best Picture, Best Director, and Best Actor (Harrison). Cukor was
also Jewish and of Hungarian background, not unlike the character Karpathy, in
the film and play. See also Dominic McHugh, *Loverly: The Life and Times of "My
Fair Lady"* (New York: Oxford University Press, 2012).

7. That rival speech expert, Zoltan Karpathy, was played in the film by Theodore
Bikel, a Jewish folk singer and actor who has recorded widely in Yiddish as well
as multiple other languages.

8. George Bernard Shaw and Alan Jay Lerner, *Pygmalion and My Fair Lady,*
adaptation and lyrics by Alan Jay Lerner, music by Frederick Loewe (New York:
Penguin Signet Classics, 1980), 189.

9. And yet, those moments of sentimentality are also of course carefully constructed. In an interview in 2008, Julie Andrews discussed how Moss Hart
worked with her tirelessly to develop the character of Eliza. (http://www.
achievement.org/autodoc/page/and0int-4). The film version featured an
even less "authentic" Eliza: the part was split between Audrey Hepburn, who
appeared on screen, and Marni Nixon, whose voice was dubbed in for the
songs.

10. For specifics on post-war Jewish mobility, see Edward S. Shapiro, *A Time For
Healing: American Jewry Since World War II,* in *The Jewish People in America,* vol.
5, ed. Henry Feingold (Baltimore: Johns Hopkins University Press, 1992).

11. *Fiddler on the Roof* was adapted by Joseph Stein from Sholem Aleichem's story
"Tevye, the Dairyman," with music by Jerry Bock and lyrics by Sheldon Harnick. It was directed and choreographed by Jerome Robbins (taking on this
project after *West Side Story* and *A Funny Thing Happened on the Way to the
Forum*) and opened on Broadway on September 22, 1964, produced by Harold Prince, and starring Zero Mostel. It was made into a film in 1971 directed
by Norman Jewison and produced by United Artists. *Funny Girl* was written
by Isobel Lennart with music by Jule Styne and lyrics by Bob Merrill. It was
directed on Broadway by Garson Kanin, starred Barbra Streisand, and opened
on March 26, 1964. It was made into a film in 1968 directed by William Wyler.

12. Joseph Stein noted, "We showed it to one producer, who shall remain anony-
mous, who said, 'I love it, but what will we do when we run out of Hadassah
benefits?'" Peter Stone, Jerry Bock, Sheldon Harnick, and Joseph Stein, "Land-
mark Symposium: 'Fiddler on the Roof,'" *Dramatists Guild Quarterly* 20, no. 1
(1983): 15.

13. In his overview of the impact of *Fiddler on the Roof* on American Jewish
culture, Stephen Whitfield notes that Music Theater International regularly
licenses more than five hundred different productions of *Fiddler on the Roof*
annually in the United States alone, and that it ranks among their top five
most successful scripts. He also details the international success of the play.
"Fiddling with Sholem Aleichem," in *Key Texts in American Jewish Culture,* ed.

Jack Kugelmass (New Brunswick, NJ: Rutgers University Press, 2003), 105–125. For more details on the history of *Fiddler on the Roof,* see Richard Altman and Mervyn Kaufman, *The Making of a Musical: Fiddler on the Roof* (New York: Crown, 1971).

14. For a recent example, see the YouTube video "To Life: Vanessa's Wedding Surprise" prepared by Lin-Manuel Miranda, writer and composer of the 2008 Broadway musical *In the Heights,* for his fiancée.

15. Alisa Solomon, "How Fiddler Became Folklore," *Forward,* September 1, 2006.

16. For more on this controversy, see Jessica Hillman, "Goyim on the Roof: Embodying Authenticity in Leveaux's *Fiddler on the Roof,*" *Studies in Musical Theater* 1, no. 1 (January 2007): 25–39.

17. Hillman and John Lahr (*New Yorker,* March 8, 2004) both note that the initial production of *Fiddler on the Roof* featured a much more demonstratively theatrical and hence more authentically Jewish Tevye than the 2004 revival.

18. Joseph Stein, Jerry Bock, and Sheldon Harnick, *Fiddler on the Roof* (New York: Limelight Editions, 1964), 93. Hereafter cited in text.

19. Referring first to Sholem Aleichem's original story, Howe notes: "God is a presence to whom Jews can turn in moments of need and urgency; in *Fiddler on the Roof* He ends up as Zero Mostel's straight man." Irving Howe, "Tevye on Broadway," *Commentary* 38 (November 1964): 73–74.

20. Isobel Lennart, Jule Styne, and Bob Merrill, *Funny Girl* (New York: Random House, 1964), 13. Hereafter cited in text.

NOTES TO CHAPTER 5

1. See Jonathan Sarna, "Renewal," in *American Judaism* (New Haven: Yale University Press, 2004) for a detailed history of this period.

2. For details on the Jewish involvement in politics in this period, see Michael Staub, *The Jewish 1960s* (Hanover, NH: Brandeis University Press, 2004); and Marc Dollinger, *Quest for Inclusion: Jews and Liberalism in Modern America* (Princeton: Princeton University Press, 2000).

3. Cynthia Ozick, "Toward a New Yiddish," in *Art and Ardor* (New York: Knopf, 1983), 153. Hereafter cited in text.

4. Ozick calls *Fiddler* an "emptied-out prettified romantic vulgarization" in her essay "Sholem Aleichem's Revolution," originally published in the *New Yorker* (March 28, 1988). Reprinted in *Metaphor and Memory* (New York: Knopf, 1989), 183.

5. Free [Abie Hoffman], *Revolution for the Hell of It* (New York: Thunder's Mouth Press, 2005), 27. Hereafter cited in text.

6. Norman Mailer, *The Armies of the Night* (New York: Signet, 1968), 139. Hereafter cited in text.

7. Ibid., 145, "one did not immerse oneself with open guru Ginsberg arms crying; Baa, baa, slay this sheep or enrich it Great Deep."

8. Ozick, "Toward a New Yiddish," 170.

9. Thanks to James Harbeck, who shared his research files on Schechner with me. His "Containment Is the Enemy: An Ideography of Richard Schechner" contains important information on Schechner's Jewish background (PhD diss., Tufts University, 1998), 26.

10. See Bial's introduction to *The Performance Studies Reader* for a discussion of Schechner's influence on the field. For a useful discussion of the legacy of Schechner's work, see also Mike Vanden Heuvel, "A Different Kind of PoMo: The Performance Group and the Mixed Legacy of Authentic Performance," in *Restaging the Sixties,* ed. James M. Harding and Cindy Rosenthal (Ann Arbor: University of Michigan Press, 2006), 332–351.

11. This concept of "site-specific" theater became commonplace in both experimental and more mainstream theater by the late 1980s, but it was still a new idea in the 1960s.

12. See Schechner's second book, *Performance Theory*, for an extensive discussion of his anthropological research into performance traditions in traditional communities.

13. Richard Schechner, *Environmental Theater* (New York: Applause, 1994), 43. The original text was published in 1973. Hereafter cited in text.

14. The Performance Group: The Jewish Piece. Proposal. October 1977. Schechner Papers, Carton 65, Department of Rare Books and Special Collections, Princeton University Libraries, Princeton, NJ.

15. See Richard DeCordova, *Picture Personalities: The Emergence of the Star System in America* (Champaign: University of Illinois Press, 1990).

16. While Stephen Sondheim and Stephen Schwartz continued to produce popular musicals, a majority of the new composers and writers on Broadway in the 1970s, such as Andrew Lloyd Weber and Tim Rice, were not Jewish and, in many cases, not American. By the early 1970s, expressions of theatrical liberalism had moved away from the theater, which was an increasingly less popular mode, and into Hollywood film, television, popular novels, and performance theory.

17. Gerome Ragni and James Rado, *Hair: The American Tribal Love-Rock Musical* (New York: Pocket Books, 1969), ix. Hereafter cited in text.

18. Scott Miller, *Rebels with Applause: Broadway's Groundbreaking Musicals* (Portsmouth, NH: Heinemann, 2001), 81.

19. Trilling, *Sincerity and Authenticity*, 2. Hereafter cited in text.

20. See Greenblatt, *Renaissance Self-Fashioning*; and Marjorie Garber, *Shakespeare and Modern Culture* (New York: Random House, 2008).

21. Matthew Jacobson, *Roots Too* (Cambridge, MA: Harvard University Press, 2006).

22. Script to *Young Frankenstein*, 26. Available at: http://www.godamongdirectors.com/scripts/young.shtml.

23. Mel Brooks is famous for creating (or some might say revealing) the Jewish aspects of countless genres of American popular entertainment. *Blazing Saddles*

(Western), *Spaceballs* (science fiction), *Young Frankenstein* (horror), *High Anxiety* (Hitchcock psychodrama), and *History of the World* (epic) are just a few examples.

NOTES TO CHAPTER 6

1. *Purple Rose of Cairo* (1985); produced by Orion Pictures, directed by Woody Allen; starring Woody Allen, Mia Farrow, and Jeff Daniels.

2. For an introduction to the voluminous material in this field, see Daniel Boyarin and Jonathan Boyarin, eds., *Jews and Other Differences: The New Jewish Cultural Studies* (Minneapolis: University of Minnesota Press, 1997); and David Biale, Michael Galchinsky, and Susannah Heschel, eds., *Insider/Outsider: American Jews and Multiculturalism* (Berkeley: University of California Press, 1998).

3. See, in particular, Judith Butler, *Gender Trouble* (New York: Routledge, 1990); and *Bodies That Matter* (New York: Routledge, 1993); Marjorie Garber's discussion of Barbra Streisand and *Yentl* in *Vested Interests* (New York: Routledge, 1992); and Eve Kosofsky Sedgwick's discussion of the story of Esther in *Epistemology of the Closet* (Berkeley: University of California Press, 1990).

4. For a comparison of the role of cross-dressing in the film and the original I. B. Singer story, see Garber, *Vested Interests*, 77–84.

5. In recent years, Butler has become increasingly vocal about and interested in Judaism and the politics of Jewish identity in North America. She has written extensively on Levinas, the Middle East crisis, and Jewish ethics. See Daniel Boyarin, Daniel Itzkovitz, and Ann Pellegrini, eds., *Queer Theory and the Jewish Question* (New York: Columbia University Press, 2003), 395–402; and "Is Judaism Zionism," in *The Power of Religion in the Public Sphere,* ed. Eduardo Mendiepo and Jonathan VanAntwerpen (New York: Columbia University Press, 2011), 70–91.

6. Judith Butler, *Excitable Speech: A Politics of the Performative* (New York: Routledge, 1997), 161.

7. For a wonderfully clear description of Butler's attitude toward censorship and resignification, see Sara Salih, *Judith Butler: Routledge Critical Thinkers* (New York: Routledge, 2002), 112–114.

8. *Zelig* (1983), produced by Orion Pictures, dir. Woody Allen, featuring Woody Allen and Mia Farrow.

9. The ending also likely references the end of *Casablanca,* a film Woody Allen parodied in *Play it Again, Sam* (1972).

10. Perhaps second only to the theater, psychoanalysis has long been seen as an explicitly Jewish practice. Indeed, psychoanalysis and theatrical liberalism can be seen as two different ways of encountering Protestantism—the first accepts that the self originates internally and involves an anxious examination of the mind in order to achieve healthy liberal modern subjectivity; the second resists the Protestant focus on the internal and argues for the self as an external performed entity. The literature on this subject is voluminous. A good introduction

for the purposes of this book can be found in Andrew R. Heinze, *Jews and the American Soul: Human Nature in the Twentieth Century* (Princeton: Princeton University Press, 2006).

11. Philip Roth, *The Counterlife* (New York: Vintage Books, 1986), 41 (emphasis in original). Hereafter cited in text.

12. Jonathan Boyarin and Daniel Boyarin, "Self-Exposure as Theory," in Jonathan Boyarin, *Thinking in Jewish* (Chicago: University of Chicago Press, 1996), 38.

13. Shaye J. D. Cohen, *Why Aren't Jewish Women Circumcised: Gender and Covenant in Judaism* (Berkeley: University of California Press, 2005), xii.

14. David Savran articulates the role of ambivalence in the play in his essay, "Ambivalence, Utopia, and a Queer Sort of Materialism: How *Angels in America* Reconstructs the Nation," *Theater Journal* 47, no. 2 (May 1995): 207–227. He shows how the play functions simultaneously as popular and radical. His interest, however, is in national, rather than religious issues.

15. Kushner has acknowledged his debt to Miller in many ways. He edited the Library of America volume of Arthur Miller's collected plays and wrote a lengthy obituary for him in the *Nation,* among others. *Arthur Miller: Collected Plays, 1944–1961,* ed. Tony Kushner (New York: Library of America, 2012); and "Kushner on Miller," *Nation,* June 13, 2005. Part of the obituary reads: "I first saw Arthur Miller in person at the 1994 Tony Awards, when I sat behind him, too unnerved to introduce myself; for the whole evening I stared at the back of his head, which was far, far more interesting to me than anything transpiring onstage. Inside this impressive cranium, inside this dome, I thought to myself, Willy Loman was conceived—for an American playwright, a place comparable in sacrosanctity to the Ark of the Covenant or the Bodhi Tree or the Manger in Bethlehem."

16. Tony Kushner, *Angels in America: Part One, Millennium Approaches* (New York: Theater Communications Group, 1993), 1:5. Hereafter cited by part number and page number.

17. Kushner, *Angels in America: Part Two, Millennium Approaches* (New York: Theater Communications Group, 1994).

18. Kushner does write, in the notes to part 2, *Perestroika,* that this section is "essentially a comedy." But he then qualifies this: "it's not a farce" and notes that only through high seriousness can a comic resolution be reached (2:8). The filmed version was, in many ways, more successful than the stage version because it dispensed with the need to "have the wires show." The Angel's entrance in the film is truly spectacular, and the realism of her appearance helps to mitigate the ironic knowingness of the text enough to allow the audience entrance into the emotional experience.

19. Belize does later hint obliquely to Louis that he might be doing drag again, but he is oddly indirect about it, raising the possibility that he has just mentioned it to get a rise out of Louis, who responds on cue: "I think it's sexist" (1:94).

20. See Savran, "Ambivalence, Utopia, and a Queer Sort of Materialism," 216. He notes the limitations of cross-dressing and the surprising stability of masculinity (but not femininity) in the play.

21. Kushner makes clear in the introduction to the play that his translation of the blessing for Jacob as "more life" comes directly from Harold Bloom's in *The Book of J.*

NOTES TO CURTAIN CALL

1. Ben Brantley, review of *The Book of Mormon*, by Matt Stone and Trey Parker, *New York Times*, March 24, 2011.

2. The 2001 musical *The Producers*, originally a 1968 Mel Brooks movie, was also made into a movie in 2005.

3. Austin, *How to Do Things With Words*, 22.

4. Babylonian Talmud, *Eruvin* 13b. This embrace of contradiction is called, in the Talmud, *mahloket*, which indicates ongoing debate. My thanks to Jonathan Sarna for making the connection between *mahloket* and theatrical liberalism.

"This Can't Be Love" (from *The Boys from Syracuse*)

"Bewitched, Bothered and Bewildered" (from *Pal Joey*)

"The Flower Garden of My Heart" (from *Pal Joey*)

"I Could Write a Book" (from *Pal Joey*)

"Free" (from *A Funny Thing Happened on the Way to the Forum*)
Words and Music by STEPHEN SONDHEIM
© 1962 (Renewed) BURTHEN MUSIC CO., INC.
All Rights Administered by CHAPPELL & CO., INC.

"Do You Love Me?" (from *Fiddler on the Roof*)
Words by SHELDON HARNICK Music by JERRY BOCK
Copyright © 1964 (Renewed) Mayerling Productions Ltd. (Administered by R&H
   Music) and Jerry Bock
Enterprises for the United States and Alley Music Corporation, Trio Music Com-
   pany, and to Jerry Bock
Enterprises for the world outside of the United States. Used by permission. All
   rights reserved.

"Matchmaker" (from *Fiddler on the Roof*)
Words by SHELDON HARNICK Music by JERRY BOCK
Copyright © 1964 (Renewed) Mayerling Productions Ltd. (Administered by R&H
   Music) and Jerry Bock
Enterprises for the United States and Alley Music Corporation, Trio Music Com-
   pany, and to Jerry Bock
Enterprises for the world outside of the United States. Used by permission. All
   rights reserved.

"Tradition" (from *Fiddler on the Roof*)
Words by SHELDON HARNICK Music by JERRY BOCK
Copyright © 1964 (Renewed) Mayerling Productions Ltd. (Administered by R&H
   Music) and Jerry Bock
Enterprises for the United States and Alley Music Corporation, Trio Music Com-
   pany, and to Jerry Bock
Enterprises for the world outside of the United States. Used by permission. All
   rights reserved.

ABOUT THE AUTHOR

Andrea Most is Associate Professor of American Literature and Jewish Studies in the Department of English at the University of Toronto. Her first book, *Making Americans: Jews and the Broadway Musical* (Harvard University Press, 2004), won the 2005 Kurt Weill Prize for the Best Book on Musical Theater.